ANNE BANCROFT

ALSO BY PETER SHELLEY
AND FROM MCFARLAND

Philip Seymour Hoffman: The Life and Work (2017)

Neil Simon on Screen: Adaptations and Original Scripts for Film and Television (2015)

Gwen Verdon: A Life on Stage and Screen (2015)

Sandy Dennis: The Life and Films (2014)

Australian Horror Films, 1973–2010 (2012)

Jules Dassin: The Life and Films (2011)

Frances Farmer: The Life and Films of a Troubled Star (2011)

Grande Dame Guignol Cinema: A History of Hag Horror from Baby Jane *to* Mother (2009)

Anne Bancroft
The Life and Work

Peter Shelley

McFarland & Company, Inc., Publishers
Jefferson, North Carolina

Acknowledgments: Thanks are offered to Barry Lowe and Kath Perry for their continued support.

LIBRARY OF CONGRESS CATALOGUING-IN-PUBLICATION DATA

Names: Shelley, Peter, 1962– author.
Title: Anne Bancroft : the life and work / Peter Shelley.
Description: Jefferson, North Carolina : McFarland & Company, Inc., Publishers, 2017. | Includes bibliographical references and index. | Includes filmography.
Identifiers: LCCN 2017030122 | ISBN 9781476662428 (softcover : acid free paper) ∞
Subjects: LCSH: Bancroft, Anne, 1931–2005. | Actors—United States—Biography.
Classification: LCC PN2287.B164 S54 2017 | DDC 791.43028092 [B] —dc23
LC record available at https://lccn.loc.gov/2017030122

BRITISH LIBRARY CATALOGUING DATA ARE AVAILABLE

ISBN (print) 978-1-4766-6242-8
ISBN (ebook) 978-1-4766-2858-5

© 2017 Peter Shelley. All rights reserved

No part of this book may be reproduced or transmitted in any form or by any means, electronic or mechanical, including photocopying or recording, or by any information storage and retrieval system, without permission in writing from the publisher.

Front cover: Anne Bancroft in *The Graduate* (author's collection)

Printed in the United States of America

McFarland & Company, Inc., Publishers
Box 611, Jefferson, North Carolina 28640
www.mcfarlandpub.com

Table of Contents

Preface   1

1. Beginning   3
2. An Independent Actress   20
3. *Two for the Seesaw* and *The Miracle Worker*   36
4. Mel Brooks   52
5. *Mother Courage and Her Children*   65
6. *The Graduate*   84
7. Max Brooks   102
8. *Fatso*   119
9. *Agnes of God*   132
10. *Neil Simon's Broadway Bound*   148
11. *Keeping the Faith*   165
12. The End   174

Appendix: Stage, Film and Television Performances   177
Bibliography   181
Index   185

Preface

I first saw Anne Bancroft in the film 'night, Mother (1986). This had significance for me since I had seen the original stage production in New York when I was there on vacation in 1983, and it had a profound impact on me. As a young man in my twenties, the pain and depression of Bancroft's Thelma spoke to me, since I had my own feelings of depression. While the film was undoubtedly stagey, I felt it had retained the play's power. Bancroft's performance was criticized but I enjoyed it.

Bette Davis once commented that she thought that acting on film should have a heightened quality and be more than naturalistic, and it appeared that Bancroft had the same notion. But she didn't start off that way. When she first came to Hollywood in the 1950s, she delivered what can be seen as naturalistic performances. Bancroft could be intense; but it was her soft voice that clued you in to how she acted. Broadway changed that. Her runs in *Two for the Seesaw* and *The Miracle Worker* seemed to stretch her thespian muscles and she returned to films with a stronger voice and a theatricality that never left her performances. She was now a different and a better actress. Bancroft had transitioned from being one of the West Coast movie stars like Marilyn Monroe and Elizabeth Taylor into what Molly Haskell defined (in her book *From Reverence to Rape: The Treatment of Women in the Movies*) one of the East Coast Theatah serious-artist actresses like Julie Harris, Kim Stanley and Joanne Woodward. She was overlooked for the film of *Two for the Seesaw* but was fortunate to be cast in the 1962 film of *The Miracle Worker* and she won the Best Actress Academy Award. But this led to few leading film roles.

Bancroft achieved box office power with a supporting role in *The Graduate* (1967), for which she was nominated for the Best Actress Academy Award. But again, additional leading roles did not come. She had more starring roles in the theater than in movies. On stage, Bancroft played the protagonist in *The Miracle Worker, Mother Courage and Her Children, The Devils, The Skin of Our Teeth, The Little Foxes, Golda, Duet for One, Mystery of the Rose Bouquet* and *The Occupant*. In movies, she had only played supporting roles until *The Miracle Worker* and then, after it, only the lead in *The Pumpkin Eater* (1964), *7 Women* (1966), *The Slender Thread* (1965) and *84 Charing Cross Road* (1987).

Part of the problem was that Bancroft didn't want to work so much. Married to Mel Brooks in 1964, she came to appreciate her private life and decided that she would only work when she found something special. Then she decided to have a child and she devoted her time to raising him. Bancroft had a comeback of sorts with *The Turning Point* (1977), for which she was again Oscar-nominated as Best Actress although she played a supporting role. She also directed a film, *Fatso* (1980)—then decided that she didn't want to direct again. After Bancroft received another Best Actress Academy Award nomination for a supporting role in *Agnes of God* (1985), her film appearances became supporting or cameos. Television, perhaps the refuge for aging stars, provided her with her last leading roles: Mrs. Cage (1992) in *Neil Simon's Broadway Bound* (1992) and the title role in "The Mother" (1994).

Whether she was enacting a leading role or a supporting one, Bancroft was always good. She had the range to play drama and comedy. Bancroft was assisted in her career by the marriage to Brooks: His company produced *Fatso*, *The Elephant Man* and *84 Charing Cross Road*. He also gave her small parts in his films and a co-starring role in his *To Be or Not to Be*. But she was a star before she met him and she also worked independently after they married. One wonders whether Bancroft would have worked more if she had not met and married Brooks, but that was the life she chose. In her *New York Times* obituary, Robert Berkvist wrote that she had a sultry voice and expressive mouth, that she could appear both tough and vulnerable, and that she eagerly sought out nearly every kind of role, maturing effortlessly over the decades.

This book is the first solo and in-depth study of the life and career of the actress. *Seesaw* by William Holtzman, published in 1979, was a dual biography of Bancroft and Mel Brooks. *It's Good to Be the King* was a biography of Brooks by James Robert Parish published in 2007 and while it mentioned the actress, the focus was on her husband.

Regrettably, this book cannot be viewed as the definitive study of Bancroft, since I could not track down all of her film and television work. Accessing a wide variety of sources allowed me to consider differing views of some of the events in her life and to highlight any apparent inaccuracies. I also reviewed newspapers and magazines interviews that the actress gave, with the archives of the *New York Times*, the Internet Movie Database's Related News and the website Fannetastic.com being particularly helpful. YouTube.com was also invaluable in sourcing interviews with the actress.

The book examines Bancroft's career, presented in the context of her life. Her work is listed in the order that they were made as opposed to when they were first publicly seen. A B movie, for the purposes of this study, is defined as a feature with a running time of less than 90 minutes, although an apparent low-budget and lack of stars are other contributing factors. I have not made new chapters for each of her film and TV appearances and stage shows. Rather, they are mixed into the text, where I have given an analysis of the work when possible. For what I have viewed, I have positioned Bancroft's place in the project, commented on her look and performance, provided notes on the character's importance to the narrative, and any comments I have found by the actress as well as comments on her by her director and co-stars. I have also given the critical reaction that the work received and information about any awards it earned.

1

Beginning

Anne Bancroft was born Anna Maria Louisa Italiano on September 17, 1931, in an apartment on St. Raymond Street, near the corner of Seddon Street and Maclay Avenue, in the neighborhood of St. Peters Avenue in the Bronx. She was the second daughter of Mildred *née* DiNapoli (known as Millie) and Michael Italiano. Their first daughter was Joanne. It was a lower middle-class Italian family and Bancroft would say it was your typical Italian Catholic family because she had 33 first cousins. They lived in a modest flat in the Westchester Square section of the eastern edge of Parkchester. Anna was born during the Depression; the family had it better than some, since Michael worked steadily as a cutter in Manhattan's garment district.

At an early age the girl liked to sing and dance and she was completely uninhibited. Bancroft said that her sisters had just as much talent as she but they didn't feel her need and she was so willing, nobody had to coax her. The girl would perform at the family gatherings which took place at summer picnics upstate. As her uncle strummed a guitar, she would sing. Hearing songs on the Hit Parade at the age of two, she could manage "Under a Blanket of Blue." At four, it was "Snap Your Fingers, Turn Around a Bit" and "College Rhythm." Later her repertoire included "Sleepytime Gal" and "It Had to Be You." Anna sang more like Sophie Tucker than Shirley Temple; she was an irrepressible performer and known as the "personality kid." When her family was not available, she would sing elsewhere: the deli, the corner WPA worksite or wherever she could find an audience. Anna also showed off for a handsome stranger whom she took to be a Hollywood producer until she discovered that he drove an ice truck.

Her parents were not always happy about their daughter's street corner acts and on one occasion when Anna stayed too long away from home, she received a spanking.

When Anna was six, her mother had a third daughter, Phyllis. Michael was laid off from his job so Millie took her daughters to their grandmother's house and found a job for herself as a switchboard operator at the main branch of Macy's Department Store in Manhattan's Herald Square. She kept the job even after Michael returned to work as a patternmaker.

Anna attended P.S. 12 grammar school. She excelled at her study exercises and was chosen to be the lead of the District of Columbia in her kindergarten pageant about the American Republics where she introduced all the other republics. Anna also starred as Mama Bear when the school performed *The Three Little Bears*, wearing a makeshift costume of a perforated paper bag over her head with cut-out eyes. Her teachers encouraged her to sing and dance between official school productions, and she now added eye-rolling to her act with an agility that rivaled Eddie Cantor. Despite the fact that money was tight, Millie allowed Anna to take tap-dancing lessons, which caused her to lose her appetite and weight. One source claims that Anna deliberately stopped eating because she wanted to transform into a lithe ballerina. Being Italian, Mille was not pleased with this new phenomenon and the lessons were terminated. During the week, Anna was restricted to the neighborhood where her principal amusement was the game of hide and seek. She was allowed to go to the movies on Sundays but only after she had attended services at the Santa Maria Roman Catholic Church. Any desire Anna had to date was discouraged when she saw how Joanne was punished after being caught doing so.

When Anna went to the circus, she was so enthralled by the jugglers that she told her mother she thought she could do that. But after Anna overheard her father confide to another relative his hope that one day she would become an actress, her fantasy changed. She had had vague fantasies of being famous and now latched onto the label "Actress" as her new objective, even scribbling "I want to be an actress" on the back of the apartment building. The only problem was that the girl did not know what an actress *was*. Anna had done three variety shows and a number of small club productions and now she entered Christopher Columbus High School and joined the Drama Society. She was a member of the theater clique and her classwork was consistently in the upper percentiles, but her shyness continued to be a problem. Outwardly Anna was confident and sophisticated, and she would later say that she got aggressive to cover up her awful shyness.

She also had a striking appearance. Her face was framed by thick black shoulder-length hair and had gone from a girlish roundness to a soft pear shape, leaving the cheekbones in relief and tapering down to a wide smile. Her figure also showed the first signs of womanhood, and she was constantly asked out for dates. (Millie's dating ban continued through her daughter's sophomore year.) But Anna's platonic friends in the theater group made her feel popular and also protected, which was necessary for the girl who munched a five-cent pickle and read plays as she walked home from school.

A neighbor friend was an announcer for a small radio station in Peekskill, a little town 40 miles north of the Bronx. Through him, Anna and her friends (calling themselves the Radcliffe Radio Players) filled a 15-minute slot on Saturday mornings with capsule dramatizations. These were streamlined versions of the work of Shakespeare, Poe and Hardy. For the occasion, she changed her name to Anne St. Raymond, a name she had taken from a corner street sign. In an amateur production of *Night Must Fall*, Anne was required to smoke a cigarette, a practice that her mother had forbidden her to adopt. When the girl's Aunt Kate saw this, she embarrassed her niece during a performance by shouting, "I'm going to tell your mother." Mortified, Anne rebelled against Millie's domination by taking her mother's modest jewelry and selling it for pennies in the street. However, if Millie was angered by Anne's behavior, she also made concessions to her daughter's age by lifting the ban on dating for her junior year prom.

The girl continued acting, appearing in the school's production of the melodrama *Curse You, Jack Dalton* using the stage name Anne Tulane. As she reached her senior year, Anne's passion for drama was replaced by a greater scholastic interest in science. She had come to believe that her love of acting revealed a need for attention, something that a career as a laboratory technician could just as easily satisfy. The girl seemed determined, until she met a boy and changed her plans.

Tall and good-looking, Jay Okin was one of the school's most sought-after boys and he was interested in Anne. They had worked together on a few plays and he told her that he had decided to enroll at the American Academy of Dramatic Arts. Anne decided to also enroll and asked her parents to provide the $500 tuition fee. Millie agreed and deducted the fee from her Macy's paycheck. Anne also made a contribution from the part-time jobs she took. These included being a receptionist at the Girl Scout Headquarters ($5 a week), selling chocolate-covered cherries at local drugstores, and giving English lessons to Peruvian singer Yma Sumac. But when she reported for classes at the Academy, she learned that Jay was not there.

Anne was 16, younger than most of her new classmates. She took her classes seriously, and even rehearsed scenes on an empty stage during lunch hours. The Academy provided lessons in voice, speech, dancing and fencing, with a focus on working from the exterior rather than sophisticated interior dramatic theory. The training was more technical than motivational, which was appropriate for students who first had to acquire the physical tools of performance before tackling Stanislavski. Anne was a standout in most of her classes although she was aware that there was a difference between learning to act and earning a living at it. This was a concern that became more important as Anne's graduation approached.

Two weeks before the end of the two-year term, she was rehearsing a scene from *Fly Away Home*, playing a Mexican girl. Frances Fuller, one of the teachers, recommended that she audition for *Studio One*, a popular and prestigious CBS dramatic anthology television series. Fuller happened to be married to Worthington Miner, the show's creator and producer. The actress contacted the show's production office and was assigned a time to read for casting director Robert Fryer. When she arrived for her appointment, Anne found that she was one of six girls auditioning for a part. Her turn came and she felt she read satisfactorily, and even imagined that she noticed a glimmer of approval in Fryer's eyes. After all the girls had read, he came out to the waiting room and announced that Anne Italiano had the part. Anna had dropped the St. Raymond surname, thinking it sounded pretentious. But, unhappy with her birth name, she chose another, which seemed to sound as if it had a hint of dark-eyed mystery. She made her professional debut as Anne Marno.

The idea that she would play in that week's production of "Walk the Dark Streets" on April 10, 1950, was changed so that she had to do a second read for Miner. He then assigned Marno a larger role in the following week's production of Ivan Turgenev's "The Torrents of Spring," to be broadcast on April 17, 1950. The 60-minute episode was directed by Franklin J. Schaffner from a teleplay by Joseph Liss. The plot concerned Dimitri Sanin (John Baragrey), a young Russian aristocrat who returns home to sell his family estate to finance a wedding to a German pastry shop girl, Gemma Rosselli. Complications ensue when he falls prey to a seductress, Princess Maria Nikolaevna. Sources differ as to which part Marno played though it would seem more likely the 18-year-old would have been cast as Gemma. For her one-week of rehearsal and one hour of performance, she was paid $125. Marno is said to have acted the part fluidly and without problems. When she arrived home after the show, a sign on the front door read "Welcome Home Star!" Inside were her family, friends and relatives, all of whom applauded as she entered.

Miner next cast Marno in the comedy *The Goldbergs*, the TV adaptation of the popular NBC and CBS radio show centering on a Jewish family in the Bronx. Arlen "Fuzzy" McQuade, who played Rosalie on the show, reported that Marno was known as Anne Italiano. She said the actress had a warm voice and a lovely quality about her and everybody loved her. McQuade and Marno became very good girlfriends, and although Marno was a couple of years older than McQuade, it didn't make a difference. They used to put each other's hair up in curlers and shop together. McQuade said Marno was very Italian in her manners and McQuade loved that because her own mother was Italian.

Not all of the *Goldbergs* episodes survive. Though it is said that Marno made more than once appearance, the exact number is unknown. One episode which she is in is preserved as a bonus feature on the DVD of Aviva Kempner's documentary about actress and screenwriter Gertrude Berg, *Yoo-Hoo, Mrs. Goldberg*. The episode "Mother-In-Law" was written by Berg (as were all the show's episodes) and directed by Walter Hart. In it Marno, uncredited, played Joyce, the new married wife of George (actor unknown) and daughter-in-law of Aunt Elka (Sarah Krohner). Elka believes that Joyce does not like her because she does not call her "Mother." Joyce reveals to Molly (Berg) that she believes Elka does not like *her* because she does not call her "daughter." Joyce is shown to be different from the three other daughters-in-law who all call Elka variations on Mother and agree to the idea of Elka moving in with them. Joyce explains to Elka that she won't let her move in to be taken advantage of, and then calls her "Ma" though Elka does not respond with "daughter."

Marno's appears in five scenes, some of them continuous. Her hair is short with a side part and she is taller than the other women in the show. Marno uses her strong voice and then her soft voice when confronting Elka. She has self-conscious body language, like touching her face and fiddling with her clothes and having her hands in her skirt pockets, to presumably show Joyce's awkwardness in the situation. Marno's over-gesturing registers as the expression of an inexperienced performer.

Between *Goldbergs* appearances, Marno continued on *Studio One*, working for 49 of the next 79 weeks. On May 29, 1950, she played Maria Cassini, an Italian hat check girl at the State Line Cafe, in Miner's adaptation of the Don Mankiewicz story "The Man Who Had Influence." Directed again by Franklin Schaffner, the story told of wealthy businessman J.C. Grant (Stanley Ridges) who attempts to bribe a judge to get a suspended sentence for his playboy son David (Robert Sterling), found guilty of manslaughter. Marno played the girl killed in an automobile accident in David's car when he was apparently driving drunk. The actors are credited after the show's title but Marno's name is only in the end credits, billed seventh. The actress acts in one scene in the show though she is seen a few times—taking hats, selling cigarettes and chatting with David. Marno uses her soft voice and, though her lines are inconsequential, we see her insulted by the idea proffered by David of him giving her money for quid pro quo and later being flattered by his flirting. The narrative does not show us the car accident or Maria in it, but this is not a surprise given the studio-bound nature of the piece.

In December 4, 1950's "Letter from Cairo," Marno played a Czechoslovakian girl used by Mitch Henderson (Charlton Heston), a young American intelligence agent in postwar Iron Curtain Europe. The episode was written by Miner, based on a story by James Robbins Miller, and directed by Lela Swift. Its CBS press releases described Marno as a "find." Schaffner considered the actress excellent because she could play comedy or drama. She commented that Heston was rugged and so brawny that he didn't know his own strength. Marno said that in the show he gave her such a smackeroo that she could hardly stand up afterwards.

Despite the high opinion of the director, she was the first to admit that she still had everything to learn about acting. When talking to another rising actor, Rod Steiger, he reportedly asked her what she thought about the Method's patriarch, Stanislavski. Marno replied that she didn't know who he was so Steiger lent her a copy of the book *An Actor Prepares*. She did not read it since she preferred to learn from on-the-job experience and the comments of those around her.

Marno felt that her technique was improving with each new role, and she took direction well. If one thing bothered her, it was the possibility of being typecast. Her youth made it logical that she was cast as ingénues, but her dark hair and soft features seemed to mark her for ethnic parts. The actress was aware of this restriction since, for the most part, TV dramatists were male and white and their ethnic female characters often stereotypes. However, the benefits of the working opportunities she was being given seemed to outweigh the potential danger of typecasting.

The actress then made the first of seven appearances on the *Lux Video Theatre* anthology, broadcast by CBS from 1950 to 1954 and then by NBC to 1957. Marno's first appearance was in the Christmas drama "A Child Is Born" (December 25, 1950). The show had a teleplay by Robert Cenadella, adapted from a story by Stephen Vincent Benet, and was directed by Fielder Cook. It was a remake of the *Actors Studio* 1949 production, and the same story would also be remade for TV in 1952, 1954, 1955 and 1956. The story was about the birth of Christ through the eyes of an innkeeper (Gene Lockhart) and his wife (Fay Bainter). In the 1950 version Marno played Leah.

The actress' next role was in "Night Break," an episode of CBS's 30-minute mystery-thriller series *Suspense*. It was broadcast on February 6, 1951. She then appeared in the *Ford Theater Hour* episode "The Golden Mouth" (February 23, 1951). This show was another 60-minute anthology series filmed live in New York and broadcast on CBS. Schaffner directed from a teleplay by Joseph Liss which adapted the play by Charles S. Belden and Frederick Stephani.

She returned to *Studio One* to play another ethnic girl, this time the Latvian Lisa Berzins, in "Wintertime" (April 2, 1951). The teleplay was adapted by Robert Anderson from a story by Jan Valtin, and was directed by Paul Nickell. Lisa, a 24-year-old refugee in 1946 in Nurdune, Germany, is befriended by a German Merchant Marine officer, Martin Helm (Patric Knowles), who comes home after four years in a Texan prisoner of war camp. He takes a job as captain of a tugboat but his Communist spy engineer Wetterman (Dennis Harrison) wants to give Lisa to the Russians, since she is believed to be a member of a band of terrorists who escaped from Camp Buchenwald. Helm hides her in the ruins of his old house and he is charged with the killing of Wetterman and imprisoned. There is ambiguity about Lisa's fate, since she appears to be freed by American MPs from the Communists, but is last seen standing behind the bars of a locked courtroom.

The narrative makes Martin the protagonist and Lisa a supporting character. Marno is first seen in male drag, since Lisa disguises herself as a soldier. Her gender is revealed when her cap is removed and her collar-length thick hair falls out of it. This androgyny continues when Lisa is given a man's long coat to wear over a dress. Marno makes you believe the gentle gratitude she has to Martin for helping her, even if the character is romanticized. Lisa is presented as more desirable to Martin than his former fiancée, 31-year-old Marianne (Leni Stengel), who is older and embittered from her war trauma.

Lisa is a morally ambiguous character, since she disguises herself to stow away on the tugboat and lies to try and obtain a passport. She offers to leave Martin's house to avoid getting him in trouble for harboring her, so she is not totally self-centered. But we never see the couple kiss, only hug to show their affection for each other despite the fact that we are told they are in love. Lisa shows an edge when she orders Martin to take her home from the black market office via the haughty look she gives the soldier who takes her arm when she is arrested, and when she spits in the face of her torturer, Oberkriminalsekretar Kurz (Kurt Katch).

The actors are credited after the show's title and Marno second after Knowles. Nickell gives the actress her best close-up after we hear Lisa being tortured and there is fake blood coming from her mouth. However he fails in the three-minute monologue she has telling Lisa's backstory, since the camerawork is clumsy and unflattering to the actress, with the staging not helping since Lisa doesn't look at Martin to whom she speaks. Marno uses an accent for Lisa as Latvian, though her delivery of it falters. Her performance has self-conscious touches like fiddling with her cap and restless walking which fits Lisa's feeling that she is initially Martin's prisoner.

The show was reportedly well-received and led to Marno being offered a role in the CBS 30-minute drama series *Danger* which was to be directed by one of television's most promising young directors, Sidney Lumet. In "The Killer Scarf," written by Walter Bernstein, Marno played young circus acrobat Heidi, in love with both her guardian (Greg Morton) and an animal trainer (Ray Danton). The show had the distinction of being filmed on location backstage at Madison Square Garden where the King Brothers and Barnum and Bailey circus was in town, performing in the Garden's main arena. A still, published in the *New York Times* on April 29, 1951, shows Marno sitting on a fence in front a lion's cage, next to Danton, Morton and Stanley Prager, who played Irving, a hot dog vendor. Broadcast on May 1, 1951, it included authentic touches like the sounds of caged animals roaring off and on camera, circus performers as extras, and Prager shuttling back and forward selling hot dogs. One downside of this authenticity was that at one point a snarling leopard stepped on one of Marno's lines. As Anne Bancroft, the actress would work again with Lumet on the comedies *Garbo Talks* (1984) and *Critical Care* (1997).

She next appeared in the mystery crime drama series *The Adventures of Ellery Queen* in the May 10, 1951, episode "The Chinese Mummer Mystery." (Some sources give the date as June 7, 1951, but this may be the date the episode was repeated.) The teleplay was by Norman Lessing.

Some sources claim that Marno was next cast in the *Suspense* episode "A Vision of Death" (July 31, 1951). She is said to have played a young woman with psychic powers in a murder plot, and co-starred with Henry Hull and Jerome Cowan. The episode appears to be the same story as that of a *Suspense* radio play broadcast on March 8, 1951. The Ronald Colman-starring radio version starred Cathy Lewis as Aurora Stone, the part that Marno presumably also played. This radio play is available to listeners. It is written by Walter Newman and based on a story by Jeffrey Hausner, and produced and directed by Elliott Lewis. In the radio play, Aurora tries to manipulate Jud Stone (Colman) into murdering the couple's manager, Harry Arnold (Larry Dobkin), because she claims she has a telepathic premonition that he is going to kill her. Her real objective is to get rid of her husband. Jud outwits her, and Aurora is shot by Harry. Marno is said to have been pleased with her casting as the duplicitous wife because it was a change from the guileless virgins she was normally cast as.

The actress next appeared in another *Danger* episode, "A Murderer's Face" (August 14, 1951) with Lumet directing. She played the consort of a gangster (Robert Pastene) who has his face altered by plastic surgery. On September 18, 1951, Marno appeared in the NBC 30-minute drama series *Armstrong Circle Theatre* episode "Flame-Out." The story concerned a jet pilot (Leslie Nielsen) dealing with his fear of dying in a crash after witnessing another pilot's death. It was written by Roger Caris, produced by Hudson Faussett and directed by Garry Simpson. On September 26, 1951, Marno was in the CBS 30-minute mystery series *The Web* episode "The Customs of the Country."

On October 22, 1951, she starred in the NBC 30-minute horror series *Lights Out* episode "The Deal." This was written by James Blumgarten, produced by Herbert Swope, Jr., and directed by Laurence Schwab, Jr. Bookseller Charlie Drome (Tom Ewell) makes a deal with the Agent (Martin Gabel) to sell his wife Helen (Marno) for $50,000 to his client, the Devil (Joseph Wiseman). However Charlie is surprised to learn that the Devil changes his mind about wanting Helen when he decides that she is no longer suitable for him after she rejects him. The change of mind comes after Helen changes her attitude to her husband. She is initially an embittered woman, unhappy with Charlie and wanting material possessions that he cannot supply. This is what makes him want to sell her, since he decides to use the money he gets to give to her. While Helen's character may seem to change because of her husband's windfall, it is suggested that there is more to her transformation. At a casino, she tries to stop Charlie from gambling since she is aware of the chance that he may lose what he has already won, and she later tells him that she no longer wants the things she thought she did and is just happy to love him. Helen also reacts without anger when Charlie tells her of the deal he had made.

Ewell is billed above the show's title and Marno fourth-billed. She wears her hair in a sculptured fashion and sports a negligee with a large hair ribbon that prefigures Bancroft's look as Ma Beckoff in *Torch Song Trilogy* (1988). Marno's voice is initially brittle and she softens it for Helen's change. Her hard surface is apparent in the way she primps and brushes her nails. The moment when she dances alone to a record in the bookstore backroom apartment suggests the romanticism to be later revealed. Schwab gives Marno an extreme close-up laughing at the casino, and has her and Ewell look directly into the camera for the episode's final shot, where the Devil warns that he may return to claim her. The actress makes her character's transition believable, so that she goes from being unlikable to sympathetic, though Helen as the shrew is a more entertaining person.

In 1951, Marno found a boyfriend. He was the actor John Ericson, an athletic all–American type with a height of 6'2". Born in Germany in 1926, he was four years older than Marno. He was also a student at the American Academy of Dramatic Arts and had appeared on some of the live television shows like *Studio One*, though not on the same episodes as Marno. It is reported that the couple met after he had returned from Italy where he had a starring role in the MGM drama *Teresa* (1951). That film had been in production from early May to mid–July 1950.

Despite the differences in their professional experience and age, it was said that Marno was the more confident one. The couple called their relationship an engagement although no wedding plans were announced. It seemed that at this time, both actors were more concerned with their respective careers. Ericson was cast by director Jose Ferrer in the Broadway production of a new comedy by Donald Bevan and Edmund Trzcinski, *Stalag 17*. Making his debut, he played the leading role of Sefton. A great success, the show ran from May 8, 1951, to June 21, 1952, at the 48th Street Theatre. Ericson stayed on for the national tour for another six months, and this job caused a separation from Marno.

In the summer of 1951, Marno was approached by Frank Gregory, a test director for 20th Century–Fox. Each year he put together screen tests to showcase New York talent for the West Coast office. For the test of an actor named Doug Rogers, Gregory asked Marno if she would assist him. Another source claims that it was Rogers who asked her for the favor. Since the actor's name is so common, it is hard to identify him and know what his prior experience was. The scene being filmed was from the Alfred Hayes play *The Girl on the Via Flaminia*, featuring an American soldier in occupied Rome during the final months of World War II with an Italian girl. The property was chosen since Fox was interested in making a film of the play, though this never eventuated. Marno agreed to participate because, although she was successful on TV, she was attracted to the idea of movie stardom. She would watch newsreels to see stars arriving at Hollywood premieres, and that's what she thought acting was. In rehearsal, Gregory saw how the actress shone. The test had been designed to favor Rogers but Gregory decided to redistribute the footage equally between the two actors. This allowed Marno a share of the camera time and close-ups. The test was sent off to the West Coast for screening. Marno never saw Rogers again.

On October 12, 1951, Marno was on Fifth Avenue watching the Columbus Day Parade when she was pulled aside by her agent, who apparently had been frantically searching for her among the crowd that lined the sidewalk. He found Marno in front of Bergdorf Goodman and reportedly pressed her against the shop's plate glass to tell her the news: Fox had passed on Doug Rogers but they were eager to sign her. She decided to accept the offer. Marno and John Ericson both considered TV a way to into movies, so they made a plan: She was to go west and start work for Fox while he finished his run of the play and then join her. They would also then be married. But this was not to be. In mid-November, Marno left New York with her mother and flew to Hollywood.

At the age of 20, the actress needed Millie's parental consent to enter into the Fox contract. The both of them stood before Judge Orlando H. Rhodes who reviewed the offer. It detailed that $20,000 was to be paid for Marno's first year of work, with a sliding scale of up to $1,500 per week should she stay for the seven-year term. Presumably the studio had the option of dropping her after one year if they were not happy. The law required a statement of expenses which Millie provided and which included a trousseau for her daughter's upcoming marriage. Rhodes made the supervisory gesture of suggesting the actress agree to invest $75 a week, or 15 percent of her salary, in government bonds. Marno accepted this idea and the contract was validated. She was now the protégée and property of 20th Century–Fox.

In late November, Marno took an apartment on Sunset Boulevard between Ciro's and the Mocambo. For two weeks she was unoccupied and the young girl said she made her own fun. Her contract became active on November 21, 1951, and her signing with the studio was reported in the *New York Times* on November 26, as was her first film assignment. This was to be the second feminine lead in *Don't Bother to Knock* (1952), to star Richard Widmark and Marilyn Monroe. The actress was required to report to work on December 3, 1951. In the interim, she had studio orientation and a meeting with Fox's production chief, Darryl F. Zanuck. She intended to begin her film career as Anne Marno, since she had found it served her well enough in television. But he did not like it, feeling that her coloring and features were already suggestive of her Mediterranean ethnicity and that having such an ethnic name as well would typecast her. She acquiesced to his better judgment and was handed a list from which to choose a new one. The names were either a variation on existing movie star names like "Lana" or "Joan" or trick ones. The actress would later tease that some of these trick names were "Candy Bar" and "Paddy

Wagon." She settled on the one that sounded Anglo-Saxon and which she thought was the only one not to remind her of a bubble dancer: Bancroft. Zanuck gave his blessing.

The thriller *Don't Bother to Knock* was an adaptation of the Charlotte Armstrong novel *Mischief*. It was designed as a dramatic starring vehicle for an actress, but not Bancroft. In 1949 *the Los Angeles Times* had announced that Dorothy McGuire had been cast in the leading female role and Jules Dassin was to direct. Then the studio passed it to their newest hot prospect, Marilyn Monroe. Five years older than Bancroft, Monroe had signed with Fox in 1946 and since then had only appeared in uncredited bit parts and supporting roles. The studio was now willing to see if she could do more, and cast her as a mentally disturbed babysitter. The producer was Julien Blaustein and shooting took place from December 3, 1951, to January 14, 1952, at Fox.

Bancroft played "High-Heeled Cowgirl" singer Lyn Lesley, who performs in the Round-Up Bar of New York's McKinley Hotel. She sings six songs, "How About You?," "A Rollin' Stone," "Manhattan," "There's a Lull in My Life," "How Blue the Night" and "Chattanooga Choo Choo." Bancroft is dubbed by Eve Marley aka Eve Marlee, which must have disappointed the actress. As well as seeing Lyn perform in the bar, we also hear her singing over the hotel room's speaker system. The narrative has her as the former girlfriend of Chicago pilot Jed Towers (Richard Widmark), who has come to see her to ask to begin their relationship again after she has written to him calling it off. Lyn tells him that she rejects his marriage proposal because of the way he treats people and because

Still for *Don't Bother to Knock* (1952).

she feels he "lacks an understanding heart." The narrative will see her opinion of Jed change thanks to his concern over Nell Forbes (Monroe), whom he initially expresses a sexual interest in.

Widmark and Monroe are credited before the film's title and Bancroft after it, billed third. She appears in five scenes. Her costumes are by Travilla. Bancroft's performance alternates between using a soft voice and some edge to demonstrate Lyn's anger at Jed. Director Roy Baker gives the actress her best close-up to show a look of anger for the rude way he treats the bar's photographer Janie (Gloria Blondell). The director also strangely has Bancroft use upstaging action in her first two scenes, fiddling with a glass and then touching her arm and then the bar as Lyn speaks. Monroe and Bancroft only share one scene, at the climax when Lyn goes to Nell in the hotel lobby. Lyn asks Nell not to use a razor blade before Jed joins them to calm Nell before she is taken away by the police.

The film was released in New York on July 18, 1952, and in Los Angeles on July 30, 1952, with the taglines "SHE'S DYNAMITE! It Opens the Door on the Screen's Most Exciting New Personality—MARILYN MONROE," "You never met her type before…" and "…a wicked sensation as the lonely girl in room 809!" It was lambasted by Bosley Crowther in the *New York Times*. *Variety* wrote that Bancroft "scores brightly." The film was a box office hit.

Bancroft commented that it was a remarkable experience because it was one of the rare times in all her Hollywood experiences where she felt the give-and-take that could only happen when you worked with good actors. The actress said that she felt in her scene with Monroe that Monroe's expression of being helpless and in pain was so real that she really reacted to her. She was so moved that tears came into her eyes, though they are not apparent in the footage. Bancroft said that such a moment occurred rarely, if ever again, in her early film work. She also commented that she never got to kiss Widmark in the film, and the closest they got was holding hands. But she said it was a promise of things to come since she couldn't wait to do a movie with him again.

Director Baker said that Bancroft was a revelation. The casting director had shown him the *Girl on the Via Flaminia* test scene and Baker thought that the actress was all right. But after she was cast in the film, he said she was *more* than all right. Perhaps in recognition of her work in the film, she would later receive the Golden Key Award as one of Hollywood's potential stars.

The actress' personal life was not going as well as her professional one: Her marriage plans were now halted permanently. In Chicago with the play, Ericson began a new relationship with a singer named Milly Coury. Though he had planned to come to Hollywood after signing with MGM, he first went back to Chicago to be with her. Ericson married Coury in 1953. Bancroft tried the Hollywood social scene, talking to the gossip columnists, going to parties and attending premieres wearing sequins and furs.

She also made more movies. The color adventure *Treasure of the Golden Condor* (1953) was shot on location in Guatemala in December 1951, which was reportedly the first time the Central American country was used as a location for a major Hollywood film. The film has a card revealing that the treasure hunt was photographed in the jungles and highlands of Guatemala, and that the native rituals and costumes were authentic. Shooting also took place at Fox from January 13 to late February 1952 with additional sequences filmed in late March and late April 1952. Producer Jules Buck reported that Otto Preminger directed a one-hour retake for the film in which a boa constrictor appeared, and other unspecified scenes. The screenplay was by director Delmer Daves and based on the 1941 novel *Benjamin Blake* by Edison Marshall. The novel had been previously made by Fox as *Son of Fury: The Story of Benjamin Blake* (1942) with Frances Farmer playing the role that Bancroft now took. Working titles for the film were *The Golden Serpent, Condor's Nest* and *The Golden Condor*. The story concerned Jean Paul (Cornel Wilde), the bonded servant of his uncle Edouard Marquis de St. Malo (George Macready) in 18th century Normandy, France. After a fight with Edouard, who has him charged with assault, he goes with the Scottish adventurer MacDougal (Finlay Currie) and retrieves Mayan jewelry from Guatemala. Jean Paul then returns to France to settle scores.

Bancroft played the supporting part of Marie, the Comtesse de St. Malo, daughter of Edouard. This duplicitous character says that she is in love with Jean Paul, then becomes engaged to someone else when he is away, and later betrays him when she tells her father where he can be located so that Edouard can attempt to have him killed. Marie is also seemingly more enamored of the ruby necklace Jean Paul brings her than of him, and only agrees to marry him to keep her privileged lifestyle. The actress is billed fifth under the title and she appears in five scenes, wearing period hairstyles and period costumes by Dorothy Jeakins. Despite playing a Frenchwomen, Bancroft does not use a French accent but then neither do the actors playing Frenchmen. She may not present as pretty as a conventional beauty like Fox contract player Constance Towers, who plays Clara MacDougal, Wilde's other love interest, but she certainly has more acting ability.

The actress uses her soft voice with a mild edge to portray Marie's haughtiness, and she is more effective in her one scene with Macready than in her scenes with Wilde. Marie shows that she has passion when she brandishes a knife at Jean Paul after he pushes her, but this passion is otherwise lacking in the love scenes with him. She gets one funny line when tells Jean Paul, "I've been a comtesse my whole life. I wouldn't want to be a nobody." Director Daves gives Bancroft a good close-up in her last scene, when Marie watches Jean Paul leave her.

The film was released on February 4, 1953, with the tagline "LOST WORLD OF THE MAYANS!" It was praised by *Variety* who commented that Bancroft looked good in her costume. Howard H. Thompson in the *New York Times* wrote that she was no less persuasive than the dialogue. The film was not a box office success.

Bancroft reported that Wilde was really a dear. Whenever he kissed her, he always made sure that she was in the best light for the photographers and that her face was in a good position for the camera. Bancroft said Wilde was very technical that way.

The actress was sought for the part of Lina Patch in the MGM western *The Naked Spur* (1953). This was reportedly because she was the then-girlfriend of screenwriter Harold Jack Bloom. However, since Bancroft was with Fox, she could not be cast in the part, which was assigned to Janet Leigh.

Filmed after *Treasure of the Golden Condor* but released before it, Bancroft's next role was in the musical *Tonight We Sing* (1953) for producer George Jessel. The film was the story of the Russian impresario Solomon Isaievich Hurok, loosely based on his 1946 autobiography. Working titles for the film included *Impresario, The Hurok Story, Heaven for Sale, Stars in My Pocket, The Music Maker* and *The Music Master*. In 1945, Jessel had read galleys of Hurok's book and reportedly Eugenie Leontovich and George S. George worked on a screenplay adaptation. In November 1945, *The Hollywood Reporter* announced that Gregory Ratoff was to direct but then the project lay dormant between 1946 and

1951 until the success of the MGM biographical musical *The Great Caruso* (1951). Interest in the film was revived with Jean Negulesco reportedly assigned to direct, though in January 1952 *The Hollywood Reporter* said it was to be Henry Koster. The movie's eventual director Mitchell Leisen cast David Wayne in the leading role, and the new screenplay adaptation was by Harry Kurnitz and George Oppenheimer.

Bancroft was cast as Hurok's wife Emma, a character older than Anne, sometimes twice and three times her age. Jessel cast Bancroft because he wanted to discover a new star, despite the fact that Bancroft had been discovered first in television and then again in film in *Don't Bother to Knock*. The film was in production from April 18 to June 12, 1952, with an additional sequence shot in late June 1952.

Bancroft is billed fifth under the title. Her character only extends beyond the cliché of the passive reactive wife when Emma leaves Hurok in the last third of the narrative. She does so because she feels neglected by Hurok, who she feels devotes his greater interest to the needs of his clients. (Hurok forgets their wedding anniversary, after he has failed to keep his promise of a honeymoon.) Emma returns to her husband, who appears to make no great effort to find her, when she learns that his company is bankrupt. She tells him, "You hurt me but not as much as I was hurting myself by being away from you." Emma's awareness that Hurok's work is more important than their marriage is confirmed as the narrative ends: After he again promises her a honeymoon, Hurok is distracted by the singing voice of the driver of the hansom cab they ride in.

Tonight We Sing was Bancroft's first film in color. There is no credit for hair with the styles changing from bangs for the youthful Emma to off-her-forehead for the older woman. Bancroft is dressed by Renie, who regrettably has her wear the same blue gown on two occasions, though perhaps this is to indicate the Huroks' limited budget for clothes for themselves. Another poor choice is the large feather on the black hat she wears in her reconciliation scenes with Hurok, since it draws attention from her face. The actress mostly uses her soft voice as Emma, and even her big scene where she tells Hurok of her disappointment with their marriage has her anger so understated as to be barely existent. Leisen does not give Bancroft any complimentary coverage when Emma cries after Hurok comes to her on their wedding night after having abandoned her for the theater. Her reconciliation scene has the actress kissing David Wayne with abandon, which is rather shocking given the lack of expression of affection between the two shown previously. And in the scene when Hurok's bankruptcy is solved by Feodor Chaliapin (Ezio Pinza), Bancroft has a moment where Emma gives her husband a sly look of disbelief when she hears how close the two men are supposed to be. A still of Bancroft wearing a long white fox piece is from a deleted scene.

The feature was released in New York on February 12, 1953, with the tagline "The greatest treasure of entertainment in your lifetime!" It was praised by *Variety*, who said that Bancroft "impresses favorably." the *New York Times*' Bosley Crowther said that Bancroft provides "one vagrant dribble of pathos" when Emma discovers that a handsome brooch held by Hurok is not for her but for his client Pavlova (Tamara Toumanova), to celebrate their professional bond.

Bancroft commented on kissing David Wayne, saying that you didn't know what to expect from him. But once they got in a clinch, she found out that here was a guy who knew it was the touch and not the pressure of the lips that counted. Bancroft reported that one kiss in the film was so sexy that it was cut out.

In his autobiography *The Good, the Bad, and Me: In My Anecdotage*, Eli Wallach reported that he made a screen test with the actress and Jean Negulesco for the part of Hurok. The actor had at this time never made a film but was a friend of David Wayne. The test with Bancroft was the scene where Hurok has forgotten to bring his wife a present on their anniversary. Darryl F. Zanuck, unimpressed with Wallach, assigned Wayne the part.

It was reported that Bancroft impressed Isaac Stern, who played violinist Eugene Ysaye in the film. Making his first (and last) film appearance, he admired her "quickness in getting inside an idea and demonstrating it cleanly before the camera." Stern also said that unlike the other performers who tended to be theatrical rather than naturalistic, Bancroft "managed to convey with some accuracy the feeling of the period and the person she was portraying."

The *New York Times* reported on October 7, 1952, that the actress' contract with Fox had been renewed after the one-year period for another year. However Bancroft had to wait almost a year to make her next film for them and it signaled a period where she was relegated to work in the studio's B movies. The new film was the black-and-white sports comedy *The Kid from Left Field* (1953) which gave the actress her first above-the-title billing, billed under Dan Dailey. It was shot on location at the baseball stadium Wrigley Field in Los Angeles and at Fox from March 3 to 30, 1953. The screenplay was by Jack Sher and the film had the working title *The Kid in Left Field*. Larry "Coop" Cooper (Dailey), an ex-ballplayer, now peanut vendor, gives strategy tips to the Bisons baseball team via his nine-year-old son, Chris "Christy" Cooper (Billy Chapin), who is hired as a bat boy but soon becomes the team's manager. Bancroft played Marian Foley, secretary to the team's owner Fred F. Whacker (Ray Collins) and the fiancée of the team's third baseman Pete Haines (Lloyd Bridges). Marian is important to the narrative for taking Christy to meet Whacker, who hires him, and for also suggesting to Whacker that the club publicize the fact that Christy is the manager. Her romance with Pete is secondary: She breaks up with him because she feels he should retire from the game and get a job as a St. Louis sporting goods salesman. Since Pete is 36, he is considered old for a baseball player, and his performance falters after she breaks up with him over his refusal to take the job. The secondary plot gets a resolution when he eventually agrees with her and decides to hang up his cleats.

For Bancroft it was a return to a contemporary role after two period films. Her hair is worn short. Her best moment is perhaps in the scene when Pete accepts Marian's notion that he should retire. Director Harmon Jones stages the action so that Bridges walks away from her and the camera stays on the face of the actress as she expresses realization of Pete's change of mind.

The film was released on July 31, 1953, with the taglines "The Grand Picture About the Grandest Game of All—You'll Love Every Wonderful Minute of It!" and "The wackily wonderful story that waves pennants in your heart!" It was lambasted by Bosley

Portrait for *The Kid from Left Field* (1953).

Crowther in the *New York Times*. It was remade in 1979 as an NBC-TV movie with Tricia O'Neill as Marion Fowler.

On May 5, 1953, the *New York Times* reported that Bancroft had been cast as a first-century Roman temptress in Fox' *The Story of Demetrius*. Another working title for the film was *The Gladiators*, with the 1954 film's release title becoming *Demetrius and the Gladiators*. Filmed in CinemaScope, the historical actioner was a sequel to the Fox's *The Robe* (1953) with Victor Mature reprising his role as Demetrius. The screenplay was by Philip Dunne, based on a character created by Lloyd C. Douglas, and the director was *Treasure of the Golden Condor*'s Delmer Daves. The film was shot at Fox from May 25 to July 1953 with additional photography done on September 16 and 17,. The story follows Demetrius of Corinth who procured the robe of Jesus at his crucifixion and is taken from the village of Cana to be made a gladiator for the amusement of the Roman emperor Caligula (Jay Robinson).

Bancroft played the supporting role of Paula, one of the women provided as entertainment for the gladiators the night before their games for the birthday of Caligula. The implication is that she is a prostitute, as evidence by the makeup that Lucia (Debra Paget) wears when Paula later takes her to the second feast. Paula is also from Corinth but is not presented as a romantic rival to Lucia or Messalina (Susan Hayward) for the affections of Demetrius. She seems kind when she goes to Cana to tell Lucia about Demetrius' upcoming second games battle and to take her back to see him the night before. Unfortunately, they decided to present Lucia as another girl to be offered to the gladiators at their feast, since it leads to Lucia being attacked by Dardanius (Richard Egan) and ending up in a coma. Paula is also shown to be brave in trying to stop Dardanius from his advance, which none of the other girls appear to do. Ultimately the role is minor but it does have some impact, since Paula taking Lucia to the feast leads to her coma and that leads to the demonstration of the supposed power of the robe to provide eternal life.

The actress is billed fifth under the title and she appears in three scenes. Her hair was worn in a sculptured short style. Bancroft is funny in her first scene as Paula eats when she flirts with Demetrius, and she uses her soft voice except later when she yells and screams when Lucia is attacked by Dardanius.

The film was released in Los Angeles on June 16, 1954, and in New York on June 18, 1954, with the tagline "It begins where *The Robe* left off!" Praised by *Variety* and the *New York Times*' Bosley Crowther, it was a box office success.

Producer Stanley Rubin proposed that Bancroft star as Kay the saloon singer in the western *River of No Return* (1954) which went into production in July 1953. Director Otto Preminger wanted Marilyn Monroe and she was cast.

Bancroft next got over-the-top billing with Cameron Mitchell for the B-level crime mystery *Gorilla at Large* (1954). It was filmed in September 1953 on location at the Nu Pike Amusement Park in Long Beach, California, and at the RKO-Pathé Studios. A Panoramic Production, it was released by Fox. It had a screenplay by Leonard Praskins and Barney Slater and was directed by Harmon Jones. The film had the working title *The Gorilla*. The gorilla of the plot was Goliath, the main attraction at the Garden of Evil amusement park run by Cy Miller (Raymond Burr), whose trapeze artist wife Laverne was played by Bancroft. Goliath is thought to be the killer of two men in the park, although it turns out that the big monkey has been framed. The climax has him escape from his enclosure and run amok. This may have had more resonance if it wasn't that the gorilla was obviously a man in a suit (George Barrows). Laverne was a femme fatale,

Still for *Gorilla at Large* (1954).

married to Cy but desirous of Mitchell's apprentice, law student Joey Matthews. Her bad girl is presented in opposition to Joey's good girl fiancée, ticket seller Audrey Baxter (Charlotte Austin). Laverne is given a backstory of duplicity: She was the girlfriend of the gorilla handler Kovacs (Peter Whitney) when he was in charge of a circus, dumped him for Cy, then dumped Cy for a new trapeze partner who was killed during their act when she literally dropped him. This all prefigures the narrative where she will try to seduce Joey although she does not do so in any overt attempt to rid herself of Cy, with whom she is still congenial. Laverne is said to have committed the two murders because both men knew she had deliberately dropped her aerial act partner, although Cy also knew and she hadn't killed him. The murders are said to have been by broken necks so it is a pity that we never see a demonstration of Laverne's physical strength, apart from her agility on the trapeze.

Bancroft is billed above the title and second after Cameron Mitchell. Her trapeze work was done by a double except for one scene where she hangs from a bar. Costumes are by Renie and include a series of body suits and shorts to show off Bancroft's legs, with a color preference of red. Laverne being a smoker suggests her duplicity and the actress provides several smoldering looks. Her adultery is limited to a single kiss with Joey, although in one scene she uses the gesture of touching her mouth. The silliness of the narrative and perhaps the height of the actress' humiliation is when she is carried away in the arms of the gorilla in the climax, although she redeems herself in her last scene: Seeing Joey again after she has been rescued, and before the police take her away for the two murders, Laverne's look to him changes from a smile to concern to one of craziness.

The film was released on May 27, 1954, before *Demetrius and the Gladiators*, with the taglines "In 3-D!," "From the highest point of the carnival midway … he unleashes a terror never known by mortal man before!," "Get out of his way—Before it's too late!" and "The hate-beast who lives to kill is loose!" Bosley Crowther (the *New York Times*) wrote that Bancroft's playing was solemn.

In her book *Tales of a Hollywood Housewife: A Memoir by the First Mrs. Lee Marvin*, Betty Marvin writes that her husband admitted to having an affair with Bancroft during the film's shooting. But since she describes Marvin as being in Mexico at the time, it is assumed that she confused this film with Bancroft and Marvin's later *A Life in the Balance* (1955). Decades later, Cameron Mitchell was told by Mel Brooks that he was the star of his favorite picture: *Gorilla at Large*. The actor laughed when he heard this and understood that Brooks' reason was that Bancroft was in it. Mitchell commented that he thought she was very good and sexy in the film.

Bancroft had reportedly grown tired of dating and was looking to get married. She later confessed that she was so primed for it that she would have married George Jessel had he proposed. She met Martin A. May, the boyfriend of a girl who had gone out of town on vacation. He was nine years older than Bancroft and a USC law student. Blonde, tall and good-looking, May was the son of a landed, oil-rich Texan family. She assumed that he began to spend time with her because he missed his girlfriend but soon the couple became involved and they eloped on July 1, 1953.

The marriage got off to a rocky start. May wanted to tell the news personally to his mother but as he waited for the right moment, he thought it best that the couple keep their separate apartments to ensure secrecy. Bancroft reluctantly complied and this pretense was kept up for six months. Even after their secret had been revealed, Bancroft still had doubts as to whether the match was going to work. She was dumbfounded as to why May kept a loaded gun under his pillow but also concerned about his difficulties passing the California bar exam. Bancroft would say that his occupation was being a rich boy. It also didn't help that May had a total estrangement from the acting profession which left the couple with little in common. The most divisive elements were the clash of their backgrounds and temperaments. May came from a moneyed WASP western rural upbringing. Bancroft's was poor Italian-Catholic eastern and urban. Friends gave the union little chance of survival.

The actress made a return to TV for the *Omnibus* episode "The Capital of the World," broadcast live by CBS on December 6, 1953. Filmed in New York, the show was an Ernest Hemingway adaptation directed by Yul Brynner. The story was about a brave young boy (Sal Mineo) who dreams of becoming a bullfighter. Bancroft played the part of The Sister. She also appeared in the *Kraft Television Theatre* 60-minute comedy "To Live in Peace" which was broadcast on NBC on December 16, 1953. This had a teleplay by George Faulkner based on the play by Victor Rietta and directed by Harry Herrmann. The story was set in a small Italian mountain village, where a relative of Napoleon Bonaparte is called to take a high office in Paris.

Bancroft said that working in pictures made great demands, with personal appearances and tests when you were not on a picture; and when you *were* working, there was no time for anything else. The actress said she was seduced by every script. She thought every picture was the best and that she was Greta Garbo. Bancroft admitted that it was the ability to accept these terrible lies that kept her going.

On January 1, 1954, the *New York Times* reported that she had been cast with Richard Boone and Van Heflin in Panoramic Productions' *The Raid*, which would go before the cameras on January 6, 1954. Filming ran until February 1 on location at Sherwood Forest in California and at the RKO-Pathé Studios with Hugo Fregonese directing. The screenplay was by Sydney Boem based on the screen story by Francis Cockrell and the short story "Affair at St. Albans" by Herbert Ravenal Sass. The film had the working title *Affair at St. Albans*.

The Civil War film was a "B" and the plot was said to be based on a true story. It concerned a band of Confederate soldiers, led by Major Neil Benton (Van Heflin), who raided the Yankee town of St. Albans, Vermont, on October 19, 1864. Bancroft played Katy Bishop, a war widow and proprietor of a boarding house where Neil lives while the raid is planned. The character has the potential to be a reason for him to question his loyalty to the cause, but although he spends some time with her, there appears to be no romantic interest in her from him. He dances with Katy at a bazaar but never expresses any desire for her, although it is apparent that she is interested in him. The one concession he seems to make in light of their friendship is to delay attacking the Yankee cavalry that comes to rescue the town because he believes that Katy's son Larry (Tommy Rettig) is with them.

Van Heflin received over-the-title billing, with Bancroft billed 2nd. Hair-wise, Bancroft wearing a sculptured style with bangs and ringlets at the back. Costumes are by Travilla; the black evening gown she wears at the bazaar is drab and unflattering. The film was released by Fox on August 20, 1954.

After this film, Fox dropped Bancroft's contract so in the future she would work freelance, independently and without studio management.

2

An Independent Actress

Bancroft traveled to Estudios Churubusco in Mexico City for her next film, a black-and-white Panoramic Productions thriller released by Fox: *A Life in the Balance*. Shot from early February to mid–March 1954, it had a screenplay by Robert Presnell, Jr., and Leo Townsend, based on a story by Georges Simenon, though other sources give the material as a novella entitled "A Matter of Life and Death." In September 1953 it was announced that Hugo Fregonese was to direct and the film was to be shot on location on location in Saville and Madrid, Spain. In the October 1953 *Hollywood Reporter* it was reported that Fregonese's wife Faith Domergue had been cast as the female lead. Working titles were *7 Rue Pigalle* and *A Matter of Life and Death*. The film was ultimately directed by Harry Horner. The plot concerned widowed musician and former music printer Antonio Gomez (Ricardo Montalban), accused of being the murderer of young women in Mexico City.

Bancroft played the supporting role of Maria Ibinia, an American who meets Antonio at a pawnshop and has a romance with him. Maria's backstory is not provided. We are only told that she has been fired from her job, which is the reason she is pawning a sapphire ring, but we do not know what her job was or why she is in Mexico. The role provides for a narrative distraction for Antonio to stop him from being with his ten-year-old son (Jose Perez), who has seen the real killer and follows him. Antonio being a widower allows for the inevitable conclusion of Maria becoming the new woman in the Gomez house, sparing Antonio from having his son taken away from home from neighbors who have expressed an interest in him.

Montalban is billed above the film's title and Bancroft is the first below it. As the narrative covers only one day, the actress has just one outfit to wear, a light-colored blouse with dark jacket and skirt and large dangly earrings; she briefly wears a festival cap. Her best moment is the long look of sadness she gives while watching Antonio play a guitar in the pawnshop. She is also appealing when she closes her eyes when dancing with him. We get to briefly hear Bancroft sing when Maria joins in with Antonio while he plays the guitar in the street.

The film was released in New York on July 13, 1955, with the taglines "A killer with the cunning of a maniac. A little boy with the courage of a lion" and "In the Shadow of the Knife.... They Formed a Strange Alliance!" Howard H. Thompson of the *New York Times* wrote that Bancroft acquitted herself commendably.

Bancroft's husband May had begun to speculate in local real estate with developments in the San Fernando Valley. Bancroft's mother had been disappointed about the

Portrait for *A Life in the Balance* (1955).

elopement and repeatedly asked for the couple to have a proper church wedding. They decided to do it and packed the family car and headed for New York. Along the way, they made a detour in Chicago so that May could study for the Illinois bar exam which he planned to take later that month. While in Chicago, Bancroft received a call from producer Edward Small, who two years prior had produced the United Artists film noir *Kansas City Confidential* (1952). Now he had secured the rights to a book which focused on the warring Mafiosi in New York. He wanted her for the film but Warner Brothers needed Bancroft to go back to Hollywood to test for the part. She refused because she didn't want her husband to go on to New York without her or disrupt their new wedding plans. Bancroft also told Small that if Warners wanted to see her on film, there was plenty of it around Hollywood. The actress and May then continued on to New York, and after a brief vacation, the pair were married with Millie in attendance. Then they returned to Hollywood.

According to an item in the April 1954 *Hollywood Reporter*, Bancroft tested for the nightclub chanteuse Karen Stephanson in the MGM crime drama *Rogue Cop* (1954). Janet Leigh was eventually cast. The *New York Times* reported on July 17, 1954, that Bancroft had signed to play the feminine lead in *New York Confidential* (1955). She would play the daughter of Broderick Crawford in the film based on the 1948 book by Lee Mortimer and Jack Lait. The crime melodrama was to go before the cameras on July 19, 1954. The screenplay was by Clarence Greene and Russell Rouse. Rouse also directed the Challenge Pictures–Greene-Rouse production that was released by Warner Brothers. Shooting took place at the Goldwyn Studios.

The plot centered on the head of the New York crime syndicate, Charlie Lupo (Broderick Crawford), and his hitman Nick Magellan (Richard Conte). Fourth-billed Bancroft played Charlie's daughter Kathy.

Kathy's character was different from the Madonna-whore dichotomy of the narrative's other women, represented by Charlie's mama (Celia Lovsky) as a Madonna and Charlie's girlfriend Iris (Marilyn Maxwell) as a whore. Kathy does not want to be the bad girl she is destined to be. She rejects the gangland life of her father and gets a job as a doctor's nurse. After her true identity is discovered and she is fired, she returns to accept her fate. Knowing that Nick is romantically interested in her, she throws herself at him, but when he rejects her, she commits suicide by crashing her car. Therefore she is ultimately a tragic figure and a victim of Nick's moral ambiguity. Kathy is shown to be more desirable to him than Iris, whose advances he rejects, but he does not romantically pursue her and he also does not tell Charlie that he knows where she has relocated.

Courtesy of costumer Ernest Newman, Bancroft sports a mink coat and some spaghetti-strap dresses. Maxwell's Iris gets form-fitting, strapless and sparkly gowns and a negligee which compliment her more ample bosom. Bancroft speaks faster than she has before, perhaps because of the Warner Brothers house style of acting. The actress gets to have arguments with Charlie; he slaps her and she slaps Nick. Her best scene has Kathy drunk and making an advance to him. It was reported that the drunk scene took 33 takes because Bancroft had difficulty playing it. She had sought the counsel of Rouse but he did not know how to help her other than to tell her to do it again. Frustration like this one ultimately motivated Bancroft to return to study her craft in New York.

The film was released on February 18, 1955, in New York. It was praised by *Variety*, who wrote that Bancroft, showing continuing progress and talent, scored with a standout performance.

Bancroft returned to TV for her second *Lux Video Theatre* appearance, "A Medal for Benny" (November 25, 1954). The teleplay was by S.H. Barnett, adapted from a story by John Steinbeck and Jack Wagner, and the show was directed by Buzz Kulik. Bancroft played Lolita. The World War II story (previously told in a 1945 Paramount Film) was set in Paisanos, a small fishing village on Santa Cruz Bay, where the people learn that the deceased villager Benny Martin is to be given a presidential medal. Bancroft next appeared in an episode of the ZIV 30-minute comedy series *Your Favorite Story*, "The Waltz," directed by Peter Godfrey and broadcast on December 26, 1954. Eugene Solow's teleplay was adapted from a short story by Gladys Hasty Carroll.

Bancroft's next film, the Edward Small/Fame Pictures black-and-white crime drama *The Naked Street*, was shot from February 2 to late February 1955 and then from mid- to late March 1955 on location in New York and at the Goldwyn Studios. It had a screenplay by Maxwell Shane and Leo Katcher, based on a Katcher story, and was directed by Shane. The film had the working titles *The Big Frame*, *The Rap*, *The Brass Ring* and *The Mobster*. New York racketeer Phil Regal (Anthony Quinn) gets Nicky Bradna (Farley Granger) out of a Death Row conviction for murder so that he can marry his sister Rosalie Regalzyk (Bancroft). Rosalie is a soul sister to *New York Confidential*'s Kathy Lupo since she comes to feel her life is doomed because of her relationship with a criminal relative. With her keeping caged pigeons on the rooftop of her Brooklyn apartment house, she might have been considered an innocent except for the fact that she gets pregnant by Nicky, which is why Phil wants him to marry her. The narrative puts a spin on Rosalie's relationship with Nicky since he leaves her and cheats with other women after he gets tired of living a straight lifestyle as a truck driver. His dissatisfaction comes after Rosalie loses the baby. His being guilty of the murder for which he originally was to be executed shows us that he is no innocent. Rosalie also has a second love interest in *New York Chronicle* journalist Joe McFarland (Peter Graves), who she ends up with.

Third-billed Bancroft's wardrobe is rather dowdy; her wedding dress is not white which shouldn't be a surprise given that she is not a virgin. When Rosalie's pregnancy begins showing, she wears a maternity shirt and pants, but after the baby is born dead, she dresses in schematic black. She has a nice moment when she defends Nicky's restlessness to Phil and intensity in Rosalie's climactic confrontation with him. Bancroft gets to kiss Granger in the same scene where she slaps him, gets her hair pulled by Quinn, and dances at Rosalie's wedding. The edge that the actress presented in *New York Confidential* is missing here.

United Artists released the film in August 1955 with the taglines "They live on the main drag of Brooklyn's jungle!" and "You fixed it so I'd marry a murderer! ... live with a murderer!" It was panned by Bosley Crowther in the *New York Times*.

In Farley Granger's autobiography *Include Me Out: My Life From Goldwyn to Broadway*, he commented that he found Bancroft to be a unique actor. They would spend their lunches together talking about the theater and life in New York. He said she was not happy about any of the films she had made, and he felt Bancroft was too special and too good for Hollywood to ever figure out how to use her well; he suggested that she go back to the theater.

At this time, her marriage was reportedly deteriorating as the couple had a series of trial separations. In response to confrontations, Bancroft was said to either retreat into stony silence or avoid her husband by spending her time with friends. May supposedly felt further alienated by the increasing number of actors that his wife would crowd their home with. He said his wife was either a hungry tiger or a lovable lap dog, and intense about everything. Bancroft would lie on the floor and watch television by the hour, or she would fry an egg leaning over the skillet staring at it as if the fate of the city depended on that egg. She attempted to have the marriage annulled on the grounds that the union was childless but the request was denied.

On March 12, 1955, the *New York Times* reported that Bancroft had made a two-picture deal at Columbia. She was to go to work the following week on *The Last Frontier* with Guy Madison and Victor Mature. From March to May 1955 she shot the Columbia historical western on location in Popocatepetl, Mexico. Bancroft reportedly replaced Kathryn Grant, who was originally cast in the supporting role of Corinna Marston. The film had a screenplay by Philip Yordan and Russell S. Hughes, based on the Richard Emery Roberts novel *The Gilded Rooster*, and was directed by Anthony Mann. Its working title was *The Gilded Rooster*; for TV it was later re-titled *Savage Wilderness*.

The story was set during the American Civil War at the Fort Shallon, Wyoming, cavalry base. Former fur trapper Jed Cooper (Mature) clashes with Col. Frank Marston (Robert Preston), husband of Corinna, over his desire to fight the Indians. Corinna, the only female with lines in the movie, exists to create a love triangle (herself, Jed and Frank). Her not having a happy marriage to Frank makes her acceptance of Jed's advance, after an initial rejection of him, unsurprising. An interesting plot point is how Jed strikes her after he thinks he has eliminated Frank by leaving him in a bear trap. Corinna is not happy about this, and Jed slaps her because he claims that she is a hypocrite. He has done what she has wanted but she now rejects him again for it. Corinna does not actively pursue Jed, and it is only when Frank is climactically killed by Indians that there is the implication that she and Jed can be together. While Corinna is a passive love object, she also works at the fort's hospital and shows some gumption when she is seen firing a gun at the Indians when they attack the fort. Apparently there was also a scene where she repeatedly stabbed an Indian but it was deleted because it was considered too brutal. Since we never see Corinna outside the fort, it is assumed that the scene would have had an Indian get into it.

Mature, Madison and Preston are billed above the film's title and Bancroft is billed fifth below it. Hairdresser Helen Hunt turned the actress blonde for the role, with long hair parted in the middle, with the length worn down at night but mostly up. Costumes are period long full skirts and dresses. The role does not give her much opportunity and lacks the dimension that the characters of Jed and Frank have.

Director Mann provides some notable staging for some of her scenes. In one, Jed talks to the back of her head as she stands with her back to him. Mann has the camera on Corinna's reaction when Frank tells Capt. Glenn Riordan (Madison) how he lost 1500 men in a Shiloh battle, and he has Mature's face in shadow during Jed's attempted seduction of her in his cabin.

The film was released on December 7, 1955, with the taglines "The Men, the Women, the Wilderness of America's Most Exciting Days" and "A Rousing Tale of Adventure, Lust and Madness." It was lambasted by Bosley Crowther in the *New York Times*.

Bancroft said that, while on location in Mexico, she had a long drive from the bottom of a mountain all the way into Mexico City. She used to get pretty bored on these drives so she would shout out the window "Hello you people—here I am! You lucky people, you!" After this, five guys in a car followed her all the way to the hotel.

The actress was profiled at home in the Beverly Hills apartment she kept with May for a magazine. She reported that she had decorated the home herself in a modern style, with paneled living room walls of painted cocoa, a taupe carpet, and blue couches with rust pillows.

She was considered for the part of Becky Driscoll in producer Walter Wanger's science fiction thriller *Invasion of the Body Snatchers* (1956) along with Donna Reed, Kim Hunter and Vera Miles. Dana Wynter was cast in the part. Bancroft made her third *Lux Video Theatre* appearance in the episode "Forever Female" (June 23, 1955), adapted by S.H. Barnett from the J.M Barrie play *Rosalind*. Directed by Buzz Kulik, the story concerned an actress who refuses to admit she is too old to play the ingénue role any more. Bancroft played the part of Sally. The play had been made into a Paramount comedy in 1953.

On August 20, 1955, the *New York Times* reported that after three weeks of filming on location in North Dakota, Bancroft had been replaced because of illness by Debra Paget in the part of an Indian maiden in MGM's *The Last Hunt*. The Robert Taylor western had begun shooting on June 27 under the direction of Richard Brooks. Bancroft is said to have been injured riding a horse filming a scene with Stewart Granger.

Granger described what happened in his 1981 book *Sparks Fly Upward*. He said that Bancroft's part was a fairly dreary one which would have given her no chance to show off her acting talents. The incident occurred during a scene that required Granger to sweep her up into the saddle and gallop off into the sunset. This was not an easy thing to do considering that the actor had to pick up a girl from the ground one-handed while trying to control a fractious horse. Granger had pointed out the danger of the stunt and suggested a double should be used but Brooks insisted that Bancroft do the shot. Granger told her to spread her legs as he lifted her, to avoid the saddle pommel. Trying to control the animal with one hand, he lifted Bancroft with the other, but the horse put in a buck at that moment and she landed hard, hitting her coccyx painfully on the pommel. Granger felt that if he had been stronger, the accident would not have happened. What was thought to be a fractured vertebrae turned out to be a severely pinched nerve. The injury would mend but required three months of bed rest; Louella Parsons reported that the actress had to wear a cast.

Bancroft's recovery was not spent with May in California but with her family in New York. Her lawyers sued MGM and got her a settlement which included cancelling her new long-term contract with the studio. Granger jokingly said he was responsible for freeing her from a career of playing thankless roles as Indian girls for MGM. A still exists of Bancroft with Granger and Robert Taylor, in an Indian outfit and long headdress, the same that Paget wears in her stills with the same leading men. Reportedly Bancroft can be seen in the completed film in some long shots. She left one Indian maiden role for another, taking on the CinemaScope biographical western *Walk the Proud Land* (1956) for Universal. Three days before leaving for location work in Tucson, Arizona, the actress announced her separation from May.

Walk the Proud Land was shot from November 21 to late December 1955. The screenplay was by Gil Doud and Jack Sher based on a biography by Woodworth Chum, which was published in 1936 as *Apache Agent* (the film had *Apache Agent* as a working title). Piper Laurie was originally cast as Mary Dennison but asked to be released from her Universal contract before shooting began.

The story—a true one, according to the prologue—concerns John P. Clum (Audie Murphy) who in 1874 was the new Department of Interior agent for the Apache reservation in San Carlos near Tucson. Clum works against the local army to give the Indians freedom and a peaceful life. Bancroft plays Tianay, a widowed Indian, who comes out of mourning to become the housekeeper for Clum. She has a greater romantic interest in him than in Santos (Victor Millan), an Indian. Tianay is rejected by Clum, who has a fiancée, Mary (Pat Crowley). Tianay offers to be Clum's second wife, as is Indian custom, but he refuses because he is a Christian. Mary comes to the reservation after marrying Clum in Tucson, and she has Tianay leave the household. Mary wants to leave the reservation when Clum goes after Geromino (Jay Silverheels), a rebellious Indian; Tianay talks her into staying because she knows Clum loves her. The red dress that Tianay wears at the end is presumably made from the red material Clum had given her, but it perhaps also suggests that she is now to be more of an Indian than a housekeeper for him.

Hair stylist Joan St. Oegger has Bancroft's hair in a medium-length style with bangs, which is meant to show that Tianay has chopped off her long hair in mourning. Interestingly, Clum tells her not to grow it back. She wears tropical makeup to play the Indian and has costumes by Bill Thomas. Tianay has an alternate blue blouse and purple skirt and purple blouse and blue skirt. The narrative is refreshing in giving Tianay more dignity than Mary, and not making her as jealous as her rival. Although she speaks in the stilted language of someone to whom English is not their native tongue, Bancroft's best scene is perhaps the one where she convinces Mary not to leave. Tianay doesn't tell Mary not to go, but rather she is smart enough to say that she will look after Clum if she does. But Tianay knows that he really loves his wife and not her. Director Jesse Hibbs ends the scene with Bancroft looking shocked when Mary hugs Tianay.

Still for *Walk the Proud Land* (1956).

The film world-premiered on August 1, 1956, in Hudson, New York and then was released on September 5, 1956, with the taglines "HE TAMED APACHE WAR-LUST WITH THE POWER OF HIS FAITH ... and conquered a savage warrior in a showdown of raw courage!" and "Out of the pages of the West's most thrilling history comes the saga of Indian Agent John Philip Clum ... whose Faith built a fortress in a wilderness of hate ... and tamed the fury of Geronimo's last desperate stand!"

Tommy Rall, who played the Indian Taglito, recalled that he and Bancroft both got sick while on location because of the heat. Another actor reported that Bancroft took ill only a few days after arriving and she required x-rays back in Los Angeles. It is not known what the malady was, but is also afflicted Charles Drake, Robert Warwick, Eugene Iglesias and Anthony Caruso. This resulted in delays in filming and pickup shots that were done back at Universal in March and April 1956. It is claimed the most of Bancroft's work was not done on location, but rather in the studio. However, a viewing of the film attests to the fact that there are an equal number of scenes where the actress was filmed on location and in the studio. After the film was completed, Bancroft was given a non-exclusive five-year contract to make two pictures a year for Universal.

Bancroft moved in with her agent Richard Powers and his wife. There were no immediate plans made for divorce, but also none for reconciliation. She returned to television for her fourth *Lux Video Theatre*, "Hired Wife" (February 23, 1956). The show was written by Ben Simcoe based on a story by George Beck, and was directed by Earl Eby. The plot concerned a secretary helping her boss Stephen Dexter (Lex Barker) out of a legal problem by becoming his wife. It was a remake of a 1940 Universal comedy with Rosalind Russell.

On March 19, 1956, the *New York Times* reported that Bancroft was to co-star with Aldo Ray in the Columbia Pictures–Copa Production *Nightfall* (1957). Filming began on March 20, 1956, and continued until April 9, 1956, on the black-and-white crime drama. It had a screenplay by Stirling Silliphant based on the novel Nightfall by David Goodis. It was shot on location on Hollywood Boulevard in Los Angeles and at the J.W. Robinson department store in Beverly Hills. The plot centered on James Vanning (Ray), a Chicago commercial artist who is pursued by thugs attempting to retrieve $350,000 missing from a Seattle bank job. Bancroft played the role of model Marie Gardner, who meets Vanning at Fallatti's Restaurant, and later has him come to her for help. Marie comes across as a woman who is cynical about men, since the ones she has been involved with have all been married; however, she is prepared to try a new romance with Vanning. His initial assumption that she has set him up to be caught by the thugs is false, complicated by the fact that she assumes that the men pursuing Vanning are policeman. Marie is not revealed to be a femme fatale, but rather an innocent who is endangered by her association with her new man. Her good nature extends to walking out on a fashion show, while still wearing a gown, to be with him and also bravely going with him to the Wyoming shack after he has asked her to stay behind.

Bancroft is billed third after Ray and Brian Keith. Amusingly, Bancroft is seen with her hair in clips and in face cream in bed. Costumes are by Jean Louis. The narrative scores a laugh when Marie runs in one the show gowns and eventually has to be carried by Vanning for speed. The screenplay provides the actress with some banter, which is refreshing after only having stock lines in other films. This allows Marie's initial cynicism to be funny although she gets another funny, ironic line when she kisses Vanning and tells him, "You're the most wanted man I know." Her role as a fashion model allows us to appreciate her figure. Director Jacques Tourneur inexplicably shoots her close-ups in soft focus.

The film was released on January 23, 1957, with the taglines "YOU COULD GO TO

THE MOVIES EVERY DAY FOR FIVE YEARS—BEFORE YOU'D SEE ANOTHER PICTURE WITH SO MANY THRILLS AND SO MUCH SUSPENSE!" and "On a night made for lovers ... and killers." the *New York Times* wrote that Bancroft was decorative and understanding.

On June 19, 1956, the *New York Times* reported that she would play turn-of-the-century opera singer Geraldine Farrar in *The Golden Age*, an original screenplay purchased by Bruce Odlum. The film had a tentative starting date of November 1956 but it would never be made.

Bancroft made her fifth *Lux Video Theatre* appearance on June 21, 1956, in "The Corrigan Case." The S.H. Barnett teleplay was adapted from a story by Larry Riley and the director was James P. Yarbrough. The story concerned a woman who is acquitted of murdering her husband, and her daughter and a tenant in the family rooming house who set out to find the real killer. On July 12, 1956, she made the first of two appearances on the CBS anthology drama *Climax!* with "Fear is the Hunter." The show had a teleplay by Arthur Rowe and was directed by Buzz Kulik. The story concerned a man who comes to the town of Brewster for car repairs, but is told to leave because the ruthless man who runs the town looks on any stranger as his potential murderer. On July 19, 1956, she made another appearance on the show when she was the intermission guest for the episode "No One to Cry With."

From July 30 to August 8, 1956, Bancroft shot the "B" mystery *The Girl in Black Stockings* for Bel-Air productions. The screenplay was by Michael Landau, based on the short story "Wanton Murder" by Peter Godfrey. The film was made on location in Kanab, Utah. It had the working title *Black Stockings*. The plot centered on a series of killings around a Utah motel, Parry's Lodge, which are investigated by Sheriff Jess Holmes (John Dehner). Bancroft played the supporting part of Beth Dixon, a motel employee and the person revealed to be the killer. Although she is dating lawyer David Hewson (Lex Barker), her resistance to his advances makes it apparent that there is something else going on with her, which turns out to be serial killing.

Beth's backstory has her as an escapee from a Pittsburgh asylum and her killing of the private detective Felton (Gene O'Donnell) stops him from exposing her past, since has been sent to find her by her former husband, Prentiss (Stuart Whitman). Her killings of the title girl, Marcia Morgan (actress uncredited), and later Harriet Ames (Mamie Van Doren) are said to be because they were loose women who insulted her employer, the paralyzed hotel owner Edmund Parry (Ron Randell). It is implied that Beth has a maniacal empathy for his condition. The narrative also has Beth attempt to murder Parry's sister Julia (Marie Windsor) although this is like the killing of Felton, as self-defense. Although we don't see Beth's action that leads to the murder of Marcia, we are told by Parry that she had rejected him, which motivated the killer. We *are* shown Beth spilling a drink over herself in a distressed reaction to Harriet drunkenly throwing herself at him at a dinner, which seals her fate. Beth's destiny appears to be back to the asylum rather than jail since the last time we see her, when she is led away by a policeman and Prentiss, she holds a flower which suggests that she will be handled with care.

Bancroft was billed second after Barker. Her wardrobe was supplied off the rack by the local Kanab dress shop, Pink Poodle. Director Howard W. Koch obscures the sight of Bancroft in a bathing suit by having her only shown in the pool from the chest up, when Beth helps Parry with his water therapy, and then wearing an Oriental-patterned robe over it when she gets out.

The horse-riding scene is interesting in light of the actress' horse accident on *The Last Hunt*, although the scene's coverage here suggests that a double could have been used for the long shot where Beth rides. Bancroft uses a child-like variation on her soft voice when Beth is caught as the killer and she repeats "Don't let them take me" to David. In this climax, the actress also uses big eyes to suggest the character's madness. However Bancroft screams in reaction to seeing the corpse of Marsha, and uses her harder voice in the scene when Beth tells Parry, "I think I understand how you feel" in regards to his expressed misogyny. This scene is perhaps one of the actress' best moments in the film, since in the same scene she is lovely when she holds his paralyzed hands to her face to fulfill a frustrated desire he has. Bancroft also impresses when Beth tells David that she has been previously married, which Koch stages so that she stands in a medium shot to camera with her back to the watching Barker behind her.

The film was released by United Artists in September 24, 1957, with the taglines "She's every inch a teasing, taunting 'Come-on' Blonde," "High Society Dames for Hire!" and "One Will Die Tonight!" It was praised by *Variety*.

Bancroft was reportedly in touch with Peter Godfrey, the author of the short story, at the time of filming seeking help with her characterization. In Mamie Van Doren's book *Playing the Field*, she comments that she, Bancroft and Marie Windsor were pals during the shoot. Van Doren says that, off the set, Bancroft never let a moment go by without having something outrageous to say or do. The actress was also said to be an incurable shutterbug, and took photographs of Van Doren when she shot her scenes. When they had nothing else to do, the three women would sit by the pool and gossip prodigiously. Bancroft introduced them to the "split-face" game which had come out of the Actors Studio. This was a game where you attempt to express two simultaneous, conflicting emotions with only your face. Bancroft would direct them to be afraid with your mouth and have an orgasm with your eyes, and the women would dissolve into gales of laughter as they grimaced and rolled their eyes. Van Doren said that Bancroft was also a talented mimic, doing Gloria Grahame's Ado Annie from the film *Oklahoma!* (1955) with chewing gum stuffed under her lip to imitate the actress' protruding lip. "Aw right, darlingsh," she would say around the wad of gum, "let's all be Gloria," and they all laughed helplessly until the gum fell out of their bulging lips.

From mid–September to October 1956 she filmed Edward Alperson Productions' "B" western *The Restless Breed* (1957), which was released by Fox. With a screenplay by Steve Fisher, it was shot on location in Victorville, California. In 1865, lawyer and gun-fighter Mitch Baker (Scott Brady) travels to the Texan border town of Mission intent on avenging the death of his Secret Service father at the hands of the gang of Ed Newton (Jim Davis). Bancroft played half-breed Indian girl Angelita, the ward of the Reverend Simmons (Rhys Williams). Her love of dancing is said to be the expression of her uncivilized Indian side which the reverend is attempting to tame. He is thwarted by the romantic overtures made to Angelita by Mitch. Aside from her dancing, the girl comes across as an innocent although she is also brave. Angelita goes to Mitch at his hotel to ask him to leave town before he gets killed and she appears in the climactic saloon shootout between Mitch and Newton as a distraction which helps Mitch win. The film features a song named "Angelita," used as a generic love theme.

Hairdresser Lillian Lashin gives Bancroft long black hair with bangs, sometimes tied back with a ribbon. Her wardrobe by Norma is a variety of period dresses and skirts, some with Indian patterned belts and sleeves. It is a pity that director Allan Dwan uses too many cutaways in her barefoot dancing scene, though the actress impresses in the footage that is shown. He also perversely has two kisses between Mitch and Angelita performed between the bars of the window of her room. Bancroft's best scene is perhaps when Angelita goes to Mitch to tell him she loves him and to beg him to leave town. The film has the cast do end credit curtain calls, though reportedly not shot by Dwan. The film was released in May 1957 with the tagline "Flaming Out of the Blazing Heart of Texas!"

One of the ward children in the film was played by Evelyn Rudie, who met Bancroft again when she was co-director of the Santa Monica Playhouse. Rudie said that Bancroft remembered the film as a very poignant moment in her life: It was reported that the actress' relationship with Scott Brady later developed into a romantic one.

In the summer of 1956, Bancroft began to see a psychoanalyst because she felt she needed help coping with her personal life. Within a week of starting the treatment, she and May were legally separated. Bancroft stated that she no longer enjoyed the life of a Hollywood bachelor girl. She said one could always be popular with the boys but the rules were different in Hollywood than the Bronx. There you played for keeps.

On October 14, 1956, Bancroft made the first of two appearances in the NBC anthology *The Alcoa Hour* which was shot in New York. This was "Key Largo," and the actress recreated the role played by Lauren Bacall in the 1948 Warner Brothers gangster melodrama. The teleplay was by Alvin Sapinsley adapted from the Maxwell Anderson play and the director was Alex Segal. Bancroft played the part of Alegre (Bacall had been called Nora Temple), one of the people at a Florida Keys hotel during a hurricane who become prisoners of a gang of criminals.

The actress was photographed for the *New York Daily News* in various poses at Idlewild Airport on October 15, 1956. She was reported to be flying to Hollywood where she was to audition for *The Helen Morgan Story* (1957), the tale of a torch singer who rose from sordid beginnings to fame and fortune only to lose it all to alcohol and poor personal choices. The part had been planned for Doris Day, who rejected it; other actresses reportedly considered for it were Judy Garland, Olivia de Havilland, Susan Hayward, Jennifer Jones, Peggy Lee and Patti Page. Ann Blyth was cast.

On October 23, 1956, Bancroft and May signed a property settlement. On December 13, May's lawyer, Bentley M. Harris, filed papers for divorce with the California Superior Court. On February 13, 1957, the divorce was approved on the grounds of extreme cruelty, since he claimed his wife had insisted he drop his study of law. Since May had filed for the action, he had to give testimony to his claim. He stated that Bancroft's professional need to travel had been a serious problem for the couple, saying she could be away from home for months on end. May said when she was at home, she could not talk after having worked from very early in the morning and he felt that the couple could not get along or have any understanding or any kind of real marriage. He described her friends visiting as "millions of people tracking into the house." Later, May said that he thought his wife had tried to combine the two loves of marriage and career but the career turned out to be the greater of the two.

Bancroft described her need for marriage as indulging a late adolescence where she used the relationship to give her a shelter that her career did not provide. Now the actress was willing to confront the frustrations of her professional life, stating she was only interested in four men: her father, her agent, her press agent and her analyst. When Bancroft was asked by columnist Sidney Fields about the failure of her marriage, she said it was due to different temperaments. Bancroft later commented that they came from two entirely different backgrounds and had lived two different kinds of lives.

Director Otto Preminger reportedly considered Bancroft for the title role in the historical biography *Saint Joan* (1957), based on the play by George Bernard Shaw. Eighteen-year-old Jean Seberg was instead cast in the film—*not* a box office success. The actress returned to television in the CBS *Playhouse 90* "So Soon to Die" (January 17, 1957), her first of two shows for the dramatic anthology series that was filmed in Hollywood. The teleplay was written by Marc Brandel from a story by Jeremy York. Set in London, the plot told of a murder for money, where down-at-the-heels actor and ex-soldier Lester Amblin (Richard Basehart) is blackmailed by Blaize (Sebastian Cabot) into murdering Isobel Waring (Bancroft), a secretary and young heiress due to inherit a fortune the day she turned 25. Isabel is a rather uninteresting character since she is a passive victim without any dimension, apart from the narcissism that is suggested by her repeated action of fiddling with her hair. This point gets an unintentional laugh after her hair is messed up when she reaches down to pick up Lester's dropped cigarette case. Bancroft has a drab, conventional wardrobe including a horizontal-striped suit and a dark one-piece bathing suit. Her British accent is inconsistent. Director John Brahm gives her a long close-up when Isobel is unconscious and John looks at her, but dwells too long on the scene of Bancroft screaming after Isobel is attacked. The actress' best moment is perhaps when Isobel holds her hand in front of her after being kissed by Lester, supposedly remembering the kiss he had given her when she was conscious.

Interviewed about the show, Bancroft spoke on the subject of being an actor. She felt that you didn't have to be crazy but it was helpful to be slightly neurotic in order to act. She then theorized that actors were all basically insecure exhibitionists, with moods, but you needed to have moods to understand and express emotion. She claimed that without them, an actor was just another normal, average person and who ever heard of a good actor who was normal or average?

The working relationship with Basehart led Bancroft to a new career challenge. She had made 15 films in five years and was not happy with the results. Television work had provided some relief although it lacked the cachet of film. Of her movies, Bancroft said that she had tried her best but, more often than not, the parts were beneath her capabilities. She had done the necessary preparation for the roles and had performed them without resistance. The actress had learned her lines and taken direction. She moved where she was told to move and did as she was told: "They said bark and I barked." But now she wanted more. Basehart had been approached by producer Fred Coe to star in a Broadway two-hander play by William Gibson, *Two for the Seesaw*. This was the comic-tragic story of Jerry Ryan, a dour and defeated Midwesterner, and a neurotic dancer, Gittel Mosca, who meet and fall in love in New York. Basehart liked the play, and though he hesitated about taking the male role, he recommended Bancroft for the female part.

In 1959, Gibson published "The *Seesaw* Log," a 138-page chronicle of the stage production covering the period from spring 1953 to July 1958. In it he reports that Gwen Verdon was suggested for Gittel and the script was sent to her but she declined. Next approached was Julie Harris, who Gibson thought was wrong for the part but a box office name. She too turned it down. Kim Stanley was then sent the script and she never responded. In his book on Stanley, *Female Brando*, Jon Krampner wrote that Stanley had been the first actress offered the part. He said Gibson went to see her in New York when she in rehearsals for *A Clearing in the Woods* which would open on Broadway in January

1957. However Gibson was dubious and said Stanley was so much a shiksa that he couldn't see how she could play the part. The actress apparently agreed and declined. Coe approached another unnamed star who was interested but Gibson vetoed her. Coe and Gibson had other actresses read for them, including Lee Grant, Barbara Baxley and Gaby Rodgers. Gibson thought the closest to the character was Grant; Penn liked her too, but Coe was noncommittal.

Basehart twice suggested Bancroft, whom Coe agreed to see. She was someone unknown to Gibson. He was concerned that Bancroft did not look Jewish, and he saw Coe's decision as a favor to the actor. Since it was not uncommon for one to promote a girlfriend, Coe might have assumed that her greatest attributes may not have been acting. But he was in for a surprise.

Bancroft agreed to meet with Coe in New York when she was going in February 1957 to attend her sister's wedding. Her co-star had shown her his copy of the play which allowed her to see that it was similar to her own background (the girl was from the Bronx). Bancroft said the first time she read the play, she skipped the stage directions because she already knew what the girl was going to do. That taught the actress that never again should she take a part unless on the first reading she could shout inside that she knew her. Bancroft said that she had decided that she would not work unless something moved her in that way, commenting that she didn't buy furs any more but she bought freedom instead.

To prepare for the meeting, she transformed herself into the part with Bronx inflection and gesture, because she had read that theatrical producers expected actors to be the part when they were interviewed. In the waiting room of Coe's office, she posed herself carelessly, with one shoe off and scratching her foot. When Coe invited her in, Bancroft stood with the dropped shoe in her hand and told him that she had to go to the john. This action was a strategy and she waited for what she thought was an acceptable length of time before returning and tossing off a casual "thanks." Bancroft kept up her performance and the meeting went well. The actress would say that Gittel came up out of her, and Coe was astounded. He telephoned Gibson, who was in Hollywood and had just worked on the teleplay for the *Playhouse 90* broadcast of "The Miracle Worker." This show, like the future Broadway play and 1962 feature film, had been directed by Arthur Penn. Coe told the writer that Bancroft was the best Gittel he had seen and asked that Gibson meet her before he returned to his Stockbridge home and she went to Hollywood, presumably to make the *Playhouse 90* western "Invitation to a Gunfighter" that Penn was to direct.

The actress returned for her second meeting at Coe's office on February 8, 1957, with Gibson attending. Bancroft again used her Bronx accent to be Gittel and asked the writer how Hollywood had been. Gibson wrote that she was a dark, quick, not pretty but vitally attractive girl with a sidewalk voice, and his mind blinked; she could have walked off his pages. Coe had arranged for an actor to read with her and the two performed. This convinced Gibson that Bancroft was perfect for the part. When she told a story minutes later, she slid into an elegant characterization and he perceived she was not a type, but a talent. After she left, Gibson was sold and he and Coe agreed that the decision to cast her turned on what Penn made of her. A source claims that Bancroft was not hired by Penn for the *Playhouse 90* show until after he had met her for the play, and that she was asked if she would meet with him first about *Two for the Seesaw*. Her agreeing to do so led to his then signing her for the TV show. Penn sent his opinion of Bancroft to Gibson and Coe by calling her "Gittel on the hoof."

Broadcast on March 7, 1957, "Invitation to a Gunfighter" had a teleplay by Leslie Stevens based on a Hal Goodman–Larry Klein story. A small town is terrorized by Civil War veteran gunfighter Matt Jeffers (Hugh O'Brian), who hires a second gunfighter known as Dancer (Gilbert Roland) to drive the first one out of town. The teleplay was later adapted into the 1964 movie of the same title. Bancroft played the part of Julie Bickford, the sheriff's daughter. In her 2000 Charlie Rose television interview, the actress said that on this show, because of Penn, she saw the light, changing her from a mindless, spontaneous person working on sheer talent and sheer energy.

It seemed that *Two for the Seesaw* had its cast with Basehart and Bancroft, with Basehart the name that would help get funding. He had done six plays on Broadway, and was felt to be the box office insurance needed. Despite her apparent perfect casting, Bancroft was a television and minor movie actress with no Broadway credit, and it didn't help that Gibson was also a Broadway neophyte. Coe and Penn had both been on Broadway but neither with much success. Coe had previously produced Horton Foote's *The Trip to Bountiful* on Broadway but it had only a month-long run. Penn had co-directed the Leslie Stevens play *The Lovers* with Michael Gordon but it only ran from May 10 to 12, 1956. Gibson was encouraged by the fact that Bancroft had been born a mile from him in the Bronx and that Basehart wanted to work with her. The writer now went out of his way to view her previous work. He was disappointed by it, and now feared she might well go up in smoke in a theater. It was all on Basehart but he proved to be elusive with his agent setting high terms and mutterings of prohibitive income taxes. Then the actor went to Hollywood, still unsigned. The project he went to was presumably the war drama *Time Limit,* shot from April 3 to early May 1957 at the Goldwyn Studios and then on location in New York from May 7 to 9, 1957. This situation only seemed to be a postponement of the play and it was hoped that Penn would be able to sign Basehart in Hollywood. The director was to stay there to shoot the western film *The Left Handed Gun* (1958) which was produced by Coe and in production from June to July 1957. However in mid–March came the news that Basehart had decided not to do the play.

Basehart's absence put the actress' prospect in jeopardy. For the moment, the project seemed like a lost cause.

On March 28, 1957, Bancroft made her seventh and final appearance on *Lux Video Theatre.* "The Black Angel" had a teleplay by Stanley H. Silverman adapted from the novel by Cornell Woolrich. The director was Norman Morgan and Bancroft played the part of Cathy. The novel had been previously made as the 1946 Universal crime mystery of the same title with June Vincent, as the wife of a man convicted of murder, who tries to prove him innocent. On April 18, 1957, Bancroft made her second *Climax!* appearance in "The Mad Bomber," from a teleplay by Adrian Spies.

If Gibson despaired of seeing *Two for the Seesaw* staged, Bancroft was equally despondent. She had run out of money and she decided to go back to New York to live with her family. Bancroft knew that this would drastically reduce her employment opportunities but she also wanted to rid herself of whatever bad acting habits the movies had given her. Ironically, she had gone to Hollywood with no clear technical understanding of how best to prepare or perform a role, and she had left no better equipped. Bancroft said she was ready to be an actress. She decided to enroll at the Herbert Berghof HB Studio. It had an excellent reputation and it seemed an advantage to the actress that Berghof himself had appeared in four films for 20th Century–Fox. To Bancroft's mind, this made the teacher both remedial and sympathetic.

After languishing without news during the spring and early summer, the actress finally heard news about *Two for the Seesaw*. In mid–June 1957, Coe contacted Gibson to advise that Henry Fonda had read the play and was interested in talking about it. The actor and Coe had worked in TV on the *Producers' Showcase* version of "The Petrified Forest" (May 30, 1955). Fonda also had Broadway chops, having appeared eight times and winning a Tony for Best Actor for *Mister Roberts* in 1948. The actor also had a Hollywood pedigree, with an Oscar nomination for *The Grapes of Wrath* (1940).

The three men met at Fonda's house in New York but he could not say yes outright and his reservation was due to his belief that the male part was underwritten. This was a notion that Gibson agreed with and a problem whose solution had eluded the writer for two and a half years. Fonda planned to return to the south of France in the next week for the remainder of a summer vacation and the writer worked on revisions. Gibson then asked if the actor would agree to do a reading of the play's first act with Bancroft. The writer learned that Coe was inching towards replacing Bancroft with an unnamed singer-dancer because of her name, despite the writer's objection to her. Fonda agreed to the reading so Gibson and Bancroft went to his house, with her under instructions to vamoose the instant the act had been read. This was fine with the actress as she had planned a shopping date with her mother. Fonda was impressed with Bancroft, saying she made Gittel come blazingly alive, and asked her to put off her date so that they could read the rest of the play together. She agreed so Gibson got a private preview of the entire play. He felt Fonda read detachedly and Bancroft beautifully and realized to an embarrassing degree how she had far more lines than he. After Bancroft left, Fonda commented that he thought she was wonderful and that you couldn't have asked for anyone better. Gibson promised Fonda that he would continue to work on the male part over the summer, after which the actor would advise whether he would do the play or not. A potential complication arose when another producer expressed interest in the play though he did not want Bancroft. He said he had seen her in Hollywood and thought she was "lousy" and "stank like a dead thing." Gibson declined the offer.

Gibson was still not convinced that Fonda was perfect casting; he lacked the ironic bite essential to the part. By September the writer had added 30 minutes to the script's first two acts solely in the man's lines, since previously the play had passages where he barely spoke. This was sent to Fonda and after two weeks, there was a cable which read "Start it rolling. I am yours." Another source claims that Fonda was still not pleased with the revisions and continued to be uncommitted. Coe supposedly sent Fonda a cable telling him that he needed a promise in order to book a theater for the coming season and then Fonda committed. Bancroft was told the news and that rehearsals were to begin on November 4, 1957.

In the meantime, the actress researched the role of Gittel. She already had a natural empathy for the character's history of unsuccessful relationships with men, and she could recall her own Bronx sensibilities and idiosyncrasies which she had repressed during her stay in Hollywood. Bancroft looked elsewhere for a woman to model Gittel on, and found in her sister Joanne the same emotional complexity that Gibson had given the character. There was an exterior of wit and earthiness and an interior of sensitivity and guilelessness. However, there was one aspect that neither Bancroft nor her sister had: Gittel's passion for modern dance. To further her research, she joined the classes supervised by Jose Limon's company. She attended regularly for three weeks, paying attention to the less gifted dancers who she felt could lend more insight into her role. Bancroft also ventured into the streets of Greenwich Village observing bohemians like Gittel. In time she would begin to act like her as she went about the activities of her own life. These strategies were in keeping with the Stanislavskian training Bancroft was receiving at the HB Studio.

Bancroft's personal life had also improved after she started seeing a man named Mario Ferrari-Ferreira, a distant relative of the famous Ferrari car-manufacturing family. The relationship became serious over a few months and the couple announced their engagement. Bancroft considered telling Coe that she intended to get married but then changed her mind because she felt that she could do so and still do the play. The actress told the producer that she was still interested in the production, with the timing of the rehearsals and the planned out-of-town tryouts coinciding with Ferrari being away, so this lessened any potential impact her working would have on the relationship.

With Fonda's name as insurance and the promise of an innovative play, financing was found. Fonda himself made a financial commitment, investing $20,000 and owning 25 percent of the play's earnings. He was guaranteed a weekly salary of $2500. Bancroft's contract was far less lucrative. He had a clause that could let him out of the play after six months, but she was bound to it for as long as two years if it was successful. Bancroft could also be dismissed before the play opened in New York. Her weekly check was $550 with regular increments of $100. Theaters were booked in Washington from December 5, 1957, and Philadelphia from December 25, 1957, for tryouts and the Booth Theatre for the Broadway run on January 16, 1958, after two previews on January 14 and 15, 1958.

In the meantime, there was other work. On July 7, 1957, Bancroft made her second *Alcoa Hour* appearance in "Hostages to Fortune," from a teleplay by John H. Secondari. Bancroft played Giselle, a Belgian girl suspected by her fellow townspeople of being a Nazi officer's mistress.

She returned to Hollywood to make her only appearance in CBS's western anthology series *Dick Powell's Zane Grey Theatre* in the episode "Episode in Darkness" (November 15, 1957). The show was written by Frederic Louis Fox and directed by John English. The story concerned cattleman Ethan Banyon (Dewey Martin), framed for a stagecoach robbery and murder by Pembroke Deputy Sheriff Roy Kelsey (John Anderson) and Joe Fletcher (Phil Pine). Bancroft played the part of blind woman Isabelle Rutledge from Willow Springs, Missouri, one of the coach passengers; her Aunt Julia Crayton (Edith Evanson) was the murder victim. Isabelle is identified by Banyon as former dancer Denver Belle, who suffers from glaucoma; the money stolen from her was earmarked for an eye operation. Defending himself at the trial, Banyon uses Isabelle as a witness to identify his voice as different from the one she heard at the robbery, and also to correctly identify the number of coins dropped in an experiment of hearing. She also identifies Fletcher's watch, amongst a group of watches she is given to listen to, as her father's that was in her purse that was also stolen at the robbery. Although a doctor has said that the operation would not have restored her sight, the trial experience has Isabelle change her mind about having it. She tells Banyon, "Sometimes blindness goes beyond the eyes. You started me thinking it's not what I lost but what I have left that matters."

Wardrobe by Robert B. Harris was one period light-colored suit with a dark collar, with the jacket removed to reveal a light blouse, and a feathered hat. Southern-accented Bancroft is first seen from the back for the robbery which delays the reveal that Isabelle is blind (which the actress expresses with a direct forward stare and stiff body language).

The condition of being blind is the only acting challenge that the role provides for Bancroft, and it prefigures her Annie Sullivan in *The Miracle Worker*.

The *New York Times* of October 2, 1957, reported that the Booth Theatre had been reserved for *Two for the Seesaw,* to open the week of January 13, 1958. On October 4, 1957, the paper said that the play was now to be known as *Seesaw*.

3

Two for the Seesaw and *The Miracle Worker*

The show's first rehearsal was in a room on 57th Street. Bancroft had an easy joviality, but she had gained close to 30 pounds, which she promised to lose by opening night. Her hair had grown and now adorned her nape, although Bancroft revealed that what she actually had was a removable fall. The first read-through was held and there was a second after lunch with Gibson's cuts made. After that, Penn and the cast discussed script interpretations. An Actors Equity representative had Bancroft as a non-union beginner sign the membership application.

Over the next few days there began a routine of scene-by-scene read-throughs and seminars. Things went well, although a timed reading had the play running 20 minutes longer than expected so more surgery was required. On the third day, the company's press agent brought in publicity photographs of Fonda and Bancroft in her detachable hair for an advance Washington ad. The set designer brought a model to discuss with the actors the proposed spots where they could make costume changes while the sets changed. What Gibson began to observe was the differences between Fonda and Bancroft. He was from the "old school" of acting and at 52 was twice his co-star's age. His approach was traditional, objective, representational and literal. He essentially read the lines and not what came between them, and was more concerned with his blocking and stage business. He required less time than Bancroft to review a given segment and therefore was left to sit to watch her and Penn go about their work, with a fixed tolerant smile. In contrast, she worked in a more modern, subjective and presentational way. Bancroft deliberately and patiently read between the play's lines and thereby investigated the submerged meanings. Rather than give her the answers, Penn allowed Bancroft to make her own discoveries. Gibson as an observer noted a friction between the director's divergent approach to the actors and mentioned it to Penn, who after then divided his time equally between the two of them. This helped considerably though it was apparent that Fonda's issues with the writing of the character of Jerry were increasing. Gibson was more than happy with Bancroft, taking her aside to tell her that he could not name another actress that he would rather see in the part.

After eight days, the company took a day off and then returned for on-stage rehearsal in a space on top of the Amsterdam Theatre. Penn blocked the play by allowing Fonda and Bancroft to move where their impulses dictated and then sharpened, contradicted or elaborated. Half of their movements had been written into the script with the rest created by the three of them. What emerged was that on the stage, the actors changed. Fonda, previously impassive and remote, now demonstrated his presence. Bancroft said he was breathtaking. But in opposition to her former marvelous performances in the readings, she became awkward, unsure and all but overwhelmed. A number of the show's lawyers and agents were unimpressed with the actress. One recommended that Penn dump her immediately. However he was confident that with time he could tone down Bancroft's over-projection and polish her gawkiness. Penn's faith in the actress came from having previously worked with her on television, as well as how she was totally receptive to his instructions, offering no resistance or temperament. Bancroft was finally getting the directorial sensitivity and seriousness she had desired but missed in films. While then it seemed asking questions and being conscientious was more frowned upon than admired since they slowed down the process, here she was respected. Bancroft improved and with work and nurturing, she adjusted to the theater's demands.

Since so much of Gittel's dialogue took place on the telephone, Penn would call Bancroft at home and they would improvise. He needed other skills to cope with Fonda, whose relationship with Gibson had deteriorated to such an extent that one day the actor stopped cold, bringing activity to a standstill. Bancroft reacted by retreating to a nearby cot as Penn talked to Fonda and Gibson listened. One time when she was confused about the inner logic of a passage of the script, Bancroft, with Penn's approval, went through it improvising her lines in lieu of the text. Fonda refused to improvise with her and he responded only with the play's lines like a shield. He also told Penn that he thought Bancroft's performance was too emotional. To his actress, the director would speak out of one side of his mouth about semi–Freudian adjustments, and to Fonda out of the other side he would speak like George Abbott. But Fonda remained unhappy. Jerry as written was alien to the actor as a man and as actor, but still something had drawn Fonda to the part. He had said that he liked the play because it was about "two charming people" and the actor certainly had charm. But Jerry was called upon to shout, weep, strike a girl, be weak, selfish, mocking and do other un-charming things that Fonda rebelled against. The actor's stage persona of simplicity, attractiveness and emotional reticence had little to do with the character as conceived and disappeared when Fonda struggled to be what was asked. He suggested that perhaps he should be replaced in the part. Penn talked him out of the idea. Coe summed up the problem when he commented that when you put Hamlet and a clown on the same stage, the audience would prefer the clown. The situation had an irony since the actor whose fame and clout the production relied upon played the lesser character, and the star role was not played by the star. The effort to restore the balance was the source of all the behind-the-scenes wrangling and Fonda's dilemma was made worse by the idea that he had the unappealing part in a most appealing play.

By the third week of rehearsal, the play had been blocked and after one more week they planned to do a dry run for an invited audience. The least troubled seemed to be the neophyte actress.

That is not to say that Bancroft had *no* worries. One was the fact of having to face a live audience. She had performed in live TV broadcasts but this was different. Penn introduced the cast and staff and the play was performed. Although she misplaced a few lines, Bancroft did well, showing no nerves or reason for despair. Fonda did not miss a word but his unhappiness was apparent. The audience responded with polite applause but did not offer one laugh in a show that was intended to have humor. A second dry run was organized for a Saturday night audience, with the response better: There was laughter and a request for a curtain call.

After a Sunday show, the company moved to Washington for the out-of-town opening on Thursday, December 5, 1957, at the Shubert Theatre. The actors, Penn and Gibson traveled on the train together on December 2, 1957. Gibson spoke of his concerns over Bancroft's overplaying and Fonda's underplaying and the need to bring them to one level. The play was felt to have structural problems, but the bigger problem was Fonda. He was still not happy and what made it worse for him was that the play was a two-hander and he was on stage for nearly the whole time. Fonda knew that any doubt or conceptual flaw would be apparent so his reaction was to retreat from the role and underplay. Offstage, the actor loudly made his dissatisfaction known. Perversely, what made Fonda feel worse was Bancroft's enthusiasm for what she knew to be the plum role of the play. Gittel was offbeat, charismatic and sympathetic and the actress inhabited her more than played her. The more lively she was, the more lifeless Fonda was, and the imbalance pushed Gittel into a non-realistic state which violated Gibson's realistic intention. She had to be toned down so Jerry could be toned up.

When the company arrived in Washington, the set was introduced. It had not been used in the New York rehearsals due to technical, financial and union reasons. The action of the play required two separate apartments that could be called into use alternately or simultaneously. However, it was still not working by the technical rehearsal on December 3. That morning, Bancroft was interviewed in her hotel room by the Washington press. The box office for the show was disappointing with the advance sale being half of that expected. On December 4, a run-through lasted from 2 p.m. to midnight, which included bog-downs of 15-minute durations. Despite frustrations, the show was slowly coming together. The dress rehearsal took place on the afternoon of the opening night. Before the show, Bancroft had anticipatory excitement. Her feeling was aided by the fact that her family came from Yonkers, where they had moved from the Bronx, to attend. She, Penn and Gibson and his wife had dinner out, while Fonda stayed behind in his dressing room.

Before the opening night curtain, Gibson went backstage to the makeup cells, where he kissed Bancroft on the cheek. The house had been papered to fill up the empty seats and the curtain was 20 minutes late but the audience remained patient. They noticeably enjoyed the comedy of the first act, the somberness of the second and third acts less so, and provided perfunctory curtain calls at the play's end. Penn, Gibson and Coe decided that muting Gittel to improve Jerry was not the way to go. They had experimented with toning Bancroft down but found this did not bring Fonda up—and with both performers down, there was no show. Gibson would say that it would take another month before they were able to fine-tune a more truthful performance out of the actress but, as she was, she played with bravura.

Bancroft's performance featured a moment when she went on without her pants. Gittel was supposed to grab her pajamas and run into a back room and put them on. But Bancroft only grabbed half of them and when she went back to change, she realized it was the bottom part she didn't get. She said if it had been the top part she didn't get, she wouldn't have able to come out. Backstage in her dressing room after the show, Bancroft was besieged by visitors, speaking so excitedly that Gibson doubted she heard what he said to her. Gibson found Fonda sitting alone, stoop-shouldered, at his makeup table and looking like a man who had been pulled out of a dishwater sea.

Richard L. Coe in *The Washington Post* wrote that Bancroft embarked on her wise, cynical homilies with contagious relish. Jay Carmody in the *Evening Star* said that Bancroft was vivacious and affecting. Tom Donnelly (*The Washington Daily News*) wrote that she sometimes overplayed her character in the preliminaries but soon settled down to give a performance that was altogether delightful.

The day after Gibson ran into Bancroft outside the hotel. She said that his face made her feel like crying. The play settled in for its 17-day Washington run and Gibson kept working on Jerry and tightening the second act. Fonda's continued unhappiness led Coe to suggest that there was the possibility of the actor leaving the show. Gibson responded that he wanted that possibility explored although he was aware that they had not fulfilled their responsibility to him. Fritz Weaver and Fonda's standby Kevin McCarthy were considered. Gibson decided he would stay away from performances, dutifully accepting rewrite requests from Coe and Penn. Confined to his hotel room, he received visitors including Bancroft, who would look in after the show and have dinner with him. Fonda again suggested he should be replaced after a *Variety* review hailed Bancroft but was critical of him. The issue of how the actor left was also contentious, since if he was fired the company would be liable for his contract but if he quit, they were not.

Penn left rehearsals when his pregnant wife went into labor and Gibson rejoined Coe and the actors. Now that the writer was directing, he found his relationship with Fonda improving. Returned after the birth of his son, Penn asked that Gibson continue to attend rehearsals as well. One morning Bancroft visited the writer, telling him she had worked all night, not on her role, but on Jerry, to justify her own opinion that Hamlet *could* dominate the clown by intensity rather than competitive charms. She took Gibson's room as a stage and somberly acted Jerry for him. The writer was both amused and impressed and felt that if she wasn't female, she would have been perfect casting. Gibson suggested that Bancroft repeat the performance for Fonda, and then the actor could work what she did into the show. Penn refused, feeling that such an action would be an affront.

Rehearsals went on hold when Bancroft became paralyzed with gynecic cramps. She was able to work again for the last performances in Washington. The director had told Gibson that Fonda had commenced to play Jerry as a "strange man" and a "sonofabitch" and Bancroft came to see the writer to tell him how her co-star was exciting and giving her much more to react to. The writer was pleased to see that Fonda was finally playing like a lion and quelling Bancroft's comedy into proportion. The minute the curtain came down, the stage hands took the set apart for the move to Philadelphia. The writer and Bancroft celebrated the Washington run by talking it over until four in the morning in her room. The next day, the company took taxis to Philadelphia in preparation for the Christmas Day opening three days later. The Washington season had resulted in a loss of over $15,000.

Bancroft had kept up her correspondence with Mario, still with the hope they would marry. But by the time she was in Washington, so involved was she in the play that she had stopped writing to him entirely. Bancroft broke off her engagement because it seemed that her need for marriage had been filled by the success of her career. When the actress had first come to the play, she was in a vulnerable period but now her confidence had grown. Another factor contributing to Bancroft's newfound resistance to marriage: religion. When she left Hollywood and its lifestyle, she reconnected with the values of her upbringing. Bancroft had not gotten a religious annulment of her marriage to May and this meant that the Church did not recognize the legality of her divorce. So for her to wed again, she would be rejecting the Church—something she did not want to do.

The December 7, 1957, *New York Times* had reported that the show was now scheduled to open in New York on January 13, 1958. The show had three weeks to go in Philadelphia. Offstage, Bancroft spent time with production secretary Jessica Levy, but in the days prior to the Philly opening she began experiencing difficulties with her voice. A tickle soon turned into an irritation and then laryngitis. At an afternoon run-through on opening night, Bancroft was whispering her part, saving her voice for the evening performance. But by curtain time she was not feeling at all well. Although her audibility was in question, the opening night still went ahead. Gibson found the performances lusterless with Bancroft audible but weak, and Fonda playing a level midway between his opening and closing work in Washington. But the reshaped play held the audience and the curtain calls were encouraging. Afterwards the company adjourned to a restaurant to await the reviews. The first one came on the radio and it was favorable. Henry T. Murdock in the *Philadelphia Inquirer* wrote that Bancroft lit up the stage with her funny, explosive, warm-hearted gamine heroine. Max de Schauensee of the *Evening Bulletin* said it was a triumph on her part and that nothing the actress had shown in her numerous movie roles gave any indication of the talent she displayed. But Jerry Gaghan in the *Philadelphia Daily News* wrote that Bancroft mugged unashamedly and her performance ranked as one of the year's busiest.

Gibson found Gaghan's claim to be true. He was concerned that her excessive acting would mar the Broadway debut of what he knew to be a remarkable talent. Gibson rationalized that perhaps she was playing so excessively because of the need for big shows in the circus tents provided for the out-of-town tryouts. But the show was destined for one of the smallest New York theaters, where this would be even more of a problem. He spoke to Bancroft about the mugging and she reacted blankly, as if she had no idea what he meant. The writer consulted Penn about it, and at the next performance the mugging had gone. Bancroft's bronchitis continued to trouble her and she was given outpatient treatment. She was warned not to go out unnecessarily because of her throat but the actress chose to see a movie one night with Gibson and Jessica Levy. No harm seemed to come from the experience, but in the new year Bancroft was ill again. Gibson felt that Bancroft's soul was made of leather but her body was not. The day after the Philadelphia opening, a boil in her throat had been lanced and now the doctor diagnosed her as being in a state of exhaustion and ordered her back to her hotel. The cross-legged postures in the play had caused a hernia in one of her knees and Bancroft would have to rehearse and act with it encased in an elastic bandage. She carried on, though being ill she was not at her best. Despite this issue and Fonda's unhappiness, Gibson felt the show was looking better and the box office was thriving on word of mouth.

The final Philadelphia performance was Saturday, January 11, 1958, and at midnight the crew dismantled the set to bring it to the Booth Theatre on Broadway. The first show in New York was scheduled to be Tuesday, January 14. On January 12, it was reported that the show would now open on the 16th. On the same date, Maurice Zolotow reported for the *New York Times* from Philadelphia on the show, with an Al Hirschfeld caricature of Bancroft and Fonda also appearing in his article "Concerning Five on a Seesaw." The five referred to Bancroft, Fonda, Gibson, Penn and Coe. Zolotow reported that a problem Bancroft experienced was keeping solid food down. She supposedly confided in Fonda about it and he suggested she break two raw eggs into a tumbler and drink it, as a good way of getting stout protein nourishment without pain. When Bancroft came down with acute laryngitis in Philadelphia, it was said that Gibson telephoned his wife, a resident physician at the Riggs Sanitarium in Stockbridge, Massachusetts. The actress was given a long and detailed therapeutic formula for her relief, which included lemon juice and glycerin in hot water. Bancroft was told that she must not speak at all except during a performance between then and New York, not even whisper since it was considered as bad as speaking.

She took up residence at the Hotel Manhattan, located a block from the Booth. The show still had rehearsals because of the continuous lines changes that Gibson supplied. The first preview went well except for Bancroft being struck by one of the set's turntables moving in the dark during a transition. The following day's rehearsal had director's notes, more line changes and frazzled nerves.

Opening night: The actress napped in the day to try and recharge herself after suffering from a new bout of insomnia. When she awoke, she had a bowl of pea soup which she hoped was mild enough not to aggravate her gastritis, then she went to the theater. Gibson visited the actors backstage, exchanging bulletins with Bancroft on the state of their thoraxes. She confided she had no nerves and just the desire to get the opening over with. Gibson wrote that the show happened brilliantly and the actors had never been better. After the performance, the audience stood and applauded for repeated curtain calls. Backstage, Bancroft called for her parents, whom she had invited, and when they found each other they all embraced. After the crowds dispersed, the actress was joined by her friend Ruby Rick, who had flown in from Hollywood. Together they went to the apartment of Coe's agent for the opening night party to await the reviews. However Fonda was not in attendance since he had gone back to his own apartment.

The show was praised by Brooks Atkinson in the *New York Times*, who said it had two extraordinarily winning actors. He wrote that Bancroft exploded with gestures that were natural and that she modulated the part with vocal inflections that were both funny and authentic. He wrote more about the show in the January 26, 1958, *Times*, adding that Bancroft's Broadway debut was beginning a career that at the moment seemed to have great possibilities.

The text of the Atkinson and Walter Kerr reviews were called in to the party before the city editions hit the newsstands, but by the time the actress left the party around 4:30 a.m. she had obtained printed copies of the *Times* and *The New York Herald Tribune* to take with her. She and Ruby went to Bancroft's hotel room and read the reviews, then talked until 8:30 a.m. when they went to sleep. The actress woke up in the afternoon to read the other New York critics' reviews, which were all complimentary towards her. Bancroft's sister, after reading the reviews and seeing that Anne's name wasn't up in lights, reportedly told the actress, "What are they waiting for, bulbs?"

Bancroft checked out of the hotel and moved into an apartment in the East 50s which she had sublet from another actress. The January 18, 1958, *New York Times* proclaimed the show a hit and Gibson confirmed in "The Seesaw Log" that by the fifth week, the show's statement of operations confirmed the success. The box office receipts less the theater share and expenses resulted in an operating profit of over $8000. The show was Tony-nominated for Outstanding Play and Director, and Bancroft for Supporting Dramatic Actress. She would be the only winner.

Three days after opening, Fonda got the flu and he was out for a week. After his return, he only lasted until June 28 when he was replaced by Dana Andrews. Fonda left

In *Two for the Seesaw* (January 16, 1958, to June 28, 1959).

the role to take a vacation. He would say that he had adored Bancroft and that she was one of the country's finest actresses. Bancroft was out of the show from September 15 until September 29 while she went on a two-week vacation and was replaced during that time by Lee Grant. Grant permanently replaced Bancroft on June 29, 1959, and the show ran till October 31, 1959.

By its last week, Bancroft was already in another Broadway play: *The Miracle Worker*, a reteaming of Bancroft, Gibson, Penn and Coe. It was an expansion of Gibson's teleplay recounting the story of Annie Sullivan in teaching the deaf and blind Helen Keller in childhood. Bancroft played Sullivan.

The actress was photographed in her home by Alfred Eisenstaedt for *Life* magazine and the pictures ran in the February 1, 1958, issue. On February 7, she promoted *Two for the Seesaw* on NBC's 30-minute talk show *The Arlene Francis Show*. Gilbert Millstein, who interviewed her for the February 9, 1958, *New York Times*, described her as a pale darkling actress of 26, a girl with a robust but peculiarly compelling voice and a slight but equally figure.

Bancroft appeared in an episode of ABC's *The Frank Sinatra Show*, "A Time to Cry," filmed in Hollywood and aired on February 21, 1958. The teleplay was written by Hagar Wilde from a story by Teddy Keller. The plot concerned Johnny Maitland (Lloyd Bridges), a murderer who holds Carol Welles (Bancroft) hostage in her frontier cabin while her husband Clay (John Archer) lies dying from a bullet wound in the next room.

The actress was reportedly considered by writer-director Samuel Fuller for the war movie *Verboten!* (1959). Fuller commented that she was ravishing and that he had never seen her in a film. But he decided that Bancroft wasn't right for the part of the German girl, Helga Schiller, so he cast Susan Cummings.

The April 12, 1958, *New York Times* reported that producer Charles K. Feldman had recently acquired the movie rights for *Two for the Seesaw* with the provision that Arthur

Penn direct. William Holden was proposed to co-star but no mention was made of who would play the female role. On April 13, Bancroft received her Best Supporting Actress Tony Award at the ceremony held at the Waldorf-Astoria Hotel. This show was not televised due to a strike by the International Brotherhood of Electrical Workers.

In her book *Tales of a Hollywood Housewife: A Memoir by the First Mrs. Lee Marvin*, Betty Marvin describes Bancroft meeting with Marvin at the Los Angeles premiere of MGM's *Cat on a Hot Tin Roof* (1958). This would have been around September 1958 when Bancroft was on vacation from *Two for the Seesaw*. Betty wrote that the couple exchanged a quick embrace and then Marvin introduced his wife to Bancroft, saying that she had single-handedly got him through that wreck of a film in Mexico.

As Bancroft continued to play on Broadway, she also continued to regularly attend acting classes at the HB studios. On one occasion she received high praise from Berghof: He said she was like a little daughter of Anna Magnani, consistent with the actress' own description of her mother's temperament being as hot as fire. Bancroft applied to audition for the Actors Studio and was accepted so that her weekly schedule included two visits to the Studio, two lessons from her vocal coach, three sessions with her analyst and one stop at the hairdresser. Her Broadway salary was reassessed and upgraded from its former modest terms. Bancroft tried to use some of her money to help out her family, but out of pride they refused her generosity. She became otherwise extravagant and commented that she would have bought the Central Park Zoo if it was for sale. Aware that she was perhaps spending too much, Bancroft hired David Cogan as a business manager and he put her on an allowance of $50 a week to cover meals, taxis and oddments. All her income and bills went directly to him and through Cogan's skill, Bancroft became as financially solvent as she was professionally successful. She rented a modest Village brownstone apartment which her mother described as a railroad flat like the ones she had grown up in, and in time was able to buy one of her own.

Some time in 1958, Norman Mailer arranged for a series of semi-staged readings at the Actors Studio of the play he had adapted from his novel *The Deer Park*. Bancroft, Kevin McCarthy and Rip Torn were in the cast and Frank Cosaro was the director. Mailer was critical of the actress' fiery, multi-level performance as the volatile dancer Elena Esposito. The role had been inspired by Mailer's exotic painter wife Adele Morales. Sources claim that the writer initially loved Bancroft in the role, but that changed after he supposedly made a pass at her offstage which she resisted. Bancroft responded to the writer's new disapproval by telling him to get Adele to play it, since that was what he had wanted all along. Mailer shot back that the actress "would never amount to anything," and then she *was* replaced by Adele in subsequent readings. (Mailer's play was staged off–Broadway at the Lucille Lortel Theatre [January 31–May 21, 1967] with Rosemary Tory as Elena.)

Bancroft received new offers for work. There was talk of a *Two for the Seesaw* sequel but nothing came of it. Another was a nightclub tour which would have allowed her to sing and dance and which might possibly have included a stint in Las Vegas which paid five figures a night. Bancroft declined because she preferred to stay in New York and continue to improve her craft. The actress seemed to be more intrigued by theater work, although the October 12, 1958, *New York Times* reported that she was one of many expressing interest in appearing on the CBS-TV show *Camera Three*. This came after producer John McGiffert had written invitations to well-known actors to play roles they had never had a chance to do. The show was a low-budget experimental program devoted to art, culture, drama and education. On the advice of her agent and business manager, Bancroft decided to exploit her new success by endorsing Rheingold Beer in magazine advertising. She was photographed at home by Walter Daran for *Life* in pictures published on January 1, 1959.

On February 20, 1959, Bancroft made her first of many appearances on the NBC talk show *The Jack Paar Show* in New York. On March 6, she appeared on the DuMont WABD late-night interview program *Night-Beat* with Mike Wallace. In the *New York Times* of March 15, 1959, Harold Clurman reviewed the published text of *Two for the Seesaw* which came with the Log describing the writer's experiences during the play's production. The article was accompanied by photographs that showed Bancroft reading the play with Penn and Fonda, rehearsing with both, and then on stage with Fonda.

The *New York Times* of April 2, 1959, reported that she was to leave *Two for the Seesaw* on June 27, 1959. After their Broadway success, Gibson, Penn and Coe didn't want her to leave the show since she was its drawing card. Coe had originally wanted her to stay for two years but he decided to reduce that time to 18 months so that she could do *The Miracle Worker*. The same article reported that *The Miracle Worker* was scheduled to open on October 15, 1959.

On May 15, the *New York Times* advised that *The Miracle Worker* would be produced at The Playhouse with a new opening date of October 19, 1959. Rehearsals were to commence on August 17, with Philadelphia tryouts from September 12 and Boston from September 29. On May 27, it was reported that Gibson's script was being put into Braille for the private use of the real Keller, and that Gibson, Bancroft and Penn would soon spend time with her at her Westport, Connecticut, residence to discuss the production. Bancroft also planned to visit the Perkins Institute in Boston to learn methods of training handicapped children. Some sources claim that Bancroft was back on *The Jack Paar Show* on June 5 and August 11, 1959, but these cannot be confirmed. On June 28, it was confirmed that Lee Grant would replace Bancroft in *Two for the Seesaw* beginning on June 29.

The actress' desire to go back on stage after she left *Two for the Seesaw* was said to come from a fear that she would be typecast as Gittel because it was assumed that she was simply playing herself. This is why she accepted *The Miracle Worker*. In 1953, William Gibson had come across *The Story of My Life*, the autobiography of Helen Keller, in the library of his home town in Stockbridge. There was an appendix, which was a series of letters written to her by Annie Sullivan, Keller's teacher and lifelong friend. Gibson decided that the material could be dramatized as a dance with an accompanying verse narrative. The dance was never produced and Gibson put aside the idea to work on other things, including *Two for the Seesaw*. When he met with Arthur Penn in Stockbridge in 1956 to discuss casting the play, he mentioned the Keller book and the Sullivan letters and suggested that he might dramatize them for television. After many rejections, *Playhouse 90* scheduled it in their 1957 season with Penn as director. Gibson's teleplay also drew upon the Nell Braddy biography *Annie Sullivan Macy*. The special starred Teresa Wright as Sullivan and Patty McCormack as Keller. When *Two for the Seesaw* was in tryouts in Washington, Gibson had been offered the prospect of a movie version of *The Miracle Worker* as well as bids to have him rework the teleplay as a Broadway play. He decided to stay with his *Two for the Seesaw* team and have Penn and Coe also work on the Broadway play.

Following the good notices Bancroft received in Washington, Gibson considered her a good choice to play Sullivan. He had a Sunday brunch with the actress and offered her the part. He wrote in his "Seesaw Log" that her reply was a wide-eyed and worried, "You think I'm right for the part?" In Philadelphia she read the first act of the play Gibson had fashioned but she disliked it. Later she would say this was due to her emotional immaturity, and she obviously would change her mind.

The actress prepared for the role, reading everything she could that was written by or about Sullivan. She also spent three weeks at the Institute of Physical Medicine and Rehabilitation at Bellevue Hospital mingling with blind children. She could only attend the Institute between mid-morning and afternoon, since her evenings were occupied by *Two for the Seesaw*. Bancroft soon began to concentrate on a 17-year-old boy who had not yet learned how to eat with a spoon. The actress was fortunate that before her time was taken up with other pre-production work, she was able to see the boy achieve this goal. Bancroft became close friends with one of the teachers, Joan Chase, and in the summer of 1958 the women flew together to Chicago for seminars and workshops with the American Foundation for the Blind at Northwestern University.

To further her studies, Bancroft arranged to be blind for one day, having adhesive tape placed over her eyelids which she hid behind dark glasses. Nina Leen took photographs (published in *Life* on July 1, 1959) of the actress with her eyes covered like this, sitting at a table, attempting to light a cigarette, and then laughing when the coverings were removed. Bancroft set out into the world with a young actor as an escort, with her eyes covered. She wanted more than just to make her way through a hallway or a city block so together they went to an amusement pier in Wildwood, New Jersey, where the actress rode the rollercoaster. After that they visited a nearby seaside diner to have ice cream, much of which melted, ran off Bancroft's spoon and onto her hand. When she returned to her hotel room, the adhesive was removed.

Bancroft also attended the Vacation Camp for the Blind in Spring Valley, New York, where she perfected the manual alphabet she had been studying for months. She reported there was a blind-deaf man nobody could understand when he tried to communicate with someone. She went up to him and spelled in his hand "What you do want?" and he spelled back "My bag." Bancroft said she never felt so important in her life; that the man was in trouble and she was the only one who understood him.

The actress also worked on the dialect to be used for Annie Sullivan, who spoke with an Irish-American brogue. Bancroft prepared for the sustained voice the way she did everything else—scrupulously and with a need for authenticity. As much as she worked solo on the character's exterior, she relied upon Gibson's play for the interior life, discarding most of what she learned in her research. After *Two for the Seesaw*, the actress had an unshakeable faith in his work and she replied upon Penn to help her make the correct interpretation.

In her memoir *As I Am*, Patricia Neal wrote that Penn approached her about the play in April 1959, wanting her for the part of Helen Keller's mother. Neal had first seen Bancroft at the Actors Studio and admired her as an actress. After that, they got to know each other socially at the Strasberg parties. Neal said Bancroft was great fun and she liked her very much, and their paths were destined to cross many times. She reported that she would be invited for a drink with Bancroft and Penn after a few days of rehearsal, and that Penn asked her quite candidly if she resented not playing the star role. Neal was equally candid and said that she did and found it tough to step down and she was trying her damnedest to be gracious. Penn and Bancroft then breathed sighs of relief and thanked her for being honest. They assured Neal that they knew how difficult it was for her and the actress wrote that she felt the fact that she adored the both of them helped her.

The hardest part to cast in the play was the six-year-old Helen Keller who had suffered an illness that left her unable to hear, see or speak. One little girl singularly trained for the part was 12-year-old Patty Duke. In her *A&E Biography* episode, she said she had two years of preparation before her audition, although in her autobiography *Call Me Anna*, she wrote that the project was spotted by her agent John Ross in early 1958 when he saw an article in the theatrical newspaper *Backstage*. On July 10, 1959, the *New York Times* reported that Duke was the leading contender to play Keller, said to have beaten out over 500 children who auditioned.

During the audition process, Bancroft joined the young actress for the breakfast-table fight scene, and the actresses slapped each other and wrestled on the floor. Duke said it was like being a boxer in the ring. Afterwards, Bancroft reportedly told her she was strong and Duke said so was Bancroft. There was a concern about the girl's size since it was felt if Duke grew another two inches, this would make her look too tall opposite her co-star. To address the height concern, Duke donned shoes that made her look two inches taller and stood next to Bancroft. After a month came the call that said she had the part but if she grew another two inches, she was out. On August 6, 1959, it was reported that Duke had been signed until August 1960, the agreement subject to a growth clause. Bancroft and Duke became pals and soon they were carrying on conversations in the manual alphabet behind everyone else's backs, cracking jokes and having themselves a time.

Miracle Worker rehearsals began in August at The Playhouse. In the first week, Duke carried around a little doll until Bancroft asked why she had it and said that she had to get rid of it so that they could work. Rather than being upset, the young actress instead felt the beginning of a sense of camaraderie with the older woman that was wonderful for her. Bancroft became a channel of energy and love for Duke and the two became close. Duke wrote that the most generous thing the older actress did was to allow her to go into her dressing room 30 minutes before the show's curtain and just hang around. She would fiddle with Bancroft's makeup while Bancroft opened her mail and got dressed. Duke said she felt the actress cared about and accepted her. She treated her the way she knew a kid of her age wanted to be treated.

The one major problem for Penn was the staging of the fight scenes. Some sources say he had to overcome their overzealousness, while he said he had to work to keep the improvisational feeling in the breakfast-room and the summer house scenes. The play's most violent scene had been taken from one of Sullivan's letters where she had described a battle royal over Keller's breakfast-table eating habits. Her parents had allowed the child to go from plate to plate taking what she wanted. This placated Helen and enabled the family to carry on a normal conversation. Sullivan was appalled when she saw this because she felt it worked against the discipline that was needed to free the child from her disabilities. When Sullivan tries to correct Helen, the child reacts violently. Penn believed if he blocked out the moves and crosses too definitely, the scene would have become an empty exercise and something for the actors to do by rote and unemotionally. Therefore he gave them free rein in this scene and in the summer house scene, so that Duke could tear around and break things up in any way she felt like. At first Duke was tentative but Bancroft reportedly taunted her to hit her and then the two of them went at it wholeheartedly. Duke reported that one special technique she learned for the effect of pulling

Bancroft's hair was that she would just hold the actress' head but make it look like she was gripping her hair. Then Bancroft would put her hands on top of Duke's wrists as she sank to the floor, supposedly in pain. What she was actually doing was pushing Duke's hands away as she was going down, but it worked so that it looked like the girl was tearing Bancroft's hair out. This was something that just evolved, because after the first two times Duke pulled Bancroft's hair and the older actress told her that they had to figure something out so as to not hurt her again. Penn reported that the actresses never played the fight scene in the same way, and both were rigged with elaborate hidden padding to protect them. There *were* inevitable bumps and bruises but the effort was worth it because the scene would always captivate the audience and end with applause for the actors. Duke said there was a similar situation when she had to smack Bancroft with her doll. It had a soft head but the timing needed to be worked out. Sometimes Duke would accidently hit her in the ears or eyes and it devastated the girl to hurt her co-star.

Bancroft reported that the rehearsal process was tough. Once during the fight scene, her foot was badly injured. Bancroft had a bone injury which disabled her for eight days after she ran full tilt across the stage and smashed into a fallen chair. Penn said they did not know that the actress was injured until the end of the scene because she played it through. They had to rehearse with Bancroft's understudy, with Bancroft sitting in a chair keeping her leg elevated. She would say the lines as her understudy walked through the part and Bancroft had to write down all of the movements that Penn was giving her. It was a very difficult period. Then she couldn't find a shoe that would fit over this enormous egg-shaped bruise. It was uncomfortable for the first six weeks, and it only cleared up the day before they opened in New York. It was tough for Bancroft during the Philadelphia and Boston tryouts. The actress said Penn taught her everything. He was more help to her in her acting than any other person. Bancroft said he was an extraordinary teacher and she was a good student just like Annie and Helen.

Duke reported that she and Bancroft would nap after matinee shows, because they were so draining. On some nights, the fight scene would go wrong. Once, Duke found that a door on the set was not locked as it should have been—it opened when she turned the knob, so she had no choice but to walk through. Bancroft found herself playing the scene alone while Duke laughed backstage. Bancroft came after her, cursing out loud backstage, "I'll kill you, you son of a bitch!" Duke got to hysterically laughing, wet her pants and had to go back onstage that way. Another time, a door that they were supposed to exit through wouldn't open. Bancroft tried to open it with one of the six keys she carried on a ring and was cursing "Goddamn son of a bitch" under her breath while Duke made guttural sounds very loudly because she was afraid the audience would hear. Finally the older actress said, "Screw it!," picked Duke up, walked her to the window, pushed her out and dove right behind.

When the show went for its tryouts at Philadelphia's New Locust Theatre, the breakfast fight, which had previously run at ten minutes, was now 12 and it brought down the house. In Boston, Bancroft made the planned visit to the Perkins Institute for the Blind, which the real Sullivan had left to work with Keller, and she saw the memorabilia on display.

On October 15, 1959, at a luncheon at the Grand Ballroom of the Plaza, Bancroft introduced the entertainment, which included a blind concert pianist and a deaf-blind comic monologist. This was to open a fund-raising campaign for the Lighthouse, the New York Association for the Blind. On October 18, 1959, Maurice Zolotow reported on the show from Philadelphia. Bancroft was interviewed in her dressing room. There were no traumas like the illnesses she had with *Two for the Seesaw*. She was eating well, sleeping soundly and her voice was unimpaired. Asked if she had any personal changes, she advised she was still living in the same apartment and she had not acquired minks, sables or jewelry. She said she didn't wear jewelry and she didn't care for diamonds. Bancroft said she was getting a bigger salary on the show and a percentage of the gross.

The show had an extraordinary number of lighting and set cues so that the company was at the technical rehearsal until 4 or 5 a.m. trying to solve all the problems. The advance sales were not good and they had about half a house but then they got a most unusual break. Melvyn Douglas was down the street doing a show and because he was a big star, the company was doing very well. It happened to be very hot in Philadelphia and on the day of *The Miracle Worker's* opening, the actor collapsed. His show was cancelled that night so they offered his audience the option of either getting their money back or seeing *The Miracle Worker*. By show time, the house was full. The audience loved the show, going bananas after the final curtain. Penn had choreographed a curtain call where Duke and Bancroft came out from opposite sides of the stage and grabbed hands. The audience stood up and yelled "Bravo, bravo." They had 18 curtain calls.

Opening night in New York, October 19, 1959, had the audience so responsive right off the bat that their reactions kicked the cast into another gear. At one point, when Duke threw a pitcher of water at Bancroft, it nailed Rosalind Russell in the front row. People around the actress tried to help her but she was so enthralled she wouldn't let anyone interrupt what was happening onstage. Duke said the actress just sat there drenched, with water dripping off her hat. Russell also got spoons thrown at her; presumably concerned that the actors would run out of them, she gently reached up and put one back on the stage. Duke said the company got 13 curtain calls which was unheard of for a straight play on Broadway. The after-party was held at the Absinthe House.

Bancroft would later say that she thought the play was a very important piece of work. She thanked God that Gibson wrote it and that she got the part and that it got the recognition that it did and the appreciation because they certainly didn't think it would. Bancroft remembered Fred Coe sitting around asking, "Who was going to go and see a play about a deaf, blind kid?" As soon as they opened in New York, she realized they were going to work for a while and have jobs because there was never an empty seat.

Brooks Atkinson in the *New York Times* wrote that Bancroft was glorious. In a subsequent *Times* article he added that Bancroft and Duke gave performances that were both fiery and illuminating and laid a powerful spell on the imagination of the audience.

The production received Tony nominations for Best Play, Best Actress in a Play, Best Director of a Play, Best Dramatic Scenic Design and John Waters for Best Stage Technician. Gibson, Bancroft, Penn and Walters won at the ceremony held at the Astor Hotel on April 24, 1960, which was broadcast live on CBS with Bancroft in attendance. Bancroft's award was presented by Helen Hayes. In her acceptance speech, she said that there were three reasons why she thought she deserved the award, which got a laugh from the audience. The reasons were Fred Coe, Bill Gibson and Arthur Penn.

In April, Bancroft took a week off for vacation and she was replaced by her understudy, Tresa Hughes. The show's run was interrupted from June 2, 1960, when the curtain stayed down on all Broadway stages. The League of New York Theatres and Actor's Equity Association failed to resolve their differences over a contract deadlock about minimum pay increases and the establishment of a pension fund. On June 3, 1960, Bancroft said she was sorry that the League was being unreasonable about such reasonable demands. On June 10, it was reported the dispute had been settled and shows would reopen on June 13, 1960.

Bancroft's run was also affected by Duke taking a vacation from July 4 to 9 where she was replaced by understudy Candace Culkin. Bancroft was replaced in the production from February 6, 1961, by Suzanne Pleshette, who stayed with the show until it closed on July 1, 1961. Bancroft had originally intended to stay only till December 1960. By February she said that she had to go, despite Duke's pleadings for her to stay, because she had to do other things. According to Duke, when they were on stage at Bancroft's final performance, she kept asking the older actress not to go, but not so anyone else could hear. Bancroft also declined to do the play on its national tour, being replaced by Eileen Brennan in the tour that began on April 12, 1961, in Wilmington, Delaware.

Portrait for the stage show of *The Miracle Worker* (October 19, 1959–February 5, 1961).

The actress told TV interviewer Charlie Rose in 2000 that doing the fight scene where she had to lift Duke, the girl was like the boy who had to lift the calf every day until it was a great big cow and he could lift it. As Duke grew, she gained weight and she was about ten pounds more at the end of the run than she was at the beginning. To try and slow her weight increase, the girl was put on a diet. Ice cream and candy were replaced by grapefruit and cottage cheese and lettuce sandwiches. Duke admitted she rebelled against this whenever she could by eating Hershey bars because she felt she was starving.

There were several noteworthy incidents during the performances. At the start of the play one night, a man seated in the front row rudely placed his gray fedora hat on the edge of the stage, topside, before the curtain went up. It was ignored by the actors all through the first and most of the second acts but Duke sensed that it was annoying Bancroft. There was a moment at the end of the second act where Sullivan felt she had achieved a victory and walked proudly downstage, blessed herself and turned around to look back at the garden house. One source claims that Bancroft, breaking from the action, pitched up a water pitcher from the set and slowly poured its entire contents on top of the hat. Then she crushed it into a pancake-like flatness without comment as the owner reportedly looked on agape. The audience gave the actress a thunderous ovation which Bancroft ignored and ordered the pitcher refilled and returned to the interrupted scene. Duke said the man was still in his seat for the third act but his hat was no longer on the stage. The actress also recalled how she and Bancroft would regularly laugh at the scene at the dinner table before the miracle. Col. Keller was slicing ham which was made of wax and Duke found the sight of the wax slices falling on a plate in a certain way the funniest thing she had ever seen. Her shoulders would start to shake and Bancroft would poke her and then she would start to laugh and *her* shoulders would shake too. The other actors would continue with the scene as the two actresses fought to control their laughter.

In October, Bancroft appeared on the cover of *Theatre Arts* magazine. The edition also featured an article by William Gibson about the play, with more photographs of Bancroft in variations of the cover pose. She was then on the December 21, 1959, cover of *Time* in a sketch of her in character as Annie Sullivan, giving her national recognition. The article by Dick Seamon was accompanied by photographs of the actress in *The Miracle Worker* with Duke, her wearing bandages over her eyes in preparation for the role, at home in her New York apartment sitting on a sofa, and in *Don't Bother to Knock*. The article traced her career and he ranked her among the top actresses of the day with Julie Harris, Geraldine Page and Kim Stanley. For the interview she wore one of her carefully careless costumes which included a thick shapeless sweater, flat shoes, coarse uncombed hair and a rugged tongue indicative of someone who sought refuge in being thought of as a kook. Bancroft also liked to demonstrate eccentricity. One night her friends teased her about carelessness with money so she pulled a $20 bill from her purse and ate it. Bancroft's salary was reported to be $150,000 a year and she was also said to own Manhattan real estate and have an interest in a California bank and a Texas oil well. She sometimes relied upon snacks her mother sent from Yonkers and she kept warm by huddling in the kitchen of her Greenwich Village apartment with both her stove and oven going full blast. The "ignorant slob" worked to make herself over with psychiatry, acting lessons and voice lessons because she hoped to do a musical next. This might have referred to the Actors Studio production of *My Fair Lady* where Bancroft played Eliza Doolittle, though another source claimed she only did a scene from the show which included singing "Just You Wait." Twice a week Bancroft still went to Manhattan's Institute for Physical Medicine and Rehabilitation to work with blind, disturbed children. She had little time left for dating although she still saw the Three Bears—Coe, Gibson and Penn—and a couple of boys from the Actor's Studio. Bancroft was still open to marriage and had recently put a piece of a friend's wedding cake under her pillow.

On December 20, 1959, the *New York Times* reported further on the *Miracle Worker* stage fight. The match was described as between Bancroft standing 5'6" and weighing 122 pounds, and Duke at 4'4¾" and 60 pounds. It was said that despite the actresses wearing pads that were meant to protect their shoulders, chests, elbows, knees and shins, there were still injuries. Bancroft was photographed in her dressing room at the Playhouse Theatre in her white bra and pantaloons over black stockings with a knee brace and adjusting the padding she wore on her left leg. The staged hostilities between the two began to seem real to Duke, so that she was afraid of her co-star and afraid to go to the theater. This made Bancroft extremely upset and she asked to go and see her and the two hugged and kissed and cried. When they went to work that night, the couple got through the fight scene with more care and it was a catharsis for them both. Bancroft reported that the fight scene's varying duration was determined by audience response—if coughs or rustling indicated that the audience was bored or impatient, she would prune the action. Depending on the audience, the scene could be played for laughs, tears or tension. Penn said on opening night it was played straight, dry, directly and bitterly but on occasion it had been hilarious because Bancroft was a natural clown.

4

Mel Brooks

On February 9, 1960, at an after-theater supper party held at the Hotel Astor, she was presented with one of the 1960 American National Theater and Academy (ANTA) awards for her performance in *The Miracle Worker*. On February 11, the *New York Times* reported that she had recently participated in a reading of a dramatization of extracts from the work of Ernest Hemingway with the overall title of "Scenes of Love and Death." The five-character cast was going to be directed by Frank Corsaro. An invitation had been received for the premiere of the show to take place in the summer at the Edinburgh Festival. In October a pre–Broadway tour was to start for a New York opening in the spring of 1961.

Bancroft made her first appearance on the NBC music show *Perry Como's Kraft Music Hall*, filmed in New York and broadcast on February 24, 1960. The episode was written by Herbert Baker, Billy Friedberg and Will Glickman and directed by Clark Jones. Bancroft's hair was by Ernest Adler worn in a shoulder-length style and her gowns were by Ceil Chapman. She is first seen when the guests for the show are individually welcomed by Como as the chorus sings "That's Entertainment." Como later introduces Bancroft by having the edition of *Time* magazine with her on the cover. When he comments on the success of *Two for the Seesaw* and *The Miracle Worker*, she replies "And would you believe it, I have a cold."

Como asks her how different Bancroft is from Gittel Mosca and the actress offers to play her. Since she was overlooked for the film version, this sequence is the only available view of Bancroft in the role. She produces a hairpin and ties up her hair, then has a jar of ointment as a bleach cream made by Gittel's friend Sophie which she applies to her upper lip (like a mustache) and to her chin. A telephone rings and Bancroft as Gittel speaks to Sophie. Bancroft's performance here shows how convincing she is acting on the telephone and also how she gestures with her free hand and uses her Bronx accent for the part. The actress is photographed for the nearly three-minute scene in an extended medium shot. Afterwards, Como wipes the cream off Bancroft's face with a towel and hands her a hand mirror so she can finish taking it off. She undoes her hair and they both sit on stools. Como plays a guitar as Bancroft sings the Italian song "Way Marie" with him. Her voice is deep and competent though without singularity.

Bancroft returns for the finale medley. Standing in front of the chorus, she asks Como, "What am I going to do? I don't have a hit number." (The other guests, Bert Lahr, the Mills Brothers and Kay Starr, had all sung signature songs in the medley preceding her.) Como replies, "Don't look at me. Neither have I," which causes Bancroft to laugh hysterically. Como then leads her into another Italian song, which he sings with her. The cast then all reprise "That's Entertainment."

On March 11, 1960, Bancroft was interviewed by Charles Collingwood on the CBS-TV news documentary series *Person-to-Person*. In the show (broadcast on June 10), the actress opened the doors of her Village brownstone to the cameras. Bancroft told of her changing names in radio, television and film, and added that if she ever went into burlesque she had another one picked out: Ruby Pepper. The actress commented that she had to get out and do more because she didn't know how long she was going to live. Bancroft said she wanted to do everything and, while that may have sounded greedy, it really wasn't. She just felt that when one limited their hopes, they also limited their horizons.

On March 26, 1960, 40 handicapped children, most of them deaf and others victims of cerebral palsy, attended *The Miracle Worker* and then were taken backstage to meet Bancroft and Duke. On April 6, 1960, Bancroft received the Comoedia Matinee Club's 30th annual award for the finest performance of the season at a ceremony at the club's luncheon at the Astor Hotel.

She participated in four special programs held at the Actors Studio from May 14 to 16, 1960, which for the time allowed the public to watch members at work on exercise scenes which was part of the studio's building-fund campaign. On May 29, the *Times* reported that it was hoped that Bancroft would join the cast of Ben Kerner's play *All Women Are One*. This was to be produced by Joel Schenker with the Theater Guild at the Astor Hotel's grand ballroom converted into a theatre for the 1962–1963 season. Hume Cronyn was reportedly interested in playing one of the two male roles in the piece, which had three characters. The chief stumbling block during the last three years had been the casting of the one woman in the script. The role required an actress who could play high comedy, caricature and farce. The play was produced at the Gate Theatre in New York in 1965.

June 27, 1960, was the 80th birthday of Helen Keller and also designated by New York's Mayor Wagner to be Helen Keller Day to honor her and to support the Helen Keller Crusade for the Blind. Bancroft attended the ceremony in the ballroom of the Gotham Hotel. Keller in turn honored a fellow worker in the same cause, Col. Edwin A. Baker, who received the first Helen Keller International Award for outstanding service to the blind. Bancroft spoke of the colonel's achievements in rehabilitating the blind and in helping them to help themselves. Keller reportedly told Bancroft that her handshake was like that of the real Sullivan.

On July 20, 1960, the *New York Times* reported that Paul Newman and Elizabeth Taylor had been signed to co-star in the film version of *Two for the Seesaw*. The Mirisch–Seven Arts production was scheduled to begin in New York in December 1960. The director was to be Delbert Mann and the screenplay adaptation would be written by Isobel Lennart. The article also reported that before she could begin the new film, Taylor was committed to star in *Cleopatra* for director Rouben Mamoulian, which had an August 15, 1960, starting date in England. Delays on that film would mean Taylor would not be able to make *Two for the Seesaw*.

On July 28, 1960, it was reported that at the Actors Studio, Bancroft had participated in a single presentational showing of a program of two short plays, "Rosemary" and "Paradise Hotel," by Molly Kazan, the wife of Elia Kazan. Because of her contract with *The Miracle Worker*, Bancroft was unable to appear in a planned off–Broadway production of the same which was to be directed by Gerald Freeman and to open in early October 1960.

On August 30, she appeared in two short plays at the Waldorf-Astoria Hotel under the auspices of the American Theater Wing's Community Play Series. The plays were Helen Menken's *Seven Steps to Living* and Eleanor Bayer' *Second Chance*. Staged by Herbert Machiz, they were designed to educate by dramatizing the rehabilitation of crippled children and adults. In the August 31, 1960, *New York Times,* David Anderson wrote that they were performed before delegates of the International Society for the Welfare of Cripples on the second day of a five-day meeting, one mostly devoted to medical discussions of disabilities. Anderson reported that Bancroft wept and barely got through her lines when she began to recite an epilogue to Menken's play but then, though drained of emotion, she managed to finish. The actress was no doubt affected by having around seven clusters of children and young men and women, all of whom had demonstrated the ability to overcome some disability.

On September 7, 1960, *The Miracle Worker* was one of the Broadway shows that tested an earlier start time for Wednesday evening shows. The usual 8:30 start was changed to 7:30 in an experiment designed to attract more commuters to Broadway's legitimate theaters. Bancroft had mixed feelings about the change. She said she missed the time she had to relax on Wednesday between matinees and evening performances. But now the actress said she was able to get home in time to see the beginning of *The Late Show*. On October 8, 1960, Bancroft attended a midnight block party in celebration of the first anniversary of Alexander H. Cohen's Nine O'Clock Theatre and in aid of the Actors Fund of America. It was held in Shubert Alley between West 44th and 54th Streets, with admittance to the occasion for the invited guests through the doors of the Shubert and Booth Theatres.

Bancroft reportedly performed on the NBC special *Gala Adlai on Broadway* (October 18, 1960) which honored Democratic Presidential nominee Adlai Stevenson. On October 27, 1960, she guested on *The Jack Paar Show* along with Jack Lemmon, who would later appear with her in the film *The Prisoner of Second Avenue*. Twenty-three-year-old college student Gordie Little reported that after the show, the actress stopped and chatted with him for what seemed like 20 minutes. He said she was humble and gracious and grateful for the success she had achieved. Bancroft encouraged him to pursue his dream of a radio career, and signed an autograph.

On November 29, 1960, she received the 1960 Award of Honorary Membership from Hadassah for her "outstanding performance" in *The Miracle Worker*. The presentation was made in the auditorium of the Seagram Building on Park Avenue.

Back on Perry Como's *Kraft Music Hall* (November 30, 1960), she wore gowns by Ceil Chapman. She was first seen sitting on a stool with Como and, as Bancroft bantered, her eye-line suggested that she was reading from an off-screen teleprompter. She sang a medley of "I Wish You Love" and "Some of These Days"; in the latter, she was supported by three male dancers. The dancers followed her as she moved up a staircase and they exited after she came back down again. Como then joined Bancroft to say how she gave every line of every lyric so much meaning, the same way she delivered dialogue. She told him that if he took a short course in Method acting, in no time at all he would learn not to say everything the same way. Bancroft demonstrated the different ways he could introduce the show, being happy and then sad where he gave her a handkerchief which she used to wipe an eye. She then tried it with anger which Bancroft made funny when she walked to the camera and told the audience to "sit back and relax." She asked Como to try introducing the show with anger and sadness expressing them the same way. In response a man was heard to say "Holy mackerel" which made Como and Bancroft laugh. She told Como to try with happiness which he did by plugging Kraft's Parkay margarine, to which Bancroft repeated her happy introduction believing she would get paid for it too.

She returned to banter more with Como and Bob Hope and then they moved to a barbershop set for a *Candid Camera*–style skit with the camera behind the shop mirror. Bancroft was a customer for a haircut. When Hope pulled her into a chair, she quipped, "My, you're strong for a hairdresser." She sat in the chair with her legs crossed and Como powdered her nose, because he said it was shining into the camera. When Hope asked Bancroft what she had in mind, she replied that she wanted to look like Brigitte Bardot but she laughed as she stumbled over the line. He then placed a big sheet over her under her chin and when Como told her she was on *Candid Camera*, she covered her face with the sheet. She then told Hope that if she used the film of her, it would cost him $25,000. Allen Funt then appeared to tell the cast that they were all on the real *Candid Camera* and Bancroft ended the skit throwing the sheet over her head. She returned with Como to sit on white boxes, and they played the guitar and sang the Italian folk song "Volare." Bancroft then joined Como and Hope to stand and sing a medley of "There Is Nothing Like a Dame" and "I Enjoy Being a Girl." The trio ended the show back sitting on the boxes singing "Three Sleepy People."

On December 4, 1960, Bancroft was given an award of appreciation by the New York Philanthropic League at the Hotel Astor for outstanding aid to the handicapped. The *New York Times* reported on January 22, 1961, that the West End production of *The Miracle Worker* was to begin in March but Bancroft would not be in it; Anna Massey would play Annie Sullivan.

Bancroft was again on the Perry Como show on February 22, 1961. This was written by Goodman Ace, directed by Dwight Hemion, and featured Selma Diamond, Jay Burton, Frank Peppiatt and John Aylesworth. The choreography was by Peter Gennaro. Bancroft's hair was by Ernest Adler and her gowns by Ceil Chapman. The show used the gimmick of a love story to devote three successive hours to present a different leading lady on three nights. Bancroft appears in the first of these, "Boy Meets Girl," with Jimmy Durante as her romantic partner. The show opens with Bancroft introduced as Anne Marie Italiano Bancroft, and she and Como and Durante sit on stools together. The show reveals the actress' strong Bronx accent and she uses her hard speaking voice. The men tease Bancroft for not being married, since they are, and she tells them she is in love with and married to the theatre. The actress' eye line suggests that she is reading this from a prompter and that she is speaking as a character and not as her real self. An optical effect has her suddenly appear next to Como on an empty soundstage and he continues asking her what she doesn't like about marriage. Bancroft says it is too confining, too precarious, and too commercial, which segues into a Kraft commercial which she prefigures by what seems like an ad lib, that married people eat too fast.

She is next seen alone lying on a round bed with a white cat sitting by her. Bancroft sings "Married I Can Always Get" before being joined by six male dancers. She dances alternately with individual dancers and then in front of the group. Her voice is revealed to be rather brassy, nasal and colorless though she can carry a tune, and when she dances she demonstrates she can move but is not a great dancer. Bancroft's coverage in the number features two odd shots. There is a medium shot of her in profile lying on the bed and the number ends in a close-up, not of Bancroft but of the cat!

Next she appears in a skit as Durante's wife, with the conceit that this is a typical day in Durante's household. The set was a furnished living room with a piano, and Bancroft's costume of a floor-length housecoat with a feathered collar and sleeves proves to be a bother as she repeatedly brushes feathers from her mouth. Durante sings "Who Will Be with You When I'm Far Away" as Bancroft serves him coffee on a tray. The skit makes jokes about Durante's nose and she tries to stop him from playing the piano by grabbing his chin and saying, "Oh, you mad passionate fool" which makes Como laugh. Bancroft does her own impression of Durante's "Who Will Be with You When I'm Far Away" and the three line dance to the song. After the men exit up stairs and out a door, she closes the door behind them and slides to the floor laughing.

Bancroft joins Como in a medley, with them sitting sideways on either ends of a love seat. She tells Como she had had chances to marry and that, only the day before, two people had asked her to get married. They were her mother and her father. In the medley, each took turns singing part of a song, with Bancroft singing "Makin' Whoopee," "A Good Man Is Hard to Find," "I Want Friendship," "By Myself" and "Biding My Time." Bancroft occasionally laughs during the number. After a commercial, she tells Como she is now convinced to get married and for the finale, the three sit on stools and sing "The Goodnight Song."

It was at this time that Bancroft met Mel Brooks. She was friends with composer Charles Strouse, whom she first met at the Actors Studio when she was doing *Two for the Seesaw*. She practiced her presentation of song numbers, wanting to prove her performing versatility and indulge her love of singing, and he accompanied Bancroft on the piano. The pair had kept in touch in the following years and for a short time Strouse apparently had hopes that they could have more than a friendship. Strouse had known Brooks from the NBC comedy series *Your Show of Shows* (Brooks was on the writing staff and the composer wrote dance music and occasionally played rehearsal piano). The pair then worked on a musical adaptation of the Robert Lewis Taylor novel *Professor Fodorski* which was retitled *All American*. Directed by Joshua Logan, this show opened on Broadway on March 19, 1962, and ran until May 26. Brooks also wrote a play he called *Springtime for Hitler*, which would later become his comedy film *The Producers* (1967).

One day Bancroft visited Strouse in his apartment to discuss song rehearsal matters, and Brooks was there. After a few minutes she supposedly swept out of the room but even from that brief glimpse, Brooks was said to have been entranced by her natural beauty and exuberance. Brooks asked his friend to introduce him to her. Sources differ as to Strouse's response to this. One claims the composer agreed, confident that doing so would not lead to anything romantic considering what he knew about the two. Another says that he did not think it was a good idea. He was said to have thought that they were too disparate to connect, partly because she was far more successful in her career than Brooks was. The comic had a crude sense of humor and a desire to be the center of attention and he would resort to any outlandish zaniness to get the spotlight. Strouse found it hard to consider them as a romantic couple or even as good friends.

But on February, 5, 1961, the composer decided to end Brooks' constant pestering and arranged a meeting. He suggested they stop by the Ziegfeld Theatre where Bancroft was rehearsing for the Como show. When they arrived, she was on stage singing "Married I Can Always Get." One source claims that, when she finished, Brooks applauded loudly and, rather than wait for Strouse, he rushed to shake Bancroft's hand and introduce himself. The actress was a little surprised but smiled and laughed, as did the surrounding crew. In an interview, Bancroft said that Brooks from way over on the other side of the theatre said, "Hey, Anne Bancroft. I'm Mel Brooks," and added that in two years, no man had ever approached her with that kind of aggression. Because she had just done *Two for the Seesaw* and *The Miracle Worker*, Bancroft said people were scared of her, especially men.

The actress said this voice came out from the dark and she thought it would be a combination of Clark Gable and Robert Taylor and Robert Redford but it turned out to be Brooks and he never left her. From that moment on! Bancroft reported he would ask where she was going and when she told him, Brooks would say he was going to the same place. She said the man never left her alone, "thank God." Bancroft also commented that she knew the minute she met Brooks she was going to marry him, though he didn't show this intuition. She said the day they met, she raced to see her analyst to prepare her because she had just met her future husband.

Bancroft told Brooks she had an appointment to see her agent at William Morris and Brooks lied and told her he did too, since he wanted to prolong their meeting. They left the theatre and he hailed a cab for them, and then Brooks followed Bancroft into the offices. He told her that he hadn't seen *The Miracle Worker* but he had heard that it was great. Since by now she had left the show, she offered to do the whole play for him, right on the spot. Brooks watched as Bancroft did a comical condensed version and he wept with laughter. He was smitten, and he spent the night phoning her. She wasn't home but he finally caught her the next day and arranged to visit her brownstone. Brooks arrived with a copy of his comedy skit album "2000 Years with Carl Reiner and Mel Brooks" and told Bancroft he would be on *The Ed Sullivan Show* with Reiner on February 12. The actress and the comic learned they had a mutual professional admiration, with Bancroft admitting to having been a Sid Caesar devotee for years. Brooks finally left her house six hours later. He soon decided that he wanted to marry her but his friends thought it was merely a fantasy, particularly since they knew he had previously married Florence Baum in haste and had regretted it.

Brooks reportedly had a rival for the affections of Bancroft in Mike Nichols, whom she found to be as audacious and bright as Brooks. She admired Nichols in particular for his talent but Brooks had a secret weapon: He could make her laugh to death. Nichols would marry Margo Callas in July 1963 but Bancroft kept her friendship with him. This would pay off for the actress in later film and theatre projects.

As his musical went into rehearsal, Brooks continued his pursuit of Bancroft. He repeatedly asked her out on dates. He was impressed by her intelligence and he took her to see foreign films, although his other reason for this choice of entertainment was that they were cheaper to see than other films. Unlike Bancroft who was relatively wealthy by now, Brooks had to live on a budget since he had alimony and child support to pay. The couple occasionally had thrifty dinners in Chinatown but even those were an extravagance for him. Brooks said that when they went to a Chinese restaurant, Bancroft would slip money under the table so he could pay the bill, and she would tell him not to leave such a big tip because it was her money. Brooks' relationship with Capitol Records allowed him free access to recording studios to which he took Bancroft. Aware of his limited financial resources, Bancroft also cooked for him at her home, which he loved because it saved him money. She was an excellent cook but seldom had the opportunity to do so for someone else and now she could make eggplant parmigiana and lasagna for him. They also enjoyed staying at home playing a board game called "Careers" with actor Jerry

Orbach and his wife Marta. Brooks and Bancroft were not a couple who needed to be seen at the chic night spots and watering holes of café society. They were true New Yorkers who preferred exploring the city's grottoes and hideaways. They liked the Village with its bistros and coffeehouses and spent time there talking late into the night. Although Brooks and Bancroft were spending more and more time together, neither was eager to formalize the relationship. Also, Brooks' divorce would not be finalized until January 20, 1962.

Bancroft said that she fell in love with Brooks instantly, because he looked like her father and he acted like her mother. In interviews she went public with her new love, calling him her boyfriend or saying that they were dating. However the actress dodged any questions about the prospect of marriage. According to Brooks, Bancroft understood him and laughed with him and loved his mind, and over time she loved his face and body. She said she had never derived so much pleasure so quickly from being with another human being. Right away, she said, she wanted him to enjoy her as much as the actress enjoyed him.

It is reported that during her *Miracle Worker* run, Bancroft had a working relationship with the acting coach Andreas Voutsinas, with whom she had also performed at the Actors Studio. The actress was supposedly uncomfortable with being newly famous and a celebrity, so Voutsinas ran interference for her, shopping for her and answering her phone. It is said that he could also be controlling and he disapproved of a romance she had with Lenny Bruce. The coach also reportedly told Bancroft to stop seeing Norman Mailer because he felt the novelist was not worthy of her. According to another source, the actress had no interest in Mailer, much preferring Bruce. Voutsinas claimed that he never controlled Bancroft, and they collaborated and shared together. The pair could be seen at Downey's, a theatrical hangout on Eighth Avenue, squeezed together in a booth and laughing their heads off. Once she met Mel Brooks, Voutsinas spent less time with her. Their break came about when Voutsinas disapproved of Brooks and told her so, and she just laughed. To humor her coach, the trio had an all-night discussion. Voutsinas gave Bancroft the reasons why he thought he was the better person for her to spend time with, then Brooks made the case for himself. At the end, she told Voutsinas that she was in love with Brooks but he would always be her friend. The coach said he remained friends with the actress till she died. And, at his wife's recommendation, Brooks memorably cast him as Carmen Ghia in *The Producers* (1967). Brooks also cast him in *The Twelve Chairs* (1970) and *History of the World: Part I* (1981).

In a March 2, 1961, *New York Times* article, it was reported that Bancroft was a friend of playwright Herb Gardner and had helped him get his play *A Thousand Clowns* produced by Fred Coe. The play opened on Broadway on April 5, 1962. The actress was photographed for the spread "Anne Bancroft Revisits the '20s" in the April 3, 1961, *American Weekly*. The photos were by J. Frederick Smith and the text for the article was by Sweeten Wood, describing her as being 35–23–35 and 5'7" in her stocking feet.

On April 16, 1961, Bancroft was a presenter at the Tony Awards which were held at the Waldorf-Astoria Grand Ballroom and broadcast live on CBS. With Sidney Poitier, Bancroft presented the award for Best Costume Designer. She was handed the envelope with the name of the winner by Patty Duke, who did the job of custodian of the medallions for all the awards that night. Bancroft pretended not to be able to read the winner's name, bringing the envelope closer to her eyes, and then announced it to be Motley for *Becket*. Host Phil Silvers accepted the award on Motley's behalf. Bancroft stayed as Poitier read the nominations for Best Featured Actress in a Musical and announced the winner as Tammy Grimes for *The Unsinkable Molly Brown*.

The *New York Times* reported that filming began on the film version of *The Miracle Worker* on May 31, 1961. It was shot at the Production Center in New York, though one source says the interiors were done at the Hyde-Brown Studio. Bancroft and Duke repeated their Broadway roles. The film was made by Playfilms, Inc., which was comprised of Fred Coe, Arthur Penn (who also directed) and William Gibson (who adapted his play). It was reported that United Artists originally offered a $2 million budget if Gibson and Penn would cast either Elizabeth Taylor or Audrey Hepburn as Annie Sullivan, and when they insisted that the part be recreated by Bancroft, UA cut the budget by $1.5 million. Another source says that $5 million was offered for Taylor. Ingrid Bergman claimed in her autobiography that she was offered the role of Annie. The story had been previously filmed in the silent biographical drama *Deliverance* (1919), made by the Helen Keller Film Corporation and directed by George Foster Platt. It included appearances by the real Keller and Sullivan, as well as actors playing their younger counterparts.

The editor of *The Miracle Worker*, Aram Avakian, attended the table read of the script before shooting began. He said that Bancroft sat knitting and delivered her lines without the use of a script.

Still for the film of *The Miracle Worker* (1962).

In an article about the production by Gene Archer, he reported that it would utilize two New Jersey exteriors. (Another source reports that an additional exterior location was the Big Sky Ranch in Simi Valley, California.) Bancroft was also interviewed for the article, although her on-camera chores had yet to begin. She was in the studio for makeup tests while awaiting her call and Archer described her as comfortably clad in a sloppy, oversized man's jacket and well-scuffed Oxfords. Bancroft reportedly made her way to the studio at 6 a.m. and found the walk an invigorating way to begin her day. She was photographed with Duke by Dennis Stock on location. In the photograph Bancroft sits on a box with the girl on her lap; according to the caption, Duke and Bancroft are resting after a physically taxing scene and demonstrating the great warmth that exists in their off-screen friendship. It was reported that at the end of filming, Bancroft was hospitalized with pneumonia after she had reported fatigue to her doctor. She stayed in the hospital for two weeks and was then ordered to Fire Island for a month's recuperation.

On October 3, 1961, the *New York Times* reported that Bancroft had agreed to star in a new comedy by Jay Presson, *Rich and Famous*, possibly in the current season. The project had blossomed rather suddenly with her being shown the script on September 27, 1961. Bancroft decided she wanted to do it but no contract had been signed. The producer was to be Lewis Allen, the author's husband. Bancroft said that the role was something she had never played before, the wife of a writer living in the New York of today. The play was said to have originally written as a film script which the author had rewritten for the stage. Arthur Penn was said to be the director. Around this same time, Random House released the book *Actors Talk About Acting* and Bancroft was one of the actors sharing her opinions with interviewers Lewis Funke and John E. Booth.

Bancroft was to have starred in a new Broadway musical entitled *The Blue Star*, set in Israel. This was to be produced by David Merrick, with a book by Joshua Logan and Alfred Palca and a score by Burton Lane and E.Y. Harburg. It is said that interest in the show was killed off after another show set in Jerusalem and its environs opened: the musical comedy *Milk and Honey*, with book by Don Appell and music and lyrics by Jerry Herman. That hit show, directed by Albert Marre, ran at the Martin Beck Theatre from October 10, 1961, to January 26, 1963.

On November 19, 1961, the *New York Times* published three photographs from the *Miracle Worker* film. The film was said to have been shot on location on a farm in Middletown, New Jersey, described in another source as an old Victorian farmhouse. The interiors were done in a Manhattan studio, and the film was to have its premiere early in 1962.

On December 4, 1961, the *New York Times* reported that Arthur Penn was now to co-produce *Rich and Famous* with Lewis Allen and that the production would hit Broadway in March 1962. The article added that the play was about a writer who strikes it rich with a popular novel, and that it was based on a screenplay entitled *First Wife*. On December 23, 1961, it was reported that the production had been delayed until early fall 1962. Allen said that some rewriting needed to be done and they had decided to have everything set before going ahead.

The December 20, 1961, *Times* reported that Robert Wise was to direct the film version of *Two for the Seesaw* for Seven Arts Productions–Mirisch Company–United Artists in the spring of 1962 with Shirley MacLaine and Robert Mitchum. The film was shot on location in New York and released on November 21, 1962. Bancroft said she would have given anything to make that film but it got away from her. Location footage was shot near the actress' apartment and she admitted she was glad she didn't chance upon the film crew, because she had she would have tried to get into the film. William Gibson had reportedly sold the film rights for a goodly sum but he was unable to help get Bancroft cast. Fonda probably had no thought of playing Jerry on film since he had been so unhappy with the stage character.

On January 28, 1962, it was reported that Bancroft was one of many actors seen boarding the elevator in the West 46th Street apartment house of Robert Whitehead, co-director (with Elia Kazan) of the Lincoln Repertory Company. He was said to be working toward having the company attached to the Vivian Beaumont Theatre to be erected in the Lincoln Center for the Performing Arts. Whitehead had told the actors that they were very much wanted for the company and asked them to hold themselves free of commitments beginning in the spring of 1963. It was Kazan's intention to start intensive preparations for the first season to begin the next fall. The aim of the directors was to put on four plays during their first season: two new American plays, a Greek classic and an American classic, probably be an O'Neill. Invitations had been extended to leading native playwrights for plays for the new company.

The actress reportedly turned down the role of schoolteacher Annie Hayworth in Alfred Hitchcock's *The Birds* (1963). Screenwriter Evan Hunter supposedly had Bancroft in mind when he wrote the part as a middle-aged woman. At the time, the actress was 31. Twenty-five-year-old Suzanne Pleshette was cast instead. On April 4, 1962, the *New York Times* reported that Bancroft was on a committee of prominent Actors Studio members who had come up with a plan for the establishment of a permanent theatre company. The plan had been presented and approved by the triumvirate who founded and directed the studio, Lee Strasberg, Elia Kazan and Cheryl Crawford, and it was outlined on April 3, 1962, to 150 members at the studio's headquarters. The company would operate on a year-round basis and the committee was contemplating starting production activity early in 1963. They said they would like initially to work on three plays although it had not been decided yet whether they would use new or proven scripts. The committee had formed in February for fundraising and to investigate the long-range financial stability of the studio. They had decided that a theatre company working as an extension might resolve the difficulties.

Bancroft was back on the Perry Como TV show (April 4, 1962) in an episode written by Goodman Ace, Selma Diamond, Jay Burton, Frank Peppiatt and John Aylesworth and directed by Dwight Hemion. Bancroft's fashions are by Ceil Chapman. She is first seen telling Como that she has just finished the film version of *The Miracle Worker*. Bancroft sings "Up the Lazy River" on a set of a rowboat surrounded by wooden fences with eight dancing boys lying on the floor holding fishing poles. The boys rise as she walks past them and Bancroft finishes in the center with the boys around her. They exit to leave the singer alone for the end of the song. Again her voice is competent but a little raw and lacking singularity.

She returned with Como, commenting that she likes being on his show because it gives her the chance to do something light and gay, as opposed to the heavy dramatic characters she plays on Broadway. Como suggests combining her dramatic talents with singing and dancing. A Music Hall player lit by a candle introduces a melodrama about a husband who tries to get his wife's money by convincing her that she is mad. Bancroft plays Gigi the wife with Don Adams playing her husband on a big living room set. She speaks with a Southern accent and flounces around in a negligee. After a knock at the door, dancers dressed as Disney characters enter. Playing the wife's maid and butler are Kaye Ballard and Paul Lynde. Bancroft sings "I Remember It Well" and "You're Just in Love," dueting with Como's voice as her invisible doctor. Later, as part of the show's celebration of the state of Illinois, Bancroft recites the Carl Sandburg poem "Chicago" from a book as the orchestra plays the song "Chicago." The music upstages the actress' reading, and then she is additionally upstaged by the showing news footage of the city.

Shot in black and white, *The Miracle Worker* repeated the stage story of the twentysomething Annie Sullivan, a student at Perkins School for the Blind in Boston, who is hired by the Keller family of Tuscumbia as the governess for their blind and deaf young daughter Helen. The location of Tuscumbia is also not given but it is said to be in Alabama in some sources. The child is bright but she has been spoiled and allowed to behave in a wild and disobedient manner. Sullivan is determined to teach the girl to be obedient and to use the sign language alphabet so that she has an understanding of words and objects. Helen's mother has revealed that the child was once able to speak. The narrative climaxes in the girl saying "Wah-wah" as evidence that she can speak again and also as a confirmation that Sullivan has been successful in teaching her what the word "water" means. The story ends with Helen expressing affection for her teacher and Sullivan admitting that she loves the girl, both things that the individuals had previously denied each other. Sullivan is presented as a woman still struggling with the remnants of her own blindness, where she wears dark glasses to protect her eyes from light and regularly washes them with a solution. The teacher has been strengthened and hardened by her childhood in the State Arms House asylum where her brother Jimmy died of tuberculosis, and her station in the house also suggests loneliness in her new surroundings and an isolation since her methods are frowned upon. The adult Kellers do not treat her as a social equal. In fact, the captain is quite hostile towards Sullivan and patronizes her when he carries her down the ladder thinking she is incapable of doing so herself. Sullivan still has empathy for Helen, since she recognizes the same appetite to learn that she herself had. She disapproves of Helen's childish tantrums and is on the receiving end of the girl's aggression and manipulation.

Sullivan's strict methods result in power struggles between her and the Keller parents, and especially between her and Helen. The latter is important to Sullivan because she believes that the key to helping the girl is to give her no pity and to first make her totally dependent on her teacher. While Sullivan's need for Keller to touch her is based on the way she teaches the girl the finger alphabet, it is also suggested that the teacher has a personal need for affection, which is met at the narrative conclusion when Helen kisses her and sits on her lap. These acts may be gratitude from the girl for what she learned but Sullivan signing that she loves Keller suggests it means more to her teacher.

Bancroft is top-billed above the title and her casting in the film version of her stage triumph is a refusal on the part of the production company to compromise for Hollywood. Her hair is by Ed Callaghan and worn in an extra-long style plaited and tied up at the back. Costumer Ruth Morley designed the clothes for the stage production and does the same for the film, with Sullivan wearing an array of drab period dresses, blouses and skirts, some with puffy sleeves and bustles. At times Sullivan's dark clothes suggest she is a gothic monster with her partial blindness adding to her intimidating demeanor. She makes Sullivan funny and strong. We see her crying and screaming awake from a nightmare and in the film's climax it is suggested that Keller wipes away Sullivan's tears but these are not apparent, perhaps because they are obscured by her dark glasses. The glasses give Sullivan a mystery but also an emotional distance and the emotion in the film tends to come from the score by Laurence Rosenthal. Our appreciation of the actress' performance is inescapably linked to the fact of her having met the enormous requirements of the role on stage. A lot of her part is observing and reacting to Keller, and perhaps a lesser actress might have feared that this would be upstaging.

Sullivan also endures physical abuse from the child, which is most apparent in the famous breakfast scene fight, here lasting for nine minutes. The actress is struck and bloodied and she has the indignity of taking food from the girl's mouth with her hands and has food spat in her face and her hair pulled. The scene also requires her to fight back in Sullivan's effort to force Keller table manners, where she will sit in her chair and use a spoon to eat from her plate. We are later told that Sullivan also had the girl fold her napkin but this is not shown since the fight is said to have lasted the hours from breakfast to dinnertime. Sullivan chases and lifts Keller and Bancroft breathes heavily from the exertion. There is the later indignity of Sullivan falling into the stream.

Director Penn provides some unflattering extreme close-ups of Bancroft used as transition for flashbacks, and also Sullivan's miming has her look grotesque when she grimaces to show Keller a bad girl face. Bancroft also has comic moments, as when Sullivan is carried on the captain's shoulders down a ladder. As impressive as the fight scene is, the credit for it must go to Arthur Penn, so the actress' best scene is perhaps the quieter one where she describes her asylum past to the Kellers.

The film had a charity preview on May 8, 1962. It opened in New York on May 23 and opened wide on July 28 with the taglines "An emotional earthquake!" and "A mighty motion picture experience ... touch it ... sense it ... feel it ... you can't forget it!" Bosley Crowther of the *New York Times* wrote that Bancroft played her role superbly. The film received Academy Award nominations for Best Director, Best Actress, Best Supporting Actress for Duke, Best Adapted Screenplay and Best Costume Design. Bancroft and Duke both won. It was remade for TV four times, the Italian *Anna dei miracoli* (1968) and *Anna dei miracoli* (1990) and the American *The Miracle Worker* (1979, with Duke as Sullivan) and *The Miracle Worker* (2000).

There was talk that Duke would not be cast in the film until finally someone said that if they were going to use Bancroft, then they had to also go with the kid. Duke said there was hardly any preparation before filming began. This is in contrast to the claim that the film had been many months in planning and preparation. She reported that the script made some trims from the play, including some lines of Bancroft's that Duke particularly liked and breaking up the last scene of the play into two scenes, but that the basic text was the same for both versions. The fact that Duke was taller was compensated for by blocking her so that she was placed next to Inga Swenson who played her mother and who was taller than Bancroft. Duke reported that the breakfast fight scene was shot over four consecutive days in the mornings. The actress said that at this time she was in great shape and at an age when she could usually refuel in five minutes, so that when she eventually got tired she realized that Bancroft must have felt much worse. But Duke said the older actress kept up with her, citing the moment when Keller ran around the table and Sullivan cut her off. Bancroft had longer legs but she still needed breathing power to do it. Duke wrote that the scene was mostly shot with hand-held cameras and the operators sitting in wheelchairs which were small and mobile enough to get into corners. At one moment Bancroft began laughing from sheer exhaustion, which was not in the script. It was decided to keep it since it was felt that it was entirely possible that Sullivan might have laughed and it showed that she had a sense of humor. Another source reports that Penn filmed the fight scene with three cameras with both actresses padded for the battle royal, after they had both prepared by getting in shape. This source said the filming took five days and that by the end of it Bancroft and Duke and the crew were all "whipped." Duke reported that Bancroft made another mistake when she supposedly said "shit" when she fell into the extremely cold stream.

On the May 23, 1962, Perry Como show, Bancroft sang "Let Me Sing and I'm Happy," "Kalamazoo" and "Hostess with the Mostess." On the same date she attended the Hollywood premiere of the film *The Miracle Worker* and was photographed in her seat in the cinema with Brooks and with Cary Grant leaning over from the seat behind them.

The *New York Times* reported on May 27, 1962, on the continuing saga of the Jay Presson play *Rich and Famous*, still unproduced. Now Hal Wallis, who had originally owned the screen rights, had decided to make a film of the property as a vehicle for Shirley MacLaine. In the article, Jay Presson spoke about her past hopes to have the play produced on Broadway with an unnamed but "noted young Broadway and screen star" but advised that commitments and time ran out for both the actress and herself. Since she couldn't get the star to play the role, the writer then sold the property to Wallis in 1961. The play was to be adapted by Edward Anhalt. It was hoped that shooting of the Paramount picture would begin later in the year. MacLaine reportedly got into a legal battle with Paramount when she refused to do the film. Hal Wallis eventually made it as *Wives and Lovers* (1963), directed by John Rich and starring Janet Leigh.

In June 1962, Bancroft attended a special benefit screening of *The Miracle Worker* at the Sutton Theatre. This was to raise money for the American Foundation for the Blind and Research to Prevent Blindness. She got overwhelming applause from the crowd of onlookers at the police barricades outside the theatre.

On July 1, 1962, Bancroft was the mystery guest on the CBS game show *What's My Line?* in New York. The show was directed by Franklin Heller, the host was John Charles Daly, and the panelists were Dorothy Kilgallen, Allen Ludden, Arlene Francis and Bennett Cerf. The actress alternated between making her voice sound husky as she attempted to disguise it and speaking in her normal voice, and the questions led to the fact that she was in a film that was in release. Ludden was the one who guessed Bancroft's identity. He said he had planned to see the film that day but when he got there it had already started and he understood that you had to see it from the beginning. To this, Bancroft responded with, "Please." Kilgallen commented that she had heard that as marvelous as the play was, the film was even better, which was hard to believe. Bancroft replied that it was the truth.

In July 1962, the actress appeared on the CBS game show *Password*, competing against Robert Goulet. Some sources give the date as July 3, others July 10. She was described by the announcer as "The beautiful stage and screen actress and star of *The Miracle Worker*." The celebrities were alternately partnered with chemistry high school teacher Douglas Smith from Rockford, Illinois, and housewife Anne Marie Renenger from Springfield, Virginia. The host was Allen Ludden. Bancroft said that she had just come back from the San Sebastian Film Festival where she had gone with the film. Goulet agreed to return to the show when Ludden asked him if he would, but Bancroft preempted his asking her with "Never. I'm never coming back," said as she laughed. But the actress may have been serious because she never did go back.

Bancroft was interviewed by Neil Hickey for the August 1962 edition of The *American Weekly* magazine in an article entitled "Miracle for Anne Bancroft." Hickey reported that during the run of *Two for the Seesaw*, she had triggered a vogue for the word "hoyden," which was defined as a girl or woman of loud, boisterous or carefree behavior. He said that characterization, good or bad, had clung to Bancroft but in truth she was less hoyden or kook than a canny, workmanlike, discriminating, ambitious woman of the theatre.

5

Mother Courage and Her Children

Bancroft occupied herself reading the scripts she was now swamped with. She had learned from her Hollywood experience that it was better to be discerning in what work she accepted. When it was suggested that Bancroft was avoiding work, she responded that she was only avoiding bad scripts.

One script she liked was the Bertolt Brecht play *Mother Courage and Her Children*. This was a story set in the 17th century in the 30 Years War about a woman referred to as Mother Courage, a petty war profiteer who peddled her wares from a rolling canteen at army camps. Asked why she chose the role, Bancroft said that it was because the audience for the first time was against her. Regarding the complaint that she was too young for the part, she commented that if you really became involved with the character, you would lose track of the age factor.

The production was first announced in the *New York Times* on May 17, 1962: They reported that it was to open on October 16 at the Ambassador with Jerome Robbins staging an adaptation by Eric Bentley of the Brecht drama. On June 8, 1962, it was said that Anna Magnani was eager and she was negotiating with producer Cheryl Crawford. She was currently in Rome acting in a film called *Mamma Roma*, and after that she was scheduled to make *S'Agapo*. In view of the uncertainty concerning what would be the actress' Broadway debut, it was not known whether the production would be held for her until the 1963–1964 season.

On June 15, 1962, it was reported that the production had been postponed since Joseph Hayes' suspense play *A Calculated Risk* was now to open at the Ambassador on June 31, 1962. That show would run until May 11, 1963. Hope was still held out for Magnani's commitment to *Mother Courage* for a later date. On November 14, 1962, Crawford confirmed that the delayed Broadway production would now open at the Martin Beck on March 4, 5 or 6. Still, however, no one was set for the pivotal role. There was a vague possibility of Bancroft assuming it after Magnani and Geraldine Page had stated they wanted the role but they could not get around to it. It was said that out-of-town tryouts for the show would be dispensed with and that Crawford was seeking a dispensation from Equity to rehearse five weeks instead of the customary four.

Bancroft was photographed by Evelyn Straus on November 15, 1962, with Mary E. Switzer, Director of Office of Vocational Rehabilitation of Dept. of Health and Welfare. Switzer presented the actress with the President's Award from the National Rehabilitation Association in recognition of her services to the handicapped. The November 1962 *Life* magazine feature Bancroft's lasagna recipe.

On November 30, it was reported that she had been signed for the role of Mother Courage and the production was scheduled to open on March 20, 1963. One source claims that Bancroft originally declined the role when first offered it. But after the actress was impressed by the off–Broadway production *Brecht on Brecht*, she read all the Brecht she could. When Crawford made a second offer, Bancroft accepted. *Brecht on Brecht* was produced at the Lucille Lortel Theatre by the Greater New York Chapter of ANTA for a season (January 3, 1962, to January 6, 1963). The actress explained that Jerome Robbins had directed the play not so much as one about war but more as a play about business and the cost of being in business. Bancroft said the company had done improvisations on business and buying and selling. She commented that, any way you looked at it, it was a far cry from "Don't Rain on My Parade," a reference to the *Funny Girl* show which she had reportedly declined. Another source claimed that Bancroft had been approached by composer Jule Styne about starring in the show before he had written the score and she had declined Lennart's draft of the script, opining that it was not good.

Mother Courage and Her Children was being done for the first time on Broadway and, given the subject matter, no one expected it to be a runaway hit. Bancroft's decision to do it was an artistic one and she did the same assiduous research as she had done for her previous theater work. She studied the pertinent history, examining the work of the 17th-century painter Brueghel and touring New York's slums to get a comparative sense of the desolation of the 30 Years War. She also visited Hortense W. Gabel of the Mayor's Housing and Redevelopment Board to talk about what she had seen in the slums.

A newspaper strike threatened to postpone the show but the strike was resolved and after previews from March 5, 1963, the show opened on schedule on March 28. It was praised by the *New York Times*' Howard Taubman, who wrote that Bancroft played the role with surface impassivity through which gleamed heartiness and cunning and, at the right rare moments, emotion. While he found that the actress' marked New York accent was odd for the period, he felt it had the context of a toughened working woman. He also noted that Bancroft sang credibly in a pleasant voice (the show included eight mood songs by Brecht and Paul Dessau).

The actress was reportedly signed for the show until January 1964 and she was even willing to go off–Broadway in order to her honor her commitment but it would only run until May 11, 1963. It received Tony nominations for Best Play, Best Producer (Dramatic), Best Feature Actress in a Play for Zohra Lampert, and Best Costume Design but won none. In the show's supporting cast was Gene Wilder, who wrote in his memoir, *Kiss Me Like A Stranger: My Search for Love and Art* that Brooks would pick up Bancroft every night. This was how the actor met the man who would later cast him in *The Producers* (1967) and other films.

Reportedly Bancroft's mother, Millie, had reservations about the show because she was upset at the sight of her daughter trudging around in heavy padding and pulling a wooden cart. Backstage she said so and warned Bancroft to take her vitamins every day and to get plenty of sleep or else Millie was going to pull her out of the play. Bancroft commented that her mother seemed to be unaware that her daughter was a goddess.

The actress was back as the *What's My Line?* mystery guest on April 7, 1963. Again directed by Franklin Heller and hosted by John Charles Daly, the panelists were Phyllis Newman, Martin Gabel, Arlene Francis and Bennet Cerf. To disguise her voice, Bancroft used a foreign accent. Her identity was guessed by Newman. Gabel commented that, like Bancroft, he had graduated from the American Academy of Dramatic Arts. She reminded him that they had also done a show together where he played the Devil, a reference to the 1951 *Lights Out* TV show.

Appearing on Broadway meant that Bancroft was unable to attend the Academy Awards ceremony on April 8, 1963, held at the Santa Monica Civic Auditorium and broadcast live on ABC. Brooks reportedly told her it was not worth going considering who else was nominated: The other Best Actress nominees were Bette Davis for *What Ever Happened to Baby Jane?*, Katharine Hepburn for *Long Day's Journey into Night*, Geraldine Page for *Sweet Bird of Youth* and Lee Remick for *Days of Wine and Roses*. Bancroft agreed with Brooks so she decided to stay in New York with the play.

When the announcement came that Bancroft won, Joan Crawford accepted on her behalf and read a speech from Bancroft that repeated what she had said when she won her Best Actress Tony Award for the play: "There are three reasons why I deserve this award. Arthur Penn, Bill Gibson, Fred Coe." Supposedly, because Crawford had not been nominated for her performance in *What Ever Happened to Baby Jane?* as Bette Davis had, she worked to ensure that Davis would not win. She allegedly contacted friends who were members of the Motion Picture Academy and urged them to vote for Bancroft. Some sources state that this is untrue and came from Davis' paranoia, and Crawford denied it. Crawford also offered to accept the award on behalf of the other three women (who were unable to attend) should they win. Bancroft had reportedly wanted Patty Duke to accept her award but the producers turned down that idea. She said then she would like one of the greats like Davis or Crawford, with Bancroft unaware of the feud that was going on between them. Since Davis was another nominee, she was ineligible to do so, but having Crawford do it reportedly made Davis angry at both her co-star and Bancroft. Bancroft said that when she later introduced herself to Davis, Davis looked at her and then walked away.

Bancroft and Mel Brooks reportedly watched the TV broadcast of the show together and when her name was called, they were elated. (In her May 1987 *Films and Filming* interview, she claimed that she heard the results on the car radio on the way home from the theater.) As Bancroft watched as Crawford accepted the award on her behalf, she was said to be struck by Crawford's appearance, saying, "My God! Joan Crawford looks like me!" This comment would prefigure Bancroft's later interest in doing the film of *Mommie Dearest*. The actress was photographed by Dan Farrell in her apartment supposedly showing her reaction upon hearing the news. Farrell also took photographs of the actress on the telephone supposedly getting the news, two showing her with Mel Brooks. Arty Pomerantz is also credited for some of the shots of Bancroft on the telephone. When the actress was asked the next day whether she thought her performance deserved the award, she reportedly grinned and answered, "Well, if that means was I better than anyone else … the answer is yes." Bancroft later said that the Oscars themselves were a race, you don't know who voted for you and actually there was very little value in it except that you won the race. The actress advised that she gave the award to her mother. Brooks said it was a tribute to Tinsel Town that they had dug two unusual performances like those of Bancroft and Duke.

Mother Courage and Her Children's publicist tried to use Bancroft's win for the show by placing a *Daily News* ad the next day that featured her on the cover with the Best Actor winner Gregory Peck. The ad read "Annie Won It, and We've Got Her." This did not help box office-wise. The actress compared her decision to do the show to a Hollywood marriage, saying you know it won't last but you wanted to experience it anyway.

Talking about being an actress with Paula Strasberg, Bancroft explained that it was not an easy thing to go down deep into herself and bring things up that if she were not an actress she wouldn't have to look at again and again. Building a character based on one's own inner point of view and your own experiences was no joke. Bancroft said that was one of the reasons she chose parts so carefully. She commented that all the big parts she had played were extremely strong women but there was another side of herself that she could play that she hadn't used. This was the part of a woman who was not a survivor. The actress also told Strasberg about her constant need for work and said when she wasn't working, she sometimes felt that if she didn't get a job soon, she would probably ruin everybody around her. Bancroft felt sorry for what her poor boyfriend sometimes had to listen to and put up with. She also confessed that she was afraid of the potential conflicts between her career and a home life, to say nothing of the complications of motherhood. However, now the actress said she could better deal emotionally with the time off between jobs, since it was a luxury she could well afford and she insisted on exercising the utmost discretion in her professional choices.

Jerome Robbins, interviewed by the *New York Times* Arthur Gelb (April 28, 1963), said it was because he could envisage Bancroft as *Funny Girl*'s Fanny Brice that he could also see her as an ideal Mother Courage. He felt that the two women had much in common, since both were earthy and looked at the world through shrewd, tenacious eyes. They were mother peddlers, fighting for survival for themselves and their families. When the issue of Bancroft's age was raised, Robbins answered that she could convey any age she wanted to. It was revealed that at one rehearsal, Bancroft copied a gesture that he had used, an exaggerated flourish that he felt looked false. When the actress told Robbins that if he did it this way it must be a beautiful movement, he ordered her to forget it.

When the press asked Mel Brooks if he and Bancroft had plans to marry, he replied that it was up in the air but they might bring it down to earth. When asked if he was in love, Brooks said that they had an affection for each other and they liked each other, then added that he was crazy about Bancroft and he would kill for her. She once accompanied him to a Gourmet Club outing; members of the club were Speed Vogel, Zero Mostel, Joseph Heller, Ngoot Lee. Brooks and their meetings were generally held at inexpensive restaurants in Chinatown. Bancroft had heard so much about the group from Brooks that she was intrigued to know firsthand what actually happened at the gatherings. She was even more interested when she learned that women were not welcome and that the location of their meetings was a closely guarded secret. One evening she came across a notepad where Brooks had written the Chinatown address of that night's meeting so she surprised the group with an unexpected arrival. Everyone was polite to her but it became clear to Bancroft that she was not to do this again.

Bancroft was reportedly considered for the part of Baroness Natalie Ivanoff in the action adventure *55 Days at Peking* (1963). Deborah Kerr, Jeanne Moreau and Melina Mercouri were also actresses considered for the role; Ava Gardner was cast. On May 19, 1963, Bancroft appeared on the ABC's *Theatre of Tomorrow*, which reported on the New York Repertory Company of Lincoln Center. Bancroft was back on *The Jack Paar Show* on June 7, 1963, where she sang "Where Are You?" and "These Foolish Things."

On August 7, 1963, it was announced that Bancroft was leaving New York that day to begin the movie *The Pumpkin Eater* (1964). The director was Jack Clayton and the Harold Pinter screenplay was based on Penelope Mortimer's highly praised allegorical novel about a modern married couple in conflict over their opposing attitudes towards children. James Mason was to play opposite Bancroft.

The Columbia release was shot on location in London and Buckinghamshire and at the Shepperton Studios in Surrey, England, from autumn to December 1963. Jo Armitage (Bancroft) is the three-times-married wife of screenwriter Jake Armitage (Peter Finch), who lives an upper middle class life in London and has six children. Jo, in a depressed state because she believes that Jake has had an affair with Philpott (Maggie Smith), sees a psychiatrist, Dr. Ingram (Eric Porter). A nanny is hired to care for the children. Although it is perhaps a wise move not to have a mentally ill mother supervise children, it also deprives Jo of her identity. We see her getting stronger and more vocal in her sessions, and are told that she is also taking pills. At one session she quips, "I come here and all you ask me about is Jake. Why the hell don't you see Jake?!" She still doesn't trust her husband and asks him never to leave her, which is not possible when he has to travel to Morocco for a film he has written. The idea of Jake's infidelity is presented without evidence. Later he will admit to having slept with Philpott but he does not confirm that he is the father of the child of Beth Conway (Janine Gray) and we only have the word of her husband Bob (James Mason) of the affair. That Jo should resent Jake's infidelity is also questionable since she had left her second husband, violinist Giles (Richard Johnson), for him, and then later she sleeps with Giles again after she has been told that Jake has impregnated Beth. Jo's belief that Jake is unfaithful becomes an obsession with her, repeating the accusation even after he has admitted it, but we can understand why Jake would cheat since he feels neglected by his wife. Only one of the children is Jake's and he resents the intrusion they are in his life with Jo and feels trapped when he learns that she wants yet another child.

Still for *The Pumpkin Eater* (1964).

Jake convinces his wife to have an abortion and also to be sterilized. The information about Beth's supposed pregnancy that makes Jo regress into her depression and anger after having made some progress. The narrative reaches a resolution when it appears that Jo leaves the family after having been rejected by Jake at the funeral of his father (Alan Webb), and then she accepts Jake and her children who find her at their house in the country by a windmill.

Bancroft's hair is by Gordon Bond and is a straight and shoulder-length style, worn loose and often up and off her forehead, and with gray at the temples. Her wardrobe is by Motley with furs by Deanfields of London and Paris, with the highlights being a sheer layered low-cut long-sleeved knee-length party dress with fringed trimmings and a fur trimmed coat with turban. Bancroft uses an English accent and is funny when she yells and swears because this breaks the controlled composure of a standard middle-class

Englishwoman. There are two demonstrations of Jo's extreme behavior: when she cries in public at Harrods department store and when she physically attacks Jake after hearing that he has impregnated Beth. The latter has the potential to recall the actress' infamous *Miracle Worker* fight scene except that in this film the scene only lasts 50 seconds. Bancroft is funny in her reaction to the verbal attack by the woman at the hairdresser's (Yootha Joyce) and the visit by the insane king of Israel (Frank Singuineau), and when she questions why Ingram is to water-ski on vacation. We also see her demonstrate physical passion when Jo kisses Jake's chest before the unseen love-making.

The film premiered at the Cannes Film Festival on May 9, 1964, where Bancroft shared the Best Actress award with Barbara Barrie for the drama *One Potato, Two Potato* (1964). It was released in Britain in June 1964 and in the U.S. on November 9 with the taglines "The Electrifying Performance That Won Anne Bancroft the Best Actress Award at the Cannes Film Festival" and "How many others? Six … a dozen … what does the number matter?" According to *Variety*, Bancroft was exceptionally good and she added a depth and understanding which put the role on a higher plane. Bosley Crowther in the *New York Times* described Bancroft's performance as over-agonized, and said that her mechanical attitudes and many melancholy expressions became monotonous. Clive Hirschhorn in *The Columbia Story* wrote that Bancroft's performance—delivered with an impeccable English accent—was extraordinary for the range of moods and emotions it encompassed. The actress was nominated for the Best Actress Academy Award but lost to Julie Andrews for the comic family fantasy *Mary Poppins* (1964).

Bancroft was interviewed in London over breakfast in a coffee shop for an October 6, 1963, *New York Times* article. The article said she was staying in a Mayfair apartment during filming and that the actress had campaigned to get her *Pumpkin Eater* role. It began when her New York agent suggested she read the Penelope Mortimer novel. Bancroft was impressed, saying she felt deeply about the lead character. The actress desperately wanted the lead role and she thought somebody had suggested her name to Clayton; but although he knew her work, he did not think she was right for the part. Another source claims that Bancroft had heard she was being considered for the part along with a dozen other actresses, and she sent a cable to Clayton saying that only she could play the role. It was also claimed that despite the actress' recent Oscar win, one of the director's objections was that she lacked the smoldering quality he sought. Clayton reportedly replied to Bancroft's cable by asking her to send him stills. She sent several from *The Miracle Worker*, showing herself in a state of dishevelment in the fight scene. Clayton asked for others, saying he still didn't know what she looked like. Unwilling to send more stills, Bancroft caught a plane to London. Apparently Clayton's head was turned when she entered the Connaught Hotel and sat down. No sooner had they begun to chat that he told her he wanted her for the film.

In a memorial booklet for a 1995 Clayton retrospective at the National Gallery of Washington, D.C., Bancroft was quoted as saying that his films were marked by a deeply felt personal vision. She added that unlike most commercial Hollywood filmmakers, he didn't tell stories about heroes. Instead, he looked for the heroism in unconventional people, which was a tougher but higher aspiration.

In her memoir, Patricia Neal wrote that she received a not-so-firm offer for the film at the same time that she received a firm offer for the thriller *Psyche 59* (1964). She preferred the first project, calling it a plum, but she said the producer wouldn't make the offer definite and the money for the other film was set so she chose it instead. Neal hoped that *The Pumpkin Eater* would wait for her but it didn't and Bancroft was cast. Neal would write that Bancroft was wonderful in the film and thought that she should have taken a chance and waited to do it.

During Bancroft's stay in London, Brooks frequently flew over to be with her. On British television on November 25, 1963, she was one of the actors who read excerpts from the speeches of President John Kennedy, assassinated three days earlier.

On February 14, 1964, Bancroft appeared NBC's *Bob Hope Comedy Special*, filmed in Hollywood and directed by Jack Shea. She appears in a ten-minute skit as the first female president of the United States with Hope as Robert, the First Man. A portion of the skit was included in the 1982 NBC compilation show *Bob Hope's Women I Love: Beautiful and Funny*. She wears a sparkly dark short-sleeved jacket and dark floor-length dress. She uses a swear word (which is bleeped out) when she comments to the press that she will only meet Fidel Castro when he gets a "fucking" razor. Bancroft smiles at the audience when they applaud this joke. The actress often laughs at Hope's lines, and at one point struggles *not* to laugh as she tries to get her next line out.

The actress presented the Best Actor Oscar at the Academy Awards ceremony on April 13, 1964. The winner was Sidney Poitier for the drama *Lilies of the Field* (1963). Bancroft shows her pleasure at his win as the couple walked off the stage together after his acceptance speech. She was also at the event to support Brooks, who had written the short *The Critic* which was nominated for Best Short Subject Animation and won the award. The couple was questioned by Louella Parsons, whom Bancroft had known from her Fox days. Asked about marriage plans, she said that she was at that time in her life where you stopped looking for the man on the white horse and settled for another human being.

Representing *The Pumpkin Eater*, Bancroft attended the Cannes Film Festival which opened on April 29, 1964, and was to run until May 14. She was a presenter at the 18th Tony Awards held on May 24 at the New York Hilton Hotel and televised live by WOR-TV. She reportedly volunteered her services to the Children of the Lexington School for the Deaf's evening of June 3, 1964, entitled "Without the Sound of Music." This was held at the Hunter College Playhouse with dance and dramatic numbers inspired by the collaborations of Richard Rodgers with Lorenz Hart and Oscar Hammerstein II. The program's aim was to deepen public understanding of the vitality and potential talents of deaf children.

On June 22, 1964, Bancroft was a guest at the champagne and caviar "Salute to the Audience" in Shubert Alley, held between 5:30 and 6:30 p.m. for ticketholders to *The Three Sisters* which opened that night at the Morosco Theater. In September 1963, Bancroft stated her intention to be in the production but this did not eventuate. Jon Krampner wrote in *Female Brando* that the actress wanted to play Masha and that when offered the role of Natalya by director Lee Strasberg, she responded angrily with, "No, no, darling. I play Masha or nothing." In his book *A Method to Their Madness*, Foster Hirsch wrote that Bancroft believed that the director had promised her the part. He also mentioned another possible Strasberg-Bancroft collaboration: She was to play Martha in Edward Albee's *Who's Afraid of Virginia Woolf?* but apparently the director lost interest when his first choice, Geraldine Page, turned the part down and the production was not done by the Actors Studio as originally planned.

Bancroft was said to have been among those considered for the lead in *Diamond Orchid*, a play by Jerome Lawrence and Robert E. Lee about a character suggested by Eva

Peron. The search for an actress reportedly took several years, and on June 23, 1964, it was announced that Jennifer West had been signed. Jose Quintero directed the show, which opened on February 10, 1965, and lasted five performances.

The relationship between Bancroft and Brooks changed after NBC's purchase of the pilot of the spy comedy series *Get Smart* that he had created with Buck Henry. He was now more secure financially. Brooks and Bancroft had been a couple for three years. They had both been affected by unhappy first marriages and both had ambitions to be professionally successful and creatively satisfied. They adapted to each other with Bancroft lessening her compulsion to work and Brooks accepting her devotion to her career, since he recognized that she was not the conventional housewife type. The actress said maybe it was her thirtyish maturity that helped her cope with her desire to work so that she only did so when the role was exactly what she wanted and it would also give her time and emotion for other things in life. Another issue was their difference in religions. The couple had no problem with an interfaith marriage but they were concerned how each of their mothers would react. Bancroft reported that when she brought Brooks home, Millie told her that she could do better, which amused the couple no end. But Bancroft would say of her mother that she was so happy her daughter wanted to get married again that she didn't care if it was to an orangutan. Brooks joked that when he and Bancroft visited his mother to tell her of their intentions, he couldn't hear her response because she had put her head in the oven. He would admit that the truth was that his mother was delighted with the news and proud that Brooks wanted to marry such a wonderful and beautiful girl. He said what most impressed her was how Bancroft was a star, so that her being Catholic and not Jewish paled in comparison.

The couple took a house on Fire Island for the summer of 1964 though they moved to separate rooms whenever family visited. Bancroft reported that she had become entranced by the island after having been invited there to spend the night when she was working on Broadway in *Two for the Seesaw*. She was tired after doing the show during the week so she went there on the Saturday after the show and slept over. Bancroft said she had never been in a home that was right on the ocean. She spent the whole day there and ate dinner (baked ham) out on the terrace facing the ocean, and the actress told herself that she had to be there. So the next year and the following years she rented a house in Fair Harbor. After Bancroft met Brooks, he would visit her on the weekends.

It was reportedly Bancroft who proposed marriage because she said it would be make it much easier for their folks to deal with their relationship. Brooks agreed and Bancroft nearly fainted. Brooks and Bancroft went to City Hall at lunchtime where they presented themselves to Deputy City Clerk Thomas F. McLaughlin. They had a license and asked to be married in a civil ceremony. She was 32 and he was 38. Bancroft used her real name Anna Marie Italiano and Brooks used his real name Melvin Kaminsky. Neither had thought to bring a ring so the actress offered one of the thin silver earrings she was wearing. Brooks said there was nobody at the ceremony except the couple and a black kid named Samuel Boone (another source calls him Andrew Boone). The kid had reportedly been seen by Brooks on the way into the office and he had stopped and asked the boy to serve as a witness, because he did not have a best man. The kid agreed but said he wanted to warn Brooks not to break up because the clerk who married his friend had a funny voice. When Bancroft and Brooks got in front of the clerk and he started to speak in a theatrical style, they fell on the floor laughing. They had to get up and face him, look away from each other and look away from Boone because he was laughing too. But the couple did get married and after the ceremony they went their separate ways. Brooks had to work and Bancroft returned to her brownstone to prepare a sumptuous wedding night spaghetti supper.

Brooks said this marriage was unlike his first where he needed more attention from the world and less from his wife. He said the second marriage took because both he and Bancroft grew up during it. They both knew what was really important and what love meant and what doing for each other meant. Some said the marriage wouldn't last. Cynics believed that Brooks got the better deal; others, equally unkind, labeled him and Bancroft Beauty and the Beast. However they would prove the scoffers wrong. They enjoyed one of the longest-lasting and, by all accounts, happiest unions in show business history and a partnership that only ended because of Bancroft's death. Patty Duke commented that it wasn't a surprise to her that the two married because she knew how much Bancroft liked that crazy man. Bancroft commented that people thought they were an unlikely couple but she felt they were perfect together. She found him terribly funny all the time and she had learned to stop trying to top his humor because she discovered early that she couldn't. Now she just enjoyed sitting back and laughing. However like any couple they had arguments. On one occasion, Bancroft saw that he began to clench his hand into a fist. This made her shout, "Don't you dare touch me, my body is my instrument." To this Brooks replied, "Oh yeah? Then play 'Melancholy Baby.'"

On October 29, 1964, she was back on Perry Como's show singing "Santa Lucia" with Como and "With a Little Bit of Luck" with Como and Stanley Holloway. The latter number had the trio wearing Cockney Pearly King and Queen costumes. On November 6, the actress returned to anthology TV when she appeared on NBC's 60-minute *Chrysler Theatre* episode "Out on the Outskirts of Town." Set in a small town in the Midwest, it had a teleplay by William Inge, was directed by Frank Corsaro, and was shot at Universal in Hollywood. Bancroft played Faye Benet Garret, a vain middle-aged society figure married to Jack Garret (Jack Warden), a coarse former ballplayer. He yearns for his past fame and she attempts suicide after her husband beats her up. The show was lambasted by Jack Gould in the *New York Times* but he wrote that it was a measure of Bancroft's artistry that she achieved fleeting moments of interest in a part bereft of convincing substance. The actress thought that the fight she had with Warden in the episode was the toughest she had done to date and at one point she was knocked out cold when her head hit the floor. Bancroft said when she came to, the first thing she asked was, "Did you get it?" because she thought it was so good. Unfortunately the cameraman had missed it.

On November 15, 1964, Bancroft was back on *What's My Line?* once again directed by Franklin Heller and hosted by John Charles Daly. The panelists were Dorothy Kilgallen, Groucho Marx, Arlene Francis and Bennett Cerf. This time the actress used a squeaky speaking voice to disguise herself. Bancroft was reportedly present to receive her Best Actress Drama Golden Globe award for *The Pumpkin Eater* on February 8, 1965.

The actress was profiled in the December 20, 1964, *National Enquirer*, in a Jim Blair article entitled "Anne Bancroft's Exclusive Story. I'm A Slob. I Burp & Slurp in Public." The subtitle was "I Used to Be a Drunk and a Liar." She was interviewed in a London hotel suite where she wore a rumpled jersey suit and had tousled hair. She makes the admissions, stating that she is not a lady. Bancroft reported that in her early days in Hollywood she drank and drank—she was a bottle bore. Bancroft confessed that she didn't know how she missed winding up on Skid Row and said that what saved her was getting the part in *Two for the Seesaw*. She recalled how the play's casting of her as a kooky dame saw her become known as the Beatnik of Broadway, who wore black stockings and regularly saw a psychiatrist. The actress felt that she kept this image alive by still wearing black stockings, and revealed that there were holes in both heels. Bancroft confessed to dressing like a scarecrow and said she ate like a stevedore, eating hot dogs in bed and not having the manners of an ape.

On February 19, 1965, the *New York Times* reported that Bancroft had replaced Patricia Neal in the MGM film *7 Women*. This was because Neal had suffered a brain hemorrhage on February 17, 1965, and remained in critical condition at the Medical Center of the University of California in Los Angeles. Neal's role was a cynical world-weary doctor imprisoned in Manchuria in 1935 with a group of Christian missionaries. The article reported that Neal had completed only one day of shooting for director John Ford on February 14, 1965, on the MGM back lot. However, in her memoir, Neal writes she completed four days. Other sources report that filming had begun on February 8, 1965, and that Neal's stroke occurred three days after filming. She wrote that Bancroft had wired her after her stroke to call her if there was anything she could do.

Bancroft stepped into the film role, at Ford's request. At the Actors Studio the actress had a reputation for being ever-prepared, ready to replace someone at the mere hint of a problem. In her May 1987 *Films and Filming* interview, Bancroft said she had originally turned the film down when it was first going to be made because she didn't much like the script. She said she did it after Neal dropped out because she was convinced that one day her friend would wake up and she wanted to be able to say to her that she did the role for her. It was like a gift. In his book Searching for John Ford: A Life, Jim McBride writes that Bancroft accepted the part without even reading the screenplay and left New York on February 19, 1965, to report to MGM that weekend for wardrobe fittings. The actress is said to have begun filming on February 24, reshooting Cartwright's arrival at the mission that Neal had done. Filming is said to have ended on April 12, with pick-up shots done on April 20 and 21. It was also reported that some filming was done in March outside the MGM lot, at Glenmoor Ranch in Sutton Canyon near Chatsworth.

7 Women was an MGM–John Ford–Bernard Smith production, in color. The screenplay was by Janet Green and John McCormick and based on the Norah Lofts short story "Chinese Finale." It is set in North China, near the Mongolian border in a mission of American citizens headed by Agatha Andrews (Margaret Leighton). Bancroft plays Dr. D.R. Cartwright, with her first name never revealed. In the March 7, 1960, *Alcoa Theatre* episode "Chinese Final," it's *Mary* Cartwright and she's played by Jan Sterling.

The doctor is summoned to the mission to attend to the 42-year-old, pregnant Mrs. Florrie Pether (Betty Field) but her presence creates tension. This occurs even before she arrives, since it is assumed by her name that she is a man and also she is not at the location to be collected by the Rev. Charles Pether (Eddie Albert) as expected. The screenplay toys further with the idea of the doctor's gender by having her arriving on horseback, dressed as a man, in brown jodhpurs with a brown leather jacket, white blouse and hat. Her hair being short is also in contrast to that of the women at the mission who all have long hair, although Bancroft's Sidney Guilaroff bouffant seems more 1960s style than period. According to Cartwright, the short hair is "all the rage back home" and also practical in her job. The androgyny is commented on by Florey ("You're a woman") when she first sees her and Cartwright's hair is exposed after having been covered by her hat. Cartwright replies, "Unless a lot of men have been kidding me." The doctor also comments

Still for *7 Women* (1966).

on the rarity of women doctors and the limited opportunities available to them, and states that she has taken the job in China to get out of the U.S. for personal reasons. These reasons will later be implied to be her affair with a married man, and this kind of morality allows for Andrews to later call Cartwright a whore when she accepts the advances of the invading bandit leader Tunga Khan (Mike Mazurki) in exchange for helping the other women.

Cartwright is therefore presented as a modern woman in the face of the traditional old-fashioned women of the missionary. She is a chain-smoker; Andrews remarks that smoking is unbecoming to a lady dedicated to the Christian endeavor. Since the doctor is not a Christian or one of the missionaries, this would seem to make it okay, but she herself comments on it by saying that "everything she does, she does too much." Her compulsive behavior then can also be applied to her work, where she toils long hours and gets little sleep. Cartwright clashes with Miss Andrews and expresses her disapproval by addressing her as "Andrews." They clash over the treatment of Florrie, since Cartwright feels that the woman should be sent to a modern maternity ward to have her baby, particularly in light of her age. When Andrews refuses to provide funds for the trip, Cartwright blasphemes, "I hope your God is merciful because He's the only one who can help her now." The doctor expresses contempt for religion because she has seen how little it has helped those she has treated.

Cartwright's inappropriate behavior also has her frequently swearing, sitting at the dinner table before Grace is said, entering Andrews' office without knocking, giving orders to Andrews' people and bringing a bottle of whisky to the dinner table. The doctor also advises Emma Clark (Sue Lyon) to leave the mission since Cartwright feels she is young enough to have a chance at a life in the real world. Her friendship with Emma provides another source of tension between the doctor and Andrews, since it appears that the mission leader has a lesbian interest in the girl and is therefore jealous.

Cartwright proves to have value, since her quick action (burning the clothes and belongings of Chinese refugees and inoculating people with an immunization serum) saves the mission from a cholera plague. She will make a deal with Tunga Khan to sacrifice herself to help the other women: To get her medicine bag and food, and to move the women from a hut to the mission and then have them sent away, the doctor agrees to be

Tunga's mistress. She also makes the ultimate sacrifice by killing herself as she murders Tunga with poison.

Cartwright delivering Florrie's baby and helping the women survive sees her become the mission leader after Andrews loses her position and has a form of mental breakdown. The doctor's doesn't plan to usurp Andrews, as she had done to beat the plague, but rather plays on Tunga's desire for her. It is also probably Cartwright's bravery, compared to the passive resistance of the other women, that attracts him. This is apparent after he sees her slap the face of the Lean Warrior (Woody Strode) who touched her.

Top-billed Bancroft appears in dozens of scenes and only has one change of costume, designed by Walter Plunkett. Apart from the white coat she wears over her jodhpurs and blouse, Cartwright gets a cream- and green-colored Chinese floor-length robe with a red sash and hair decorations, to please Tunga Khan. The actress uses her hard voice and sensual body language. Bancroft's anger is funny, especially when she toasts Tunga with "So long, you bastard." In her drunken scene she amusingly bangs her hip into Jane Argent (Mildred Dunnock) and hits Andrews for emphasis. Cartwright is given some nice reflective moments, like seeing herself in the mirror in her room and sitting alone in the hut where the women are imprisoned. Bancroft's best moment is perhaps the scene where she agrees to Tunga's deal. Her silent reaction is a surprise, since other choices are expected. Director Ford doesn't give Bancroft any close-ups but then he doesn't give the other actors any either. He also retains Cartwright's dignity to the end, since while Mazurki is shown to topple over from the effects of the poison, Bancroft remains seated.

The film was released on January 5, 1966, with the taglines "Seven who dared what no man dared, each for a reason that was hers, alone!" and "A Story of Flame and Fury, Faith and Fear, Love and Adventure." *Variety* opined that Bancroft endowed her character with some authority. Howard Thompson (the *New York Times*) wrote that Bancroft gave a sizzling, earthy performance. The film was not a box office success.

Bancroft reported that she envisioned Cartwright to be a female John Wayne and that Ford often called her "Duke" on the set. She said that Ford was the first really wonderful, powerful director she worked with. He was a funny fellow and very ornery. They would all sit around reading the script and if he didn't like the page, he would just rip it out. It was outrageous and Bancroft couldn't figure out how anybody was going to put that film together. She said Ford wasn't really looney but he appeared to be because he took advantage of the power that he had. He would simply leave whenever he wanted to. If he was tired in the middle of the day, he would leave, which of course was very pleasant for the company since they too would go home. Bancroft said it was all interesting and she was glad she did the film.

In his book on Ford, Ronald L. Davis wrote that the director was unhappy with the actress, saying he had had difficulty getting her to expand her performance and called her "the mistress of monotone." Bernard Smith said in Scott Eyman's book *Print the Legend: The life and Times of John Ford* that they got the wrong girl to replace Neal. He said Bancroft was a wonderful actress, but she once described herself as a guinea from Brooklyn, and what they needed was an austere lady. It was felt the story was a much more of a tragic leap that way. Smith also said that Ford shot the film carelessly because he lost interest. In his Ford book, Tag Gallagher writes that Bancroft's last line "So long, you bastard" was not in the original script and came out of improvisations that the director encouraged the actors to do. Gallagher quotes the actress as saying that the company realized why Ford was considered one of the world's greatest directors. He would arrive each morning knowing exactly what he intended to film and with every scene visually worked out on his mind. Bancroft said Ford was never in a hurry, yet he didn't waste a minute. His rehearsals were so thorough that more often than not he would film the most difficult scene in one take, and rarely more than two. She said if there was any difference of opinion about how a scene should be played, the actor would invariably end up agreeing with Ford. Bancroft added that the director could be infinitely patient in explaining the reasons for what he wanted and at the same time he was in command and could be firm when necessary. It is reported that the scene where Cartwright slaps the Lean Warrior required a number of takes, since Woody Strode kept obscuring Bancroft's face during the strike. Once they got an acceptable take, Ford told Strode to count his teeth.

On February 8, 1965, Bancroft reportedly attended the 22nd Annual Golden Globes ceremony. She won the Best Actress in a Motion Picture Drama award for her performance in *The Pumpkin Eater*. On March 7, the *New York Times* reported that she was one of the celebrities who had rallied round with great fervor to help the play *The Sign in Sidney Brustein's Window*. It had opened on October 15, 1964, and received disappointing reviews and appeared certain to close. Bancroft and Viveca Lindfors held meetings at which plots were hatched for drumming up publicity, financial support and customers. But this and other efforts were undermined by two disasters that hit: a weekend snowstorm that reduced the audiences to almost nothing, and then the death of its writer Lorraine Hansberry, who had been in hospital during the show's run. The play had closed on January 10, 1965, but then recovered its costs after a run at the Mineola Playhouse.

Bancroft's friendship with Lindfors led them to do August Strindberg's *The Stronger*, directed by Lee Strasberg, as an actors' exercise at the Actors Studio. This is described in Foster Hirsch's book on the Studio, *A Method to Their Madness*. In the play, Bancroft played the silent character and Lindfors was the talker. Hirsch writes that Strasberg criticized Bancroft for giving away the ending of the play at the beginning with unconscious anticipation. The moment caused tension in the room and the actress reportedly had a mischievous glint in her eye. Strasberg then accused her of responding too vulnerably and he encouraged her to make a sound if she wanted to speak. Hirsch described the director as moving back and forth between the two actresses and Bancroft was visibly chafing under the restriction. As Lindfors goaded and challenged her, the actress began to emit a series of grunts and growls, low moans and wheezes, and then there was an eruption. She struck Lindfors, who was stunned, and then struck back at Bancroft. The women struggled, the observers gasped, and Strasberg was delighted.

In March 1965, Bancroft was photographed by Horst in Pauline Trigere spring fashions for a spread for an unidentified magazine. She wore five outfits with coiffures by Ingrid of Michael Kazan. On April 5, she attended the 37th Annual Academy Awards at the Santa Monica Civic Auditorium. She was nominated for the Best Actress award for *The Pumpkin Eater*. Julie Andrews won for *Mary Poppins*.

It was announced that Bancroft had signed to appear as Hollywood star Merle McGill in the crime comedy *The Honey Pot* (1967). The screenplay was by Joseph L. Mankiewicz based on the play *Mr. Fox of Venice* by Frederick Knott, the book *The Evil of the Day* by Thomas L. Sterling and the play *Volpone* by Ben Jonson. Then Bancroft withdrew to do a theater show instead, and was replaced by Edie Adams. On May 11, 1965, it was reported that Bancroft and Jason Robards were set for a Broadway run of *The Devils*, to open on November 9. Adapted by John Whiting from Aldous Huxley's book *The Devils of Loudon*, the play was to be directed by Michael Cacoyannis. The show first ran in London in 1961 with Dorothy Tutin and Richard Johnson in the leads; its U.S. premiere was in Washington at the Arena Theatre, and producer Alexander H. Cohen decided to bring it to Broadway. It was reported on August 14, 1965, that he had signed the two American stars until June 30, 1966. Rehearsals were scheduled to begin on September 9, with the Broadway opening set for November.

The film *The Slender Thread* (working title: *Call Me Back*) was first announced on March 30, 1965, when Stirling Silliphant was said to be preparing the screenplay for Paramount. At this time, the film was to star Sidney Poitier and Elizabeth Ashley. On June 13, Poitier said in an interview that his co-star was now Bancroft and that the film—a fictionalized version of a true story—was the anatomy of a would-be suicide. It involved a telephone conversation between a hospital worker and a woman who has taken an overdose of barbiturates and then called the hospital because she didn't want to die without talking to someone. As they talk, the hospital and the police try and locate her. Poitier added that she never knew that the man she spoke to was an African American. A source claims that the film's title was at one time *Cross My Heart and Hope to Die* and that Ashley dropped out due to a contract dispute. In the chapter on Sydney Pollack in his book *The Directors: Take One, Volume 1*, Robert J. Emery said that Pollack got the job for his directorial debut because of Ashley. She had been a student of his when he taught at the Neighborhood Playhouse and he thought she had brought his name up to Paramount.

The Slender Thread reportedly began shooting on June 7, 1965, on location in Seattle and at Paramount. The Silliphant screenplay was suggested by a *Life* magazine article by Shana Alexander, "Decision to Die." Bancroft plays 30-year-old Inga Dyson, a secretary for the vice-president of a contracting firm. Inga is the wife of fisherman Mark Dyson (Steven Hill) and the mother of 12-year-old Chris (Greg Jarvis). The Dyson marriage suffers when Mark learns he is not Chris' biological father. Inga books a room at the Hyatt House hotel and takes an overdose of sleeping pills, then calls the Crisis Clinic 24-hour hotline and speaks with psychology student volunteer Alan Newell (Poitier). The man who had fathered Chris is now said to be dead but Mark still sees the fact that Inga has not told him the truth about it as a betrayal. Inga is shown to be mentally unstable even before she takes the pills, when we see her attempting to drown herself at the beach. But she also tries to get help by going to a hospital to say that she is "going to pieces" and to ask for someone to talk to. Her depression worsens in a scene where she tries to save an injured bird on the beach by getting it brandy, but finds that in between the time she has left it and when she returns, it has either died or been buried by the kids who brought her attention to it. Another factor that leads Inga to attempt suicide: Her boss, Mr. Hampton, has the day off, which leaves her with a feeling of uselessness.

Second-billed Bancroft wears her hair in a bouffant short style, and her clothes are by Edith Head. While the movie includes flashback scenes, the main action is the extended telephone call between Inga and Alan which relies upon the sound of Bancroft's voice. Inga's speech slowing down and slurring due to the pills is measured by a technician at the clinic over the one-hour duration of the call. Bancroft's Bronx accent sometimes comes through and she occasionally makes Inga on the phone funny. The actress mostly underplays Inga's anger and emotional response to Mark's rejection. Pollack supplies some extreme close-ups of her in a fantasy scene where Mark kisses Inga. In one of her best moments, Bancroft shows shock and tenderness in response to Mark's reaction to

Still for *The Slender Thread* (1965).

the news about Chris. Other good moments: her shocked and amused reaction to the discotheque dancers, her sudden rage at the bird's burial mound on the beach, and her transition from wonder to cynicism at the hospital's attitude to her cry for help.

The film was released on December 23, 1965, with the taglines "Two Academy Award Winners Are Giving the Performances of Their Lives," "When a woman's emotions sway on a slender thread, expect anything…" and "A Motion Picture Experience Rarely, If Ever, Surpassed In Suspense." *Variety* wrote that Bancroft was compelling and the *New York Times'* A.H. Weiler called her performance tender, knowing, graduated in intensity and convincing in its understatement even in occasional humorous asides. John Douglas Eames in *The Paramount Story* cited Bancroft's portrayal as bravura. In *Kiss Kiss Bang Bang*, Pauline Kael wrote that Bancroft wasn't bad in the film but that she couldn't seem to help looking and acting like a big movie star, although she really wasn't one quite yet. Kael added, "Not yet a queen, she already carries herself like the queen-mother." Kael also had a funny story in her review. In the moment in the film when Alan is asked whether he would like to meet Inga after she had been saved, he says no. Kael reported that at this moment, a voice behind her in the theater said, "They already met at the Academy Awards show," referring to Poitier and Bancroft as real people and not in their roles in the film. The film was not a box office hit but it received Oscar nominations for Best Costume Design and Best Black and White Art Direction-Set Decoration.

Poitier wrote in his memoir *This Life* that Bancroft was fantastic to work with, and

Pollack said she did a magnificent job. According to Janet L. Meyer's book *Sydney Pollack: A Critical Filmography*, Inga's first suicide attempt on the beach had Bancroft wearing the bottom of a wetsuit under her costume. As she waded into the sea, the suit became saturated and pulled her underwater and Pollack and other members of the film crew had to rescue her.

Interviewer Hedda Hopper asked Bancroft about her marriage, telling the actress of the rumor that it was an unhappy union, and that stories had circulated that the actress was pregnant. Bancroft advised her that she shouldn't believe everything she read. The actress said she was hard to live with and that Brooks was the same. She didn't know how they stayed together but perhaps it was due to the fact she felt he was one of the funniest men who ever lived. Bancroft said that sometimes she laughed at him until tears rolled out of her eyes.

On August 8, 1965, the *New York Times* announced that Bancroft would appear in a new Broadway play in spring after finishing her run in *The Devils*. This was to be an adaptation of the Lucille Kallen novel *Out There, Somewhere!* in which young housewife Ruth Bernard digs her comic way out of laundry piles, dishes and wall-to-wall tedium into a writing job with a TV producer. The play would deal with the double standard problem in American society. When Ruth rejoins the outside world, she discovers that her husband, whom she believed to be wonderful and broad-minded, is actually a wash-and-wear Victorian firmly committed to the dignity of man and the indignity of women. Bancroft had been responsible for initiating the project after reading the book in the summer and asking the author to make a play of it for her. The producer was to be David Black, and Arthur Penn was being sought to direct. Kallen had worked with Mel Brooks on television's *Your Show of Shows* but this was the first time she spent time with both him and Bancroft. When Kallen visited their 11th Street brownstone, she reportedly was impressed with the actress' warmth and informality. The writer felt that the couple came across as if Brooks was a younger brother who had married the Queen of England.

Kallen would find that she was unable to write the stage adaptation, despite her experience as a playwright, composer and lyricist. It was felt that the problem was that she was too close to the material and needed professional distance from it. The play was apparently never staged.

A September 11, 1965, article said that the first rehearsal of *The Devils* was September 10 and it was scheduled to open on November 16. Bancroft was to play the part of Sister Jeanne, a young 17th-century nun and an erotic hysteric hunchback. She experiences fits of spiritual possession and is responsible for the charge of diabolism against a libertine priest (Jason Robards). Bancroft was billed as Sister Jean of the Angels, the Prioress of St. Ursula's Convent. The show was reported to have pre–Broadway tryouts in Boston from October 18. In Boston, the actress missed 11 performances for health reasons.

After 12 previews from November 3, 1965, *The Devils* opened on Broadway at the Broadway Theatre on November 16. It was praised by the *New York Times'* by Howard Taubman, who wrote that Bancroft was particularly affecting when the prioress recalled her childhood and its loneliness, and said her bursts of hysteria communicated the hint of hollowness which was dramatically right.

The show ran until January 8, 1966. Bancroft was reported to have missed some performances, some because of an on-stage accident. This occurred on December 29, 1965, when Bancroft fell from a ladder and injured her back in the play's first act. She was taken to Lenox Hill Hospital and Zoe Caldwell was said to have been called upon that night to finish the second act. (It was reported that Caldwell had been hired on December 13, 1965, to replace the actress for four performances, with Bancroft to return on December 27.) Bancroft's injury was painful enough to keep her out of the show for at least ten days.

On January 5, 1966, producer Alexander Cohen announced that the season would end prematurely as a result of the actress' illness and also because of the transit strike impacting the theater district. The show's cancellation came despite there being considerable advance ticket sales. One source claims that the decision to close was also made because the actress played what would be her last performance in the show in such a low-key manner that she infuriated the rest of the cast. In 1970, the play was later made into a British film directed by Ken Russell. The part of Sister Jean was played by Vanessa Redgrave.

In late 1965, the Brookses purchased a summer home at Lonelyville on Fire Island. After they married, they had rented houses all over the island until they found one that looked like a long, all-glass shoebox. It was set apart from the other communities on the island, though later the community of Dunewood was built next door. Bancroft said that she liked the island because there were no cars and few phones. She said if she had stayed in Manhattan, she wouldn't have gotten any rest, but here she could do nothing. Bancroft felt it had the best beach she had ever seen. The narrow island had a bay on one side and the ocean on the other, and from the house she could see both.

In Bosley Crowther's *New York Times* article "Where Are the Women?" (January 23, 1966), he asked what happened to the intelligent and promising screen actresses, like Bancroft, and why we saw so little of them. In an article on Mel Brooks dated January 30, he described his wife as a "divine and splendid person and a nice girl." On May 1, Bancroft attended the funeral of the drama coach, actor and director Paula Strasberg, at the Riverside in New York City. The wife of Lee Strasberg, the director and head of the Actors Studio, she had died of a heart attack.

Directed by Arthur Penn, *The Skin of Our Teeth*, with Bancroft as Sabina, was set to open on June 21, 1966, in Stockbridge, Massachusetts. The play ran for a two-week season which means it presumably closed on July 5, 1966. Also in the cast was Frank Langella, who wrote in his memoir *Dropped Names: Famous Men and Women as I Knew Them* that in Stockbridge, he, Bancroft and Brooks became inseparable friends, and that her nickname for her husband was Mibby. Langella said they spent almost every waking hour together that summer, and then for the next five years. After performances, they would gather around a large table on a sun porch at the home of William Gibson, president of the Berkshire Festival. Langella said those gatherings were about as full of consistently riotous laughter as any he had ever known. Brooks entertained the group with humor which would make Bancroft react with hopeless, helpless laughter and then she put on music and would dance for the group. Langella said that the production was a giant success and sold out mostly due to the box office draw of the actress.

In a *New York Times* article on Arthur Penn (December 21, 1969), Bancroft commented said that the *Skin of Our Teeth* company rehearsed for three weeks and simply did improvisations, doing scenes but never using the dialogue. Bancroft said this led to a deeper understanding of what was in herself and what she had to bring to her part. She left Stockbridge after the production, not to appear in any of the other plays the ensemble troupe did that summer. She wanted to continue her sabbatical for the rest of 1966. The actress said she had not stopped looking at scripts but nothing she read had excited her or inspired her to return to work. One source claims that Bancroft was seeking a very specific sort of character, especially after the series of ones she had played that demanded various types of physical or emotional handicaps. She wanted one that was a good role and also allow her to look good.

Interviewed by Larry Siegel in the October 1966 *Playboy*, Brooks joked that Bancroft was earning more money than he at the moment, since she was not sitting for free interviews. Bancroft also reportedly encouraged her husband to write a musical number for his upcoming film *The Producers*. Brooks had considered finding a songwriter to create the original song for the stage show within the film, but his wife told him that he could do it himself. Bancroft said that he was musical and a good singer, and also that he had talked his head off ever since she had met him about how much he wanted to be a songwriter. The actress ordered Brooks to take a pad, a pencil and go into a room and she bet that within an hour he would come out with a nice song. Brooks said it took him a month to come up with the words and music for the song "Springtime for Hitler" as well as another one, "Prisoners of Love."

Bancroft participated in a radio tribute to playwright Lorraine Hansberry, broadcast on WBAI-FM on January 12 and 19, 1967. She was one of several actors who read from the late author's published and unpublished works. Bancroft reportedly volunteered her services without pay. The American Federation of Television and Radio Artists claimed that the show had not been cleared with the union board. This meant that those who participated could be charged with prejudicial conduct with the union. The director of the program, Robert Nemiroff, was the former husband of Hansberry and the executor of her estate. He stated that he did not think it was necessary to clear the program with the union because it was a non-commercial venture. On January 22, 1967, the *New York Times* reported that the radio station and the union had settled their differences and, by mutual agreement, the show "Lorraine Hansberry in Her Own Words" was to be broadcast.

On January 28, 1967, it was reported that Bancroft would appear in a two-character musical for the anthology TV series *ABC Stage 67*. "I'm Getting Married," to be broadcast on March 16, was an original work by Betty Comden and Adolph Green with music by Jule Styne. Bancroft was to co-star with Dick Shawn. The show was said to be her first performance in a musical although she had sung several times on Perry Como's shows. Comden described it as more of a musical play than a full-blown musical comedy and said it concerned the fears and fantasies of an engaged couple. It was said to be told from the girl's point of view: She thinks she knows the boy, until he makes an announcement which starts her wondering and fantasizing. Comden advised that the story had a happy ending because nothing could keep the couple apart. A photograph of Bancroft appeared in the *New York Times* on March 12, 1967, accompanying an article by Comden and Green about the show. The authors said that Bancroft initially refused to play an 85-year-old peasant whose back was to the camera the whole time. The role was changed so that now the actress played her role as a young American girl facing the camera, talking directly to the audience and singing solo, as well as acting and singing with Dick Shawn. They describe her voice as deep, reminiscent of Dietrich, Bankhead and Chaliapin ... but beautiful.

On March 17, 1967, the show was lambasted by George Gent, who wrote that it was a witless pastiche that was incredibly dull and a poor advertisement for the institution of marriage. Gent said that Bancroft and Shawn were fine professionals caught in a credibility gap with a wickedly perceptible wink which destroyed whatever mood the authors might have sought to create.

The actress was interviewed by Frank Judge about the show for *The Sunday Star* TV magazine for March 12–18, 1967. Bancroft reported that she had been offered musicals every year, on Broadway as well as on television, but she never liked any of them. Then she said Comden and Green came to her house and went through this new show and she liked it at once. Hubbell Robinson, the executive in charge of *ABC Stage 67*, said Bancroft was perfect for the role, since it required an actress who could sing rather than a singer who could act, and he said there weren't any of those around.

6

The Graduate

On March 13, 1967, it was reported that Bancroft was to appear opposite Dustin Hoffman in *The Graduate* with Mike Nichols directing for Embassy Pictures. Production reportedly began on April 24, 1967; Nichols was said to have rehearsed his actors in March 1967 before filming began. In one source, Nichols said the rehearsal period was three weeks, in another, he said it was four. Co-writer Buck Henry was worried about Bancroft in the rehearsals. He said she seemed lost, disconnected from her character's intelligence and suffocating ennui. Henry also said he wasn't seeing upper middle class in her performance. But then he came to admire her for having to climb out of someplace to get there. In rehearsals she became irritated and asked Nichols whether he liked her character. The director said he didn't because she sounded much too nice. When the actress asked why Mrs. Robinson wasn't nice, he couldn't tell her, but he said he could show her. Nichols read one of her lines with frosty, deadpan neutrality and Bancroft said that was anger, which she could do. The actress later told the director that she was never quite able to get rid of the anger in her performances. Filming is said to have completed on August 5, 1967.

This comic romance had a screenplay by Calder Willingham and Buck Henry based on the novel by Charles Webb. It was shot on location in California, including the University of Southern California campus. Ben Braddock (Hoffman) is a disillusioned 20-year-old college graduate who has an affair with Mrs. Robinson (Bancroft). (Her first name is never revealed but Bancroft told Frank Langella, perhaps facetiously, that it was "Queenie"!) She is the wife of his father's business partner (Murray Hamilton) and is twice Ben's age. The affair ends when he dates her daughter, Berkeley college student Elaine (Katharine Ross).

Mrs. Robinson is shown to be different from the other women who attend Ben's graduation party, perhaps because she has her own agenda with him. We see her sitting away from the others, not socializing, and smoking. It is suggested that she is a chain-smoker, and she admits to being neurotic and alcoholic. Director Nichols also makes her different by presenting most of the other older women as grotesques. The exception is Ben's mother Mrs. Braddock (Elizabeth Wilson) who happens to have the same hairdo of dark hair with blonde streaks that Mrs. Robinson has. Mrs. Braddock wears an animal-print skirt and an animal-print blouse, which is a style that Mrs. Robinson also favors. Mrs. Robinson makes an obvious advance to Ben at the party when she asks him to drive her home. When she throws his car keys, that he has thrown to her, into a fish tank in his bedroom, it suggests that he has unwittingly insulted her and it is also a sign that she is going to be trouble. However Mrs. Robinson has the sensitivity to see that he is upset at the party, which no one else does, even if she adds to his sense of discomfort. She sits in the parked car outside her house waiting for Ben to open her door for her, but her having him go inside the house with him, offering him a drink, playing music, and exposing her thigh to him continues her advance. She questions his assumption that she is trying to seduce him, even laughing at the idea, but continues her advance when she undresses in front of him and tricks him into seeing her naked. This is when Mrs. Robinson tells Ben that she finds him attractive and that she is available to him. She will later tell Ben that she and her husband have separate bedrooms and no longer sleep together, and that they married only because he had gotten her pregnant when they were college students.

While Ben tells Mrs. Robinson that he finds her desirable and takes advantage of her offer (he has no other love interest), his feeling of shame over the affair also seems real. He urges her to have a conversation with him, which reveals that she was once an art major. Ben calls her a broken-down alcoholic, and says he only meets with her out of pure boredom, and that what they are doing is sick and perverted. When she threatens to leave, Ben admits that he likes her, enjoys being with her, and looks forward to it. He jokes about asking Elaine for a date but this leads Mrs. Robinson to attack Ben. She pulls his hair and has him promise that he will never date her daughter. Mrs. Robinson says that he is not good enough for Elaine, though later denies this and changes to saying that Ben is not right for Elaine. The better choice is Carl Smith (Brian Avery), a medical student whom Elaine will eventually marry but then leave at the altar for Ben. Ben will agree to date her to pacify his parents who offer the alternative of a dinner party between the families. Mrs. Robinson warns Ben not to see Elaine again, threatening to tell her daughter about their affair, although Elaine guesses it when she seems them together. Mrs. Robinson will claim that Ben raped her, rather than admit the truth that Ben discloses, and we are not sure what she tells her husband. When Mr. Robinson confronts Ben, he says the couple are to divorce, and Ben tells him that the affair meant nothing and he does not love Mrs. Robinson. This scene also shows Mr. Robinson to be a physical coward towards Ben, and adds to the rationale for his wife's unhappiness with their marriage. Mrs. Robinson's revenge also extends to telephoning the police when Ben comes looking for Elaine, describing him as a burglar.

Bancroft is top-billed, despite her playing a supporting role. Stylist Sidney Guilaroff has her hair shoulder-length and brunette with blonde streaks, worn

Portrait for *The Graduate* **(1967).**

sometimes in a bouffed ponytail and sometimes with the back clipped together. Costumes are by Patricia Zipprodt and the actress has a tan so that the pale outline of her bikini is shown. The scene where it is suggested that Mrs. Robinson is nude when she exposes herself to Benjamin at her house features flash-cuts of breasts and tummy that are reportedly not those of the actress. Nichols' coverage of the sex between Mrs. Robinson and Ben is implied rather than shown, and the actress is spared any indignity.

Bancroft makes Mrs. Robinson elegant but also reptilian in her advance upon Ben, with Nichols often photographing her unflatteringly. She also shows the woman's nastiness in mouthing "son of a bitch" to Ben when he storms Elaine's wedding, and when she slaps Elaine for running away with him. The actress shows the woman's bemusement at Ben's inexperience when they meet at the Taft Hotel for their first tryst, and supplies a pause after he suggests they go to a movie rather than have sex. There are two long-held shots of Mrs. Robinson's displeasure at Ben's date with Elaine. Her scene in the car when she comes out of the rain to talk to Ben is disappointing since it does not let us see enough of her rage. Bancroft's best scene is perhaps her hotel room confession to Ben since she provides a range of emotion. We see her physical desire for Ben, her humor in frustration about his delaying more physical contact, and the character's sadness about a life she might have lived and the life she has.

The film was released on December 21, 1967, with the tagline "This Is Benjamin. He's a little worried about his future." The leg of Mrs. Robinson in the poster for the film does not belong to Bancroft. Though the image comes from a scene in the film, it was reported that the then-unknown model Linda Gray provided her leg for a recreation shot. Grey would later play Mrs. Robinson in the stage version of *The Graduate* in London in 2001 and on Broadway in 2002. The producers wanted Hoffman and Bancroft to do a pose for a different kind of shot to help the film appeal to the art-house audiences. Supposedly she would have been sitting on a bed with Hoffman facing her, standing up—naked—and she was to have her hands around him, holding his buttocks. However Bancroft refused to do it and Nichols vetoed the idea. The actress was said to have amended her contract billing privilege and insisted that Hoffman be accorded credit commensurate with his role as her co-star. This meant that his name would appear on all ads, posters and marquees beside hers in like-sized letters.

A.D. Murphy in *Variety* wrote that Bancroft was feline and slinky in a manner very much like Lauren Bacall, and excellent. Bosley Crowther of the *New York Times* said that she gave a sullenly contemptuous and voracious performance. Roger Ebert wrote that, in a tricky role, Bancroft was magnificently sexy, shrewish and self-possessed enough to make the seduction convincing. A box office hit, it was Oscar-nominated for Best Picture, Best Director, Best Actor, Best Actress for Bancroft, Best Supporting Actress for Katharine Ross, Best Adapted Screenplay and Best Cinematography. Nichols was the only winner.

A sequel was proposed but never made. Dustin Hoffman had an idea that he told Nichols about, where Ben and Elaine were still married, though not happily, and they had grown kids as well as a 16-year-old boy. Mrs. Robinson would go to their house for dinner once or twice a week. Ben started having an affair with the boy's girlfriend, so that he became a Mrs. Robinson figure. Nichols added the idea that Ben should be a director of television commercials. Co-screenwriter Buck Henry reported that a sequel was never seriously talked about. However in the Robert Altman–directed comedy *The Player* (1992), Henry appears in one scene as himself and pitches the sequel to the Hollywood studio executive played by Tim Robbins. His idea is supported by the fact that,

25 years later, the three principal actors are still alive. Henry imagines that Ben and Elaine are still married and living together in a big spooky house in Northern California. Mrs. Robinson lives with them but she has had a stroke which has made her unable to speak, though she hears what transpires in the house. The daughter of the couple is now 22 and a college graduate, ideally to be played by Julia Roberts. Altman reported that Henry's lines were improvised, and we don't hear whether the pitch is successful or not in the narrative.

Bancroft advised that she wasn't the first choice for the part, saying that they were down to Doris Day before they got to her. The actress would be incredulous about the notion of Day's casting. A number of actresses were said to have been offered the part, and even more considered for it. Some sources reported that Day was Nichols' first choice, but she turned it down because of the sexual content. One rumor says the property was acquired with her in mind as Mrs. Robinson. When the novel was sent to her manager-husband Martin Melcher, he was supposedly so disgusted by the thought of Day in the role that he refused to even mention it to her. She wrote in her 1975 memoir that she was actually offered the role, but "I could not see myself rolling around in the sheets with a young man half my age whom I'd seduced." In his book on Day, *A Reluctant Star*, David Bret wrote that the actress claimed that she could never get away with being the older, sexually liberated woman after years of playing the hard-to-get virgin. In his book *Doris Day: Sentimental Journey*, Gary McGee says that the actress' reason was that the nudity offended her sense of values. Producer Lawrence Turman reported that he had thought about Day because he liked casting against type but that Bancroft was the only actress they offered the part to. Buck Henry said that Day was considered for the role of Ben's mother.

One source claims that Nichols' actual first choice was Jeanne Moreau. The idea behind this was that in the French culture, the older women tended to train the younger men in sexual matters. But the producers were completely opposed to the idea. Patricia Neal wrote in *As I Am* that Nichols offered her the part but she declined as she was still recovering from her illness. She also commented that she didn't think anyone could have touched what Bancroft did. Susan Hayward reportedly refused the part because she wanted to avoid modifying her screen image. Another source claims she was offered the part of Mrs. Braddock. Geraldine Page and Natalie Wood also supposedly turned down the part of Mrs. Robinson.

It was said that Joan Crawford, Lauren Bacall, Audrey Hepburn and Angela Lansbury inquired about it. Nichols met with Ava Gardner but he felt that at 44, she was older than the person he wanted, and she also told him, "I don't take my clothes off for anybody." Even though Nichols told her that that would not be required and he considered her a great movie star, he said he recognized the impossibility of working with her and an offer was never made. Other actors considered for the part included Claire Bloom, Angie Dickinson, Sophia Loren, Judy Garland, Grayson Hall, Rita Hayworth, Anouk Aimee, Jennifer Jones, Deborah Kerr, Eva Marie Saint, Rosalind Russell, Simone Signoret, Jean Simmons, Lana Turner, Eleanor Parker, Anne Baxter and Shelley Winters.

Sam Kashner wrote the *Vanity Fair* article "Here's to You, Mr. Nichols: The Making of *The Graduate*" (February 25, 2008) in which he reported that Bancroft was really the only actress Nichols had in mind. Kashner quoted the director who said that he didn't offer the role to anyone except her. Nichols claimed that everyone she knew advised her to turn it down as being too risky. Mel Brooks persuaded her to do it because he liked the script.

Interviewed in Mark Harris' *Pictures at a Revolution: Five Movies and the Birth of the New Hollywood,* Nichols said that it took him a long time to think of Bancroft for the film. He considered her too young for the part (she was 35) but then decided it didn't matter. The director had turned the 33-year-old Elizabeth Taylor into a hard-bitten, middle-aged drunk for *Who's Afraid of Virginia Woolf?* and he figured he could do the same for Bancroft. Also, she was a name; not a blockbuster name, but a name Hollywood knew and a name he could get for a price. In Harris' book *Scenes From A Revolution: The Birth of the New Hollywood,* he wrote that it was production designer Richard Sylbert's idea to give Mrs. Robinson a wild stripe in her hair. This would literalize the character as a wild beast in the jungle, with leopard underwear, zebra-striped things and jungle plants. Sylbert also thought up her tan and the idea of seeing the bra straps marked, which required elaborate and careful makeup to be applied to the actress. Harris wrote that the wedding scene was filmed in June 1967 on a scorchingly hot day and that Bancroft fainted filming the moment when the crowd was pushing to get out of the church. She had to be given oxygen and sent home. Harris also reported that Bancroft's mood darkened as the filming progressed. He said some mornings she was hung over, and on others she had such painful menstrual cramps that she couldn't get out of bed, so the company had to reschedule around her.

Bancroft said that she was always in the market for a challenging role and Mrs. Robinson was just what she had in mind. After she read the script, she immediately wanted the part. But it was not an easy job. She knew that she was required to appear in various states of undress but when it became time to stand on set in her bra and slip, the actress said she thought she would die. She chased everyone away. Thereafter Nichols was more sensitive to Bancroft's sense of modesty and, when scantily clad scenes were going to be filmed, the set was closed to all but essential personnel. He also erected partitions screens for an added measure of privacy. Bancroft initially thought she had the nerve to do a nude scene but then refused to do it, which forced the filmmakers to bring in a body double. Dustin Hoffman reported that Nichols and the actress had a last-minute misunderstanding about whether she would show her breasts in the film. She said she had not agreed to it so the company had to get someone with the same dimensions as Bancroft, who *would*. On the Sunset Strip, they found a stripper who was prepared to be topless but when it came time to shoot, it was revealed that under her bathrobe, she had pasties on her nipples that she refused to remove. Another stripper was then procured. Bancroft also had contractual veto power over whose nudity would be used and how long they would appear on the screen. Apparently she and her lawyers watched the footage in a Los Angeles screening room and were given copies so that if anything changed, what they had in their vault would be the evidence required to take the appropriate legal action.

Nichols commented that Bancroft was not Mrs. Robinson because she was very different from her but the actress had this tremendous real anger and power. He felt that she was brilliant and a great actress but that their relationship was very emotional, perhaps because he had dated her for a little while in New York before she met Mel Brooks. The director said he saw the actress change. He became a little scared of her and found her to be someone new as Mrs. Robinson. In a way, Nichols played Ben to her Mrs. Robinson and after making the film they could never quite get rid of that dynamic. He reported that she always did something new or different, and in the bedroom scene where Ben asked Mrs. Robinson to talk, she upset Hoffman by pulling his hair too hard. Bancroft initially forgot to incorporate the character's sadness over the loss of art in her life, and when Nichols reminded her of it, she apologized and they reshot the scene. He felt that her genius put you on Mrs. Robinson's side. This partly came from how she was so much fun and partly because she a beautiful woman. You felt for her and also admired her for the risk she took in her life. After Bancroft died, the director asked himself why he hadn't made ten films with her, why he hadn't used her in the films he did make, and why he didn't go to her and ask her what she wanted to do. Nichols reported that she was initially furious about the way she was photographed in the film, but then at one of the anniversaries, he asked her if she felt the same. Bancroft replied that she thought the woman she saw on the screen was the most beautiful she had ever seen.

Dustin Hoffman loved Bancroft but said he didn't enjoy working with her as much as with Katharine Ross, because their scenes together were difficult. He said it was the actress' idea that Ben should kiss Mrs. Robinson impulsively in the hotel room in their first meeting after she had just taken a puff of a cigarette, and that she should blow out the smoke after he lets go. Bancroft told Frank Langella that the idea was Hoffman's, and Nichols claimed it came from him. She thought it was a stupid idea but Nichols liked it. Hoffman said that in the television room, the actress came up with the idea of Mrs. Robinson resting one leg on another chair, provocatively exposing her underwear and making it possible for Benjamin to see up her skirt. This led Nichols to create the moment where Ben says she is trying to seduce him, with him framed under her leg. Hoffman also said that Bancroft's irritation as Mrs. Robinson in the bedroom scene where Ben wanted to talk was based on the actress hoping to finish the scene early. This was because she wanted to get back to New York to be with Mel Brooks. Hoffman said he was afraid to ever touch Bancroft since he knew Brooks and wondered whether her husband would approve.

Co-star Elizabeth Wilson observed that Bancroft was tough and not aloof on the set. She wanted to be left alone to work on her character and to think whatever she had to think. Wilson felt it made sense for Bancroft to be like that but it wasn't easy.

In his book, Frank Langella reported that Bancroft rented a house with him in Beverly Hills while she made the film. He said that they were joined by Mel Brooks who came out on weekends while he was editing *The Producers*. Langella said that it was in the house that he began to see patterns in Bancroft's behavior that would rule her life and that she never seemed able to conquer. Most evenings the two actors would have dinner together after her day's shoots and before she would have to leave to do *The Devils* at the Mark Taper Forum. Bancroft had stories about her co-stars and her director. She felt that Nichols was giving Hoffman and Katharine Ross most of the attention because they were really nervous, but he felt that Bancroft did not need it. Langella wrote about when the actress had her accident during the church scene, and said that following the ambulance that carried Bancroft were Nichols and Hoffman in another car. He said they both jumped out looking terrified and worried, and when the actress was being carried upstairs to her room, Nichols told Langella that she had fallen backwards while shooting. X-rays were taken, pills dispensed, and Bancroft stayed in bed for a few days. The writer said that the event took place in one form or another on most every project the actress did through the years.

After she returned to work, one night Arthur Penn came to visit her and Langella talked with him until she came back home. After making a drink, Bancroft told the men about the scene shot that day, which was the one in the Taft Hotel bar. That night at 11, the telephone rang. It was Nichols who told the actress that they had to re-shoot the scene because there was a technical problem with the film. This made Bancroft go into a rage, particularly as she now had to go back and do it now, and she repeatedly swore. She took two Valium out of her bag and Langella said the actress was in a hostile panic because she felt she would never be able to do it again the way she had done. Penn assured Bancroft that she would, and advised her to forget what she had done and do it fresh. The actress replied, "What the fuck. Mike's only watching Dusty anyway." Bancroft sat in an armchair to await the car that was coming to collect her, and she spat out a series of slights she felt she had endured during the shoot. Langella said she then began to sob uncontrollably, like a little girl who'd been told by her mother to stand in the corner before she could explain that whatever had happened was not her fault. Penn remained sympathetic and comforting, and after the car arrived and Bancroft re-shot the scene, Langella said the result was superb. The actor wrote that in 1991, he reminisced about that night—and Bancroft became furious and denied that the events ever happened. When Langella insisted that it did, he said the actress claimed it was "a fucking lie" and she flung her napkin across the table into his face. She continued that she knew it probably made a great story for Langella to tell his friends. He was so angry with her that he told the actress that nobody cared about Anne Bancroft stories any more and walked out of the restaurant. She later phoned him and apologized, though (according to Langella) her apology was typically non-introspective and self-serving. Bancroft explained that she had been going through a rough time; the actor said he was unsympathetic and their friendship never fully recovered after the incident. However, Langella wrote that she and Brooks subsequently and loyally came to every play he was in and saw every movie he made.

Bancroft said she was not happy at the time with the attention the role of sexual aggressor brought her, but she found as the years went on that she was beginning to have fun and take pleasure in it. In later life when men met her, Bancroft thought *The Graduate* was always in the backs of their minds. Sometimes it made them uncomfortable to be in her presence. It all depended on what age they saw it at. If they were comfortable with their own sexuality, it was okay. Bancroft knew there were plusses to forever being known as the older woman who seduced her daughter's boyfriend. She recalled the time a woman in a restaurant in Italy told a group of young men that Bancroft was Mrs. Robinson. They threw her in the air and kissed her hands and head and feet. Bancroft said that the behavior was so unbelievable, how could she not love it?

On the 2000 Charlie Rose show she said that she came to love *The Graduate* but when they were doing it, she found so many problems with it and she was conflicted. Everybody was telling her it was beneath her and she shouldn't do it. The actress thought it would be very easy to take off her clothes and be naked but when she got to the day when she had to do it, she couldn't. That left Nichols up a creek but she also got pneumonia so she really couldn't do the nudity so they sent her home and they got someone else. Bancroft said she didn't know she couldn't do it till she got there. Nichols was upset but she didn't care because she was going to abide by her instincts and Bancroft thinks that's probably why she got sick. She said she couldn't have been replaced in the part because there was nobody else who could have played it like she did, and the problem was only over one little scene because she could do everything else. The actress felt that Mrs. Robinson was misunderstood. She had dreams and the dreams could not be fulfilled because of things that had happened. And she had talent because she probably was a gifted artist or thought that she was so she spent a very conventional life with this conventional man in a conventional house.

Bancroft said she was exhausted after making the film and then she went right into *The Little Foxes*, another enormous job for her. After *The Graduate*, Bancroft did find out of the corner of her eye a lot of guys looking at her in a strange way. She would even know in the future when it was played on TV because the next day a lot of the eyes were on her.

Bancroft said because the film made a lot of money, she became more popular than she had been after winning the Academy Award for *The Miracle Worker*. She was now bankable and so from all over the world she got offers. She was insulted by many of them because she thought they were only made now that she was box office. She received an award like "Head Box Office Star of the Year" which confounded her. Bancroft agreed that the film of *The Miracle Worker* was all artistry and she didn't think she was ever paid for it because it was all deferred money and she didn't think it made a profit. Arthur Penn would say that she actually earned a salary of $37,500, the same amount he, Fred Coe and William Gibson all received. Bancroft said that film did nothing for her and the Academy Award did nothing for her in comparison to what *The Graduate* did for her. The actress was not approached for the Broadway play version (April 4, 2002–March 2, 2003) with Kathleen Turner as Mrs. Robinson. Bancroft said that she tried not to think about it and didn't think that she could see it.

At the American Film Institute Salute to Mike Nichols, held on June 26, 2010, at Sony Pictures Studios, three clips were shown from *The Graduate* that featured Bancroft. These were the famous "Mrs. Robinson, you're trying to seduce me" scene, Mrs. Robinson on the phone with Ben in the hotel lobby, and their first hotel room love scene. One of the speakers at the event was Dustin Hoffman who talked about the first hotel room scene in the film and described the actress as a genius.

On April 9, 1967, it was reported that William Gibson was at work on a musical about the character of Gittel from *Two for the Seesaw*. It was not an adaptation of his play but rather a new script where she would now sing and dance. Again Arthur Penn would direct. It was hoped that the project would be ready for the spring of 1968 but Bancroft was not yet set to play that part. Barbra Streisand and Barbara Harris were said to be candidates. There would be no more news about the show until January 2, 1972, when the *New York Times* reported that the musical was now to open on Broadway in the fall. There was no name attached to star as Gittel. The book was to be written by Michael Stewart, with Dorothy Fields writing the lyrics and Cy Coleman the music. Rehearsals were to begin in the summer. On May 19, 1972, the show was said to be opening around Christmas after tryouts in Washington and Detroit. Robert Moore was the director. On November 3, 1972, it was reported that the show was now called *Seesaw* and the female star was Lainie Kazan. The show opened on March 18, 1973, at the Uris Theatre with Michele Lee as Gittel; the director was Michael Bennett. It was a hit that transferred to the Mark Hellinger Theatre from August 1, 1973, until December 8, 1973.

Bancroft appeared at the 39th Annual Academy Awards ceremony on April 10, 1967, at the Santa Monica Civic Auditorium. She accepted the Best Actress award for Elizabeth Taylor who won for *Who's Afraid of Virginia Woolf?* Footage of the event is available on YouTube. As she approached presenter Lee Marvin on stage, she mouthed "I'm not her," although the announcer had already said that Bancroft was accepting on Taylor's behalf. The actress said that Miss Taylor regretted not being able to be at the awards and Bancroft was sure that she must be very proud but not as half as nervous as she. Her being nervous is suggested by the way she repeatedly turns away from the camera as she speaks, as if something off-stage is capturing her attention.

On May 15, 1967, producer Saint Subber announced that Bancroft had been signed to play Regina in the Lincoln Center Repertory Theater production of Lillian Hellman's *The Little Foxes*. The actress replaced Margaret Leighton, who relinquished the role because of her concern that American performers might resent the use of a foreign actress. Leighton's concern was a legitimate one since it was reported that in recent months an Actors' Equity faction opposed to foreign performers had picketed the Vivian Beaumont Theater where British actor Anthony Quayle starred in the repertory company's production of *Galileo*. The faction had demonstrated despite the fact that the company had gained the approval of the union to employ the alien actor. This disturbance may have cost that show some box office, since it only ran from April 13 to June 17, 1967. Leighton had offered to withdraw from the production altogether but was persuaded to stay when told that the venture might be abandoned without her. She now would play the supporting part of Birdie. The British actress denied Saint Subber's claim that she switched parts because of complaints by Actors' Equity. Rather she felt she was better suited to the "lesser" role because of her conversations with director Mike Nichols. Leighton expressed puzzlement over the reported objections to her playing the lead, since she had been a U.S. resident for seven years. The production was scheduled to open at the Vivian Beaumont on October 26, 1967, for a seven-week run.

Rehearsals began on September 19, 1967, in the little Forum Theatre, downstairs from the Vivian Beaumont. There were four previews, the first on October 20. The show opened on schedule and ran until January 20, 1968, transferring to the Ethel Barrymore Theatre on December 19, 1967.

Frank Langella felt that Bancroft was totally unsuited to play Regina and the actress covered her anxiety with an imperious disdain. He reported that the actress had his girlfriend at the time, Kathleen Eric, as one of the understudies. Eric told him that at the dress rehearsal, as Bancroft stood on the stage in full costume, nobody was paying attention to her. Finally, in a thunderous voice, she shouted out across the footlights, "Well?" There followed a deafening silence and Mike Nichols told her that he wasn't sure about her eyebrows. Bancroft reportedly replied, "Yeah! I know. They've held me back," and stormed off.

The production was praised by Clive Barnes in the *New York Times* on October 27. He wrote that Bancroft left a series of unforgettable visual and aural images. The review was accompanied by a photograph (by Martha Swope) of the actress with George C. Scott, who played Ben in the play.

On November 2, it was reported that Margaret Leighton would play the role of Regina after all. She was to succeed Bancroft when the production moved to the Ethel Barrymore Theatre.

Bancroft's run in *The Little Foxes* meant that she was unable to accompany her husband to a test screening of *The Producers* in Philadelphia in November 1967. The event was a disaster: The Lane Theatre was nearly empty since the distributors Joseph E. Levine and Avco Embassy were said to have put all their interest in *The Graduate*. When Brooks returned to Manhattan that night, he said Bancroft observed, "You look white. What happened?" Brooks told her about the screening, and then the couple stayed up all night reciting passages from books to each other, because Brooks was unable to sleep.

Bancroft was a guest on NBC's 60-minute *Bob Hope Comedy Special*, broadcast on March 20, 1968. The show was directed by Stan Harris and written by Mort Lachman and Bill Larkin, and featured Lester White, John Rapp, Charles Lee and Gig Henry. Bancroft was in a 14-minute sketch with Hope, Paul Lynde and Jack Benny. Her Kate Drain Lawson gown was a floor-length pink sleeveless outfit with a sparkly top and pants and a pink sheer overlay. Bancroft played Raquel Anthorpe, a film actress and patient of heart surgeon Dr. Frederick Myron (Lynde), whom she calls Harvey. He has a transplant heart for her—that of actor Rod Tiger (Hope), who is diagnosed with two weeks to live. Myron brings Rod to meet Raquel. Bancroft having Lynde as an acting partner is a seemingly odd choice but they work well together. She has what appears to be a spontaneous laugh when Hope has trouble getting up off a couch, and she has a funny bit when Raquel offers Rod a cigarette and then knocks it out of his mouth, saying, "They're very bad for you." The sketch uses a point of self-reference for the actress. Raquel feels the room is depressing and on the pretext of getting more light into it, she pulls back curtains to reveal a portrait of herself, saying it is so much better when you let the sun shine in. This is a close-up photograph of Bancroft with short hair, with the photograph colored pink to seemingly match Raquel's dress.

On April 10, 1968, the actress, Oscar-nominated for *The Graduate*, appeared at the 40th Annual Academy Awards, which was held at the Santa Monica Civic Auditorium. The Best Actress award was presented by Sidney Poitier to winner Katharine Hepburn for *Guess Who's Coming to Dinner* (1967). Dustin Hoffman reported that he sat behind Bancroft and Mel Brooks at the ceremony. That year the early winners were European, and Hoffman reported that every time a foreign nominee or winner was announced and they would come down the aisle, Brooks would say out loud, "Wacko. Another wacko!" Hoffman reported that Bancroft was literally sinking in her seat, telling him to stop. On April 21, Bancroft was a presenter at the 22nd Tony Awards at the Shubert Theatre in New York. She was introduced by Peter Ustinov and presented the Tony for Best Play. The winner was Tom Stoppard for *Rosencrantz and Guildenstern Are Dead* but the award was accepted by producer David Merrick (Stoppard was in London).

On May 26, 1968, it was announced that Bancroft was to return to the Berkshire Theater Festival of Stockbridge for William Gibson's play *A Cry of Players*. It was scheduled to open on July 24 and then to be restaged in the fall for the Repertory Theater of Lincoln Center. Gene Frankel was to direct both productions. The Broadway production was planned to run for 27 weeks until February 15, 1969. The play was set in the 1580s in a small English town. Frank Langella was to play the leading character of Will, based on William Shakespeare, and Bancroft was to play his wife Anne, based on Anne Hathaway. Bancroft at 36 played the 29-year-old wife of the 21-year-old Shakespeare.

In his book, Langella wrote that after the first preview performance he received a note that at the second performance the order of the curtain calls would be changed. Previously Bancroft had the last call and he had the one preceding her. Now this would be reversed so that Langella would take the final bow. Bancroft was playing a supporting role because of a loyalty she felt towards William Gibson, but Langella knew she was still a big star. He went to see her in her dressing room and protested since the actor felt chagrined at this change. When Langella arrived, Bancroft was putting on her makeup and brushing her hair and he said she generally avoided his gaze as he stood over her. Finally the actress told him that the new order was how it was going to be. Apparently Langella had received the bigger hand on the first night and since she felt it was his show, Bancroft wanted to look like the gracious star giving it up to the new guy. Then she added, "Now get the fuck out of here and let me get dressed." That night the actress took her bow, turned and flung both her arms out to the wings and presented Langella with a giant smile to the audience. The actor reported that this power play did not hurt their friendship but he learned a valuable professional lesson in how to understand and survive the playing field.

Langella wrote about one moment in the play when Bancroft played with her eyes oddly placed. In the second act, it becomes clear that Shakespeare is going to leave his wife and Anne tells him that she loves him. Langella reported that she played it with heartbreaking honesty every night, with her voice quivering and eyes welling with tears as she stood about two feet from him. But Bancroft resolutely never looked him in the eyes, rather focusing deeply on the second button down on his shirt. After the play closed, Langella asked the actress why she did that, to which she replied, "Oh, that's about where Mel comes up to on you."

The actor also wrote about the time after the play's run when he and Bancroft decided to go to William Gibson's home after he had been absent from the theater for several days. They feared for his safety since he claimed to have received threatening telephone calls from his cousins who supposedly had been offended by things he had written in his 1959 memoir "The Seesaw Log." The couple was concerned when they approached the house in their car and saw that there were no lights on. When they parked in the driveway, the doors on both driver and passenger side of the car were suddenly flung open, men's hands grabbed their necks, and guns were held to their temples. The men said they were FBI and asked the pair to identify themselves. Bancroft was so scared that she said she nearly yelled out "Anna Maria Italiano from Class 2B2" as if she were still six years old.

On August 14, 1968, the *New York Times* reported that she was interested in playing Margo Channing in a musical version of the film *All About Eve*. The show was being written by Sidney Michaels, Charles Strouse and Lee Adams and was listed as a spring entry for Broadway. On July 10, 1969, it was announced that Lauren Bacall would play Margo Channing, with the book now being written by Betty Comden and Adolph Green, and the director being Ronald Field. The show was to go into rehearsals in late November and open on Broadway around Christmas after engagements in Boston and Philadelphia. Rehearsals actually began on December 22, 1969, with the show now called *Applause,* to open on Broadway on April 2, 1970, after a Philadelphia trial run. On March 22, it was reported that the show would open on Broadway at the Palace Theatre. The show opened on March 30 and ran till July 22, 1972. Bacall's performance earned her a Tony for Best Actress in a Musical.

On September 1, 1968, it was confirmed that *A Cry of Players* was to open on Broadway the week after November 7, 1968, at the Vivian Beaumont Theatre. It was to run in repertory until mid–February 1969. On September 6, the opening was confirmed to be November 14, 1968. On September 14, 1968, it was reported that Bancroft's name was one of those appended to a letter from a group of 20 Americans prominent in the film industry who had expressed concern for Czechoslovak filmmakers. The letter had been sent to Anatoly F. Dobrynin, the Soviet ambassador to the United States.

After four previews, *A Cry of Players* opened. Clive Barnes of the *New York Times* wrote that hardly any praise was too great for Bancroft. He said that her accent could have been more regional-specific but added that she had all the troubled, careworn qualities the part required. Walter Kerr wrote about the show on November 24, 1968, commenting on the wintry, frost-crisp smile Bancroft uses to take the Will character down a peg or three at a time. The show ran until February 15, 1969. It was reported on December 5, 1968, that both Bancroft and Langella had been felled by flu during the run, although it is not known whether they were replaced by their understudies for performances.

Interviewed by Judy Klemesrud for the *New York Times* (December 1, 1968), Langella said that he and Bancroft didn't attend the opening night party for the show. Rather they sweated out the reviews at the Brookses' apartment in the Village. Langella believed that very few actresses of her stature and ability would have agreed to work in a play that was not a vehicle for themselves, especially in Bancroft's case after the success of *The Graduate*.

The actor wrote that Bancroft had not attended the 41st Academy Awards ceremony held at the Dorothy Chandler Pavilion on April 14, 1969; instead she stayed in New York. She supposedly told Langella that she didn't go because Brooks had been nominated for Best Original Screenplay for *The Producers*, and she couldn't have faced it if he lost. (Brooks won the award.) Other sources claim that Bancroft was there and after the ceremony both she and Brooks attended the Governor's Ball, the official post-award party.

Earl Wilson reportedly asked Brooks whether he would ever produce and direct a film with Bancroft. Brooks answered that his wife was his best friend and he wanted to keep it that way. Bancroft said she again encouraged her husband to write a theme song for his next film *The Twelve Chairs* (1970), telling him not to come out of his room until it was done. The song was "Hope for the Best (Expect the Worst)." She was also said to have suggested that Brooks cast Langella and Dom DeLuise, who she had seen on television. The actress would later cast DeLuise in the leading role in *Fatso* (1980), the film she directed.

The April 20, 1969, *New York Times* reported that Bancroft was to appear in another William Gibson play at the Berkshire Theater Festival: She was to play Abigail in *John and Abigail*, about John and Abigail Adams. The opener for the Festival in Stockbridge, Massachusetts, the show was to open in early July. Gibson advised that the play would cover the couple in the period from 1774 to 1778. The writer said he had planned to ask the Festival producers for a few actors with whom he could workshop the play in the summer but then decided to give it a regular production in the schedule instead. The play, also known as *American Primitive,* was directed by Frank Langella.

Bancroft appeared on NBC's *Kraft Music Hall* on April 30, 1969. Filmed in London in color, the episode was co-hosted by Peter Cook and Dudley Moore. In a May 18, 1969, article, the actress was listed as one of the actors who did TV commercials but whose voice was not recognized doing so. The article did not mention what commercials Bancroft voiced.

The Twelve Chairs had a screenplay by Brooks, based on the Ilf-Petrov novel which had been translated by Elizabeth Hill and Doris Mudie as "Diamonds to Sit On," and was also directed by Brooks. The novel had been previously filmed as the Czech-Polish *Dvanáct kresel* (1933), the British *Keep Your Seats, Please!* (1936), the German *13 Stühle* (1938), the Italian *L'eredità in Corsa* (1939), United Artists' *It's in the Bag!* (1945), the Swedish *13 stolar* (1945) and *Sju svarta be-hå* (1954), the Brazilian *Treze Cadeiras* (1957), the German *Das Glück liegt auf der Straße* (1957), the Cuban *Las doce sillas* (1962), the Russian made-for-TV movie *12 stulyev* (1966) and the Italian-French *12 + 1* (1969). The plot: In 1927 Russia, former General Ippolit Matveyevich Vorobyaninov (Ron Moody) learns from his dying mother-in-law Claudia Ivanovna (Elaine Garrero) that she has sewn her jewels into the upholstery of one of the chairs of her walnut dining room suite.

The chairs were left in their house in Stargorod from which they fled during the revolution; it's now a Soviet government office. When he learns that the chairs had been sent to Moscow, Vorobyaninov is joined by con man Ostap Bender (Langella) in searching for them. They compete with the local priest Father Fyodor (DeLuise), to whom Claudia has presumably also confessed her action. The film was shot in Yugoslavia in the late summer of 1969. The company was stationed in Belgrade.

Bancroft is said to have appeared in the film uncredited. Brooks sneaked her into a take with Langella and Moody, done as a practical joke on the editor, Alan Heim. The actress cannot be positively spotted in the film. There are over a dozen opportunities for her, with crowd scenes featuring women and one of a single woman walking with a man. It seems likely that it is Bancroft is the woman walking behind Moody as he sits on a bench in Moscow. Wearing a red hat and brown jacket, the woman is seen in three separate shots as she passes.

The film was released on October 28, 1970, with the tagline "A wild and hilarious chase for a fortune in jewels." It was praised by *Variety* and Roger Ebert. The film was not a hit. Subsequent versions of *The Twelve Chairs* include the Greek *I Loved an Armchair* (1971), the Russian *Twelve Chairs* (1971) and the TV miniseries *12 stulyev* (1977), the Austrian made-for-TV movie *Mein Opa und die 13 Stühle* (1997), the German *Zwölf Stühle* (2004) and the Russian made-for-TV movie *12 stulev* (2004).

Bancroft had to arrange her work schedule, which included a future television special, to allow her to accompany Brooks on location. She told a reporter that since marrying Brooks, she had consciously reordered her life and after doing a role, she always took a rest. This could range from six months to a year. Bancroft commented that it took a month to adjust back to being a homemaker. By her admission, she was no fire-breathing feminist but an old-fashioned woman. However, her recent projects had left her little homemaking time.

Langella wrote how Bancroft was a great and loving pal throughout the shoot, warming his feet in the dressing room when he would come in from the cold, watching dailies, giving great notes to DeLuise and himself, and generally keeping everyone's spirits up.

Martin Charmin reportedly wanted Bancroft to star in her own television special for some time. Bancroft had repeatedly rejected his offer, then finally accepted. The actress rehearsed in installments which left her time for expeditions to Yugoslavia. She would gather together a batch of new material, fly to Belgrade and rehearse days at the Hotel Yugoslavia while Brooks worked at the Studios Kosjutnat. Then Bancroft would return home for a fresh batch of material and the process would be repeated. She would say that the arrangement was absolutely perfect and it kept her marriage together so she was very happy.

She was reportedly offered the title transsexual role in the Fox comedy *Myra Breckinridge* (1970) but turned it down, as did Elizabeth Taylor. The film went into production with Raquel Welch playing Myra. It was a box office flop.

On February 15, 1970, the *New York Times* featured a photograph of her from her television special. The caption revealed that the show was called *Annie, the Women in the Life of a Man*, it was being broadcast on February 18 on CBS, and in it Bancroft acted, sang, danced and clowned. The 60-minute Joseph Cates production was directed by Walter C. Miller, conceived and produced by Martin Charnin, with additional material by Gary Belkin, William Gibson, Reginald Roe and Jacqueline Susann. Mel Brooks is credited as being one of writers of additional material but his name is not featured on screen as being attached to any of the individual sketches. However, other screen credit is given to the writers Judith Viorst, Herb Sargent, Peter Bellwood and Thomas Meehan. Additionally there are sketches with the songs "The Night Was Made for Love" with music by Jerome Kern and lyrics by Otto Harbach, "I Don't Want to Walk Without You, Baby" with music by Jule Styne and lyrics by Frank Loesser, "Stay" with music by Richard Rodgers and lyrics by Stephen Sondheim and "Change Partners" with music and lyrics by Irving Berlin. The special closes with "Ev'ry Time We Say Goodbye" with music and lyrics by Cole Porter. Bancroft's also sang the special's first number "Look at Us Now," which is not credited to any composer or lyricist.

Sketches had female names as their titles. "Valerie" is the bride to Dick Shawn's groom, about to be married in the presence of her father (John McGiver). "Joanne" is a housewife who delivers three blank-verse poems by Judith Viorst. "Katherine" is a medieval lady joined by knights in armor for a song-and-dance routine. "Libby" is the lover of Jack Cassidy, and they lie together on a rug in front of a fireplace. "Phyllis" has Bancroft reclining on a giant rug singing "I Don't Want to Walk Without You, Baby." "Eugenia" is a wealthy matron packing to leave Robert Merrill. "Bebe" is a young hopeful asked to sight-read the song "Let's Call the Whole Thing Off" for theater producer David Susskind. "Trixie" is an aging lady who sings "Change Partners" with dancers as the decades shift from the 1930s to the 1960s. "Lillian" is a mother reading a letter from her son, a soldier—an anti-war number with the song "Maman" sung by Dick Smothers. Finally, "Paula" is the glamorous patient of a psychiatrist, relating the details of a nightmare.

The actress is billed last, below the names of eight of her nine male co-stars. Bancroft is heard in voiceover before she is seen and she appears in all the 14 sketches. Her hair by Ernie Adler is now a length that falls half-way down her back but she has it in various styles, including worn up and off her forehead with loose strands at the back, worn under a wedding veil with the hair loose at the back, in a ponytail, in a plait tied with a white ribbon under a medieval headdress, loose with a side part, and in a bun. It is colored gray for the "Lillian" sequence. She wears a series of blonde wigs for the "Trixie" number. Bancroft's gowns are by Patricia Zipprodt, with furs by Reiss and Fabrizio.

The quality of the sketches is variable, with the musical and comic pieces more successful than the dramatic ones. The best are perhaps "Katherine," "Trixie" and "Paula." "Katherine" has Bancroft as a medieval woman who sings to a stuffed bird which falls to the floor after she throws it in the air, and then dances with a group of male dancers dressed as knights. Another comic moment comes when one knight's glove comes off in Katherine's hand after she dances with him. "Trixie" is perhaps the special's most ambitious production number, where Bancroft dances with a group of male dancers to "Change Partners" and ends up with Arthur Murray. The actress dances in a variety of period styles; it's a better showcase for her dancing skills than previously seen on television. What makes both these sequences a stand-out is the choreography of Alan Johnson. However, as in other TV appearances where she sings, Bancroft's vocals are competent but not extraordinary. She perhaps does best in "Phyllis" where she sings "I Don't Want to Walk Without You, Baby" as she lies on a giant red pillow, and at the end for "Ev'ry Time You Say Goodbye." The best of all the sketches is "Paula" where, as a patient of psychiatrist Lee J. Cobb, she lies on a couch telling him about her dream in which she introduces the guests at a cocktail party. The humor comes from the similarity of the first names of the celebrities.

The show has some references to Bancroft's past, as in "Bebe" where theatrical agent David Susskind auditions her and she sings "Let's Call the Whole Thing Off." The set has a play poster for "Jane Street in *The Pumpkin Worker*, a musical based on *The Miracle Eater*," obviously a play on Bancroft's titles *The Miracle Worker* and *The Pumpkin Eater*. The sketch is hard to read since we don't know whether she sings the song deliberately badly, given some of her bum notes at the end of "Trixie." "Lillian" features an odd moment where Bancroft's apparent tears upon reading a letter from her soldier son (Dick Smothers) are undermined by director Miller's use of superimpositions. He has the actress' close-up covered by the long shot of her sitting in the chair reading the letter and also a shot of Smothers singing the song "Maman" with the lyrics supposedly the words she is reading.

The show was broadcast with the tagline "Bancroft funny. Bancroft sad. Bancroft singing and dancing. Watch and be dazzled." Jack Gould (the *New York Times*, February 18, 1970) wrote that it was truly a tour de force for Bancroft, of such multiplicity of charms, humor and talent that it was almost hard to believe. The show won Emmy Awards for Outstanding Writing Achievement in Comedy, Variety or Music and the Outstanding Variety or Musical Program—Variety and Popular Music. The latter award included Bancroft's name with Joseph Cates and Martin Charnin.

On May 24, 1970, the *New York Times* reported that the actress was returning to the Berkshire Theater Festival on July 12 to perform a single night of singing and dancing. The event, *An Evening with Anne Bancroft*, was one of the commercial hits of the festival.

On June 7, 1970, Bancroft attended the 22nd Primetime Emmy Awards, carried simultaneously from the Century Hotel in Hollywood and from Carnegie Hall in New York. She was photographed by Bettman holding the Outstanding Variety or Musical Program—Variety and Popular Music Emmy she had won for *Annie, the Women in the Life of a Man* alongside fellow award winners Peter Ustinov and Walter Cronkite.

Another film role Bancroft reportedly rejected was that of Golde in *Fiddler on the Roof*, the 1971 adaptation of the Broadway musical. The director was Norman Jewison, who would later direct Bancroft in *Agnes of God*. Bancroft supposedly turned down the part on the grounds that the character was too small next to the leading role of Tevye. Other actresses reportedly considered were Anne Jackson, Claire Bloom, Maureen Stapleton, Geraldine Page, Colleen Dewhurst, Zoe Caldwell, Dorothy Loudon, Marian Seldes, Beverly Sills and Lee Grant. Norma Crane was cast.

On September 17, 1970, it was reported that director Joseph Hardy hoped to have Bancroft in a revival of *Mourning Becomes Electra*. She was a guest on ABC's music show *This Is Tom Jones* broadcast on September 25, 1970. The show was filmed in Los Angeles and Bancroft is said to have appeared twice, in a dramatic sketch reciting the poem "A Woman's Liberation Movement Woman" by Judith Viorst and in a comedy sketch. In her book *Tom Jones Close Up*, Lucy Ellis describes how for the comedy sketch the actress sits in a bathtub where the bubbles began to sink at an alarming rate and soldiers on with a forced smile as she debates the ideals of feminism against respectful chivalry. Then there is a kitchen scene where Bancroft plays the wife to Jones' exaggerated chauvinistic husband. She pretends to gratefully agree with everything he says, evidently happy to spend her life cooking and cleaning for him. After Jones exits, Bancroft rejoices in the appearance of several ladies who enter the kitchen exclaiming, "Ban the man! Women unite! Girl power!" One of her lines is reportedly "First we eat and then we picket Hugh Hefner!"

The actress was offered the chance to play the title role in an off–Broadway revival of the play *Colette* by Elinor Jones. The role was taken by Fenella Fielding in a production directed by Gerald Freedman. Bancroft did participate in the five-day non-stop reading of Leo Tolstoy's *War and Peace* for radio station WBAI-FM from December 1 to 6, 1970. On March 16, 1971, she was a commentator of a fashion show lunch at Tavern on the Green in Central Park. The affair had been planned by Mrs. Andrew Heiskell and Mrs. John V. Lindsay to aid New York's Mayor's Council on the Environment.

The actress was interviewed for the 1970 documentary *Arthur Penn, 1922–: Themes and Variants*. This 86-minute special, made by the British Film Institute, was written, produced and directed by Robert Hughes and broadcast on PBS. The date of broadcast is unknown but sources report that the airing was just before the release of Penn's comic western *Little Big Man* which opened on December 14, 1970. Another source claims that the show was to have a repeat television airing on May 24, 1970, but that it was disrupted because of Bancroft. She had not given a release on a film segment which featured her on location, presumably for *The Miracle Worker*. The source claimed that WNET promised to edit out the offending sequence. The show won the Emmy for Outstanding Achievement in Cultural Documentary Programming—Programs.

In 1970, producer Joseph Janni reportedly bought the rights to the novel *The Driver's Seat* by Muriel Spark for director Luchino Visconti, and Bancroft was supposedly the first choice to play the role of the mentally disturbed spinster Lise. The resultant film, *Identikit*, was directed by Giuseppe Patroni Griffi and starred Elizabeth Taylor as Lise. Bancroft was reportedly considered for the role of Mama Corleone in the Paramount crime drama *The Godfather* (1972). It was said that she turned it down, as did Anna Magnani, and the part went to Morgana King. King also played the character in *The Godfather: Part II* (1974).

The actress was reportedly wanted by Charlton Heston to play Cleopatra opposite his Antony in the historical drama *Antony and Cleopatra* (1972). Heston was also the director and adaptor of the Shakespeare play. Other actresses in the running were Diana Rigg, Irene Papas, Glenda Jackson and Suzanna York; Hildegard Neil was cast.

On June 15, 1971, the *New York Times* wrote that Bancroft was on the organizing committee for a new theater organization, Solar Theater, Inc. The non-profit membership company had been formed by a group of actors with recognized ability and distinguished accomplishments to deliver quality theater product without financial sacrifice on the part of the participating actors. They also planned to become a self-sustaining producing unit operating in films, television and the burgeoning video cassette industry. The group hoped to someday have their own permanent theater. The organizing members had been meeting roughly every ten days for the last 18 months to work on the idea. The name Solar stood for Society of Loose Actors Revolving. The company's first play, David E. Robison's *Promenade, All!*, was to be produced by Fred Coe and to star committee members Hugh Cronyn, Eli Wallach and Anne Jackson. The play was to open on June 30, 1971, at the Berkshire Theater Festival with other engagements to follow, although a Broadway season had yet to be decided upon.

Bancroft next appeared in a supporting role in Columbia's biographical war drama *Young Winston* (1972). The screenplay by Carl Foreman was based on Winston Churchill's book *My Early Life: A Roving Commission* and it was directed by Richard Attenborough. It was shot on location in England and Wales and at the Shepperton Studios in England from June 21 to September 24, 1971. The story covered the life of Churchill (played at seven by Russell Lewis, at 13 by Michael Audreson and as an adult by Simon Ward) till his age of 26, when he was elected as a British Member of Parliament.

Bancroft played his mother, Lady Jennie Randolph Churchill; she was the former American heiress Jennie Jerome who married Lord Randolph Churchill (Robert Shaw). Jennie is supportive of her husband's political career, helping him to get votes; her wealth is another plus for him. It is suggested when he is diagnosed with syphilis that he has contracted it from her, since she is accused of having an extramarital affair with an Austrian count. It's also suggested that her society life has her neglect her son's wellbeing but this plot point is not clarified. We see how she is shown that the boy has been caned on the buttocks at his school but we do not see Jennie take action about it. We do see her ask her husband whether he thinks he has overreacted to the boy Winston when he makes a lot of noise collecting his breakfast, and we are told that later Jennie contacts General Kitchener (John Mills) to use her influence in an effort to get Winston out of India and advanced. When questioned about this, she will rationalize her behavior by saying that it is a natural action of a mother. We are told that Jennie loses her wealth in a stock market swindle and that she then is supported by Winston; this does not to inhibit her lifestyle or wardrobe. Jennie also tries to talk Winston out of his policy on military economy, since she thinks going against the popular opinion of Parliament is what destroyed her husband's career. This advice proves to be wrong when she witnesses how popular her son's speech on the matter in parliament makes him.

Bancroft's hair (by Biddy Chrystal) is in a long style which is mostly worn up in a sculptured style. Her costumes are by Anthony Mendleson, with the most striking a period high-collared purple dress with white lace trimming and matching hat with feathers, flowers and ribbon. Jennie is an American but Bancroft uses a British accent. She uses her soft voice to present a privileged woman except when she expresses anger in reaction to the news of her husband's fatal illness and when she confronts Winston at a restaurant for not agreeing with his policy on military economy. Bancroft also expresses Jennie's anger at the unseen interviewer but she is understated because she has the sense to know that a raised voice would be counterproductive when dealing with a reporter. This last might have been a triumph for the actress but director Attenborough upstages her with his editing where alternate camera angles keep occurring in her coverage. Attenborough gives her a nice silent scene when Jennie slowly walks up and around a staircase after she has been told how her husband has

Still for *Young Winston* (1972).

resigned from Parliament. Bancroft is funny when Jennie tells Winston that Lloyd George (Anthony Hopkins) has the most annoying way of looking at women, and in the look of disdain and how she does not reply when Lloyd George wishes her a good evening as a greeting at the restaurant.

The film was released in London on July 20, 1972, and then given a wide release in Britain on July 29. It opened in the U.S. on October 10 with the tagline "Rebel Soldier Hustler Prisoner Fugitive Firebrand." *The New Yorker*'s Pauline Kael was very hard on Bancroft, saying it was an appalling performance from a reputable actress. The film received Oscar nominations for Best Adapted Screenplay Based on Factual Material or Material Not Previously Published or Produced, Best Art Direction–Set Decoration, and Best Costume Design. It won none.

A source claims that Bancroft had to submit recordings of her voice to the widow of Churchill for endorsement before she landed her part. Attenborough reported that he had no hesitation in trying to get the actress for the film; he thought of her as probably the finest of her generation.

7

Max Brooks

Bancroft said that she and Brooks had tried and tried to have a baby so it must have been good news when she learned that she was pregnant in August 1971. The actress felt she was at the peak of her career and her looks but having a baby occurred in what she called the last possible moment. Bancroft said the couple considered calling the child Nick for "in the nick of time."

She was reportedly in the running for the part of actress Chris MacNeil in the supernatural horror *The Exorcist* (1973), based on William Peter Blatty's eponymous novel. Blatty said the character inspired by Shirley MacLaine. MacLaine had reportedly interested producer Lew Grade in making a film of the 1971 novel, presumably with her to star as Chris, but the plans fell apart. When interest in the film was revived, William Friedkin was the director. In his memoir *The Friedkin Connection*, he writes that he did not want MacLaine, partly because she had since made another, similar horror title *The Possession of Joel Delaney* (1972). Some sources say that MacLaine had chosen to make that film instead of *The Exorcist*, but it was released on May 24, 1972, before the new film went into production on August 14, 1972. Other choices for the part were said to have been Carol Burnett, Audrey Hepburn (who wanted it to be filmed in Rome), Jane Fonda (who turned it down because she didn't believe in fairy tales) and Geraldine Page. Ellen Burstyn wrote in her autobiography *Lessons in Becoming Myself* that Friedkin told her he would choose between her and Bancroft after a meeting with Bancroft in New York. He reportedly rang Burstyn and told her Bancroft was out after he had run into her in the street and he thought that she looked rotten. Other sources say that Bancroft was dropped from consideration because she was in her first month of pregnancy. Friedkin wrote that Bancroft asked him if he would wait a year for her, but he said no. He would later work with the actress on the Broadway play *Duet for One*. Burstyn was cast and she was nominated for the Best Actress Academy Award for her performance.

Maximillian Michael Brooks was born on May 22, 1972. Bancroft insisted on a baptism, even though neither she nor Brooks had been terribly religious in recent years. The couple made a bargain that Max be baptized and bar-mitzvahed when he was 13. The actress now pulled back on her career to raise her son. She knew that one of the perks of show business, and perhaps the reason actors went into it, was not having to work every day. Bancroft felt this was especially true for women but when she became a wife she felt there were certain demands put on her. While she believed that work was important for a man's identity, the actress said it wasn't that important to women so this gave them a choice. Bancroft said she tried very hard to be a mother and that both Max and

Brooks really took up her time. But she later realized she had a lot of conflict about motherhood. Bancroft knew it would be a tremendous responsibility, but on the other hand, she wanted and needed it. The actress was quoted as saying, "Motherhood, what an assignment!" She also reported that she would not discuss Max publicly; while her work was public, her other life was not. However, Bancroft did later describe Max as Mel in miniature.

Around July 1972, Brooks moved his family from New York to California so he could work on the script of his next film *Blazing Saddles* (1974). They bought a house at 1718 Rising Glen Road in West Hollywood, a spacious mansion with huge glass walls overlooking a swimming pool, 12-foot iron gates and a long entrance driveway. The living room was so large that it accommodated a billiard table and massive overstuffed couches.

The comic western *Blazing Saddles* was made on location in Santa Clarita, at the Vasquez Rocks Natural Area Park in California, and at Warner Brothers. It had the working titles of *Tex X, Black Bart* and *The Purple Sage*. Alan Arkin was originally set to direct, but eventually co-writer Brooks took the helm. In the Old West (1874), Attorney General Hedley Lamarr (Harvey Korman) attempts to profit from the railway being built for the town of Rock Ridge. He hires the country's first African American sheriff, Bart (Cleavon Little), thinking it will destroy the town and enable him to make his land grab.

Bancroft was said to visit the set with her infant son and is said to have been an extra in a church congregation scene; she cannot be found in the film. *Blazing Saddles* was a box office hit and received Academy Award nominations for Best Editing, Best Original Song and Best Supporting Actress (Madeline Kahn).

In late 1973, Bancroft signed for a part in the film version of Neil Simon's hit play *The Prisoner of Second Avenue*. The Mike Nichols–directed play, starring Peter Falk and Lee Grant, ran at the Eugene O'Neill Theatre from November 11, 1971, to September 29, 1973, and had won Nichols a Tony. Grant was replaced at various times by Barbara Barrie, Phyllis Newman and Rosemary Prinz.

The Warner Brothers–Melvin Frank production was scripted by Neil Simon and produced and directed by Frank. It took three months to shoot, with two weeks of exteriors on location in New York and the rest in Hollywood. Mel Edison (Jack Lemmon), a 48-year-old New York advertising executive, is fired after 22 years during a summer heat wave. Bancroft plays Mel's wife Edna, a housewife and the mother of two unseen children. Edna takes a job as a TV production assistant when Mel is unable to find a new job. She loses the job when the company goes out of business.

Edna is initially shown to be a reactive character, responding to Mel's troubles, and she is sympathetic until she feels that he takes out his anger on her. She defends Mel when he has water thrown on him on their balcony by the upstairs neighbor, Mr. Jacobi (Ed Peck), and tells Mel that she is prepared to move to wherever he wants to go. Edna suggests the couple can start a summer camp or that she can work if Mel cannot, telling him she doesn't want to live in the world without him. By taking a job, Edna becomes the breadwinner, and her previous position with Mel is reversed. He initially resents this and appears not to be the housekeeper that she was. This is evident when we see Edna bringing home meals or the couple eating a TV dinner. This seeming inaction of Mel is rationalized by his having a nervous breakdown (he is under the care of a psychiatrist who medicates him). Edna glares at Mel when he expresses his misery and frustration at not working through sarcasm, but she is patient and interested in hearing his conspiracy theory about how he is being deliberately kept from working. When she becomes aware that he is veering into craziness, Edna shows pity and then fear for him. Mel's brother Harry (Gene Saks) with his sisters Pearl (Elizabeth Wilson) and Pauline (Florence Stanley) offer money to help but Edna suggests that instead they borrow the $25,000 deposit for a Vermont property she thinks can be used for the summer camp. Edna loses her job at a time when it appears that Mel is no longer medicated though still unemployed. Her anger at her situation grows when the building's water is out and she wants a bath. The narrative reaches a resolution with the couple united in their plan for revenge upon the Jacobis, after Mrs. Jacobi (Patricia Marshall) throws water on Mel on the terrace. The water was intended for Edna, with whom she had an argument. The couple are last seen laughing together, with Mel holding a snow shovel and snow seen falling outside the window.

Bancroft's hair is by Sherry Wilson and worn in a short sculpted style that is down to her neck at the back. Her clothes are by Joel Schumacher. The actress over-gestures in her performance and uses a New York accent. She is funny in her anger, particularly when she explains to Mel what being robbed means and in the way she shakes her body when asking where Mrs. Jacobi is going to get the water that she threatens to throw. Bancroft is also touching in showing Edna's understated compassion for Mel, and she screams when he unintentionally brandishes a knife at her. We see her cry when Edna finds her money has been stolen from a cookbook. Bancroft's best scene is perhaps the one with Harry and the sisters, where she shows a range of emotions from anger at the relatives' refusal to loan the money and comic pride when offering homemade cookies that Mel has made.

The film was released on March 14, 1975, with the tagline "…and you think you've got problems." Clive Hirschhorn in *The Warner Bros. Story* wrote that Bancroft was far too attractive and sophisticated for her role. *Variety* said that she demonstrated a fine versatility in facing the script demands.

Still for *The Prisoner of Second Avenue* (1975).

In the making-of documentary *Urban Living: Funny and Formidable*, Bancroft, interviewed on the set, comments on the balance of comedy and drama in the film. The documentary also shows two goofs, with Bancroft laughing when Lemmon stumbles over one line, and then her laughing again in another scene when he forgets his line.

Frank commented that he always admired Bancroft and felt she was a great actress. Quoted in Don Widener's book on Jack Lemmon, Bancroft reported that in the scene where he had to carry in the snow shovel, she had tears in her eyes because the actor had accidentally hit her in the shin with it. Frank saw something was wrong so he stopped shooting. Bancroft had a big bump on her leg. This occurred on a Friday.

When they came back on Monday, they began with a retake of the shovel scene. When Lemmon brought it in, she anticipated getting hit again because he was so full of energy. However this time the actor didn't touch her and the take was fine, but Bancroft saw Lemmon limp away. To avoid hurting her, he had cut himself. Lemmon's leg was bleeding and it had to be bandaged. Bancroft saw that his wound was much worse than hers and she felt that he was so kind that he had hurt himself rather than injure someone else. She said that was a little crazy but it was the nicest crazy she knew and she knew a lot of crazy people.

Neil Simon wrote in his memoir *The Play Goes On* that he was thrilled at the prospect of working for the first time with the wonderful Bancroft. He said once the company gathered around the table and listened to Bancroft and Lemmon read the script, Simon felt an enormous sense of relief and gratitude. He said he had two major stars who would carry the day.

Bancroft was reportedly set to play the title role in the Warner Brothers romance *Alice Doesn't Live Here Anymore* (1974). But ultimately Ellen Burstyn played it and won a Best Actress Oscar. Bancroft returned to television for another musical variety special, ABC's 60-minute *Annie and the Hoods,* broadcast on November 27, 1974. It was directed by Martin Charnin and the writers were Charnin, Gary Belkin, Bob Ellison, Thomas Meehan, Gail Parent, Bob Randall and Kenny Solms. Bancroft's co-stars included Mel Brooks. The Hoods of the title referred to eight segments which all had "Hood" in the title. In "Womanhood," she acts opposite Tony Curtis as a male chauvinist. In "The Other Womanhood," she sings "Guess Who I Saw Today" and she and Brooks have a discourse on extramarital relations. In "Likelihood," Bancroft sings Noël Coward's "Mad About the Boy" wearing her hair in a waved 1930s style. "Unlikelihood" had five different segments. These included her singing Cole Porter's "Night and Day"; as Mrs. Dorian Gray in a picture frame with changing period outfits as she stands in front of a bust; wearing a blonde wig and a dress with a bare midriff as she sings and dances to "Some Sunny Day" to audition for producer David Merrick; as the gum-chewing Bambie Levine and soon-to-be bride of Prince Charles, interviewed by Carl Reiner; and as the patient of psychiatrist Jack Benny, lying in his couch telling him of her dream. In "Bachelorhood," Bancroft has "Strangers in the Night" sung to her by Robert Merrill. In "Parenthood," she and Alan Alda recall bringing up babies in poetry by Ogden Nash. In "Adulthood," Bancroft and Gene Wilder play a husband and wife in bed who are turned on by books about the stock market and French cooking. And in "Motherhood," she sits in a chair and sings Hoagy Carmichael and Ned Washington's "The Nearness of You" to a baby.

Bancroft was interviewed by Tom Burke about the show for a November 1974 edition of *TV Guide*. Doing the interview, the actress was nearly decapitated by stagehands as they removed a tall pedestal. Bancroft said about her singing that she was no Beverly Sills but that she always sang. Bancroft warned Burke not to start her on women's lib as she said she had so much to say that it would be enough to fill the magazine and a book. Bancroft felt the movement did one bad thing: It could force out into the marketplace women who'd really prefer to stay at home with the kids. Otherwise she says it led to sheer freedom which the actress had been fanatical about since she was a kid.

The star commented about working with Brooks, saying that this was the first time and that it could be the last. At this time she didn't know how their segment would work out, since it had yet to be taped. When asked why that hadn't collaborated before, the actress said that Brooks was always terribly busy and she didn't like to burden him with her career problems. Bancroft reported that they had kept their careers separate; she felt that Brooks hadn't done a script for her because he had relatively few women in his work. She didn't know why but she said she would have to ask him about it. She said she never cared for cooking but because he loved Chinese and Italian food, she learned fast how to make them. When asked about her son, Bancroft said that she does not discuss him publicly because the world is too full of maniacs and hostility. Burke also interviewed Brooks, who suggested that he could omit any reference to their son, despite the fact that his existence is public information. The comedian said, "I ask you: who'd have had anything against Martin Luther King's mother? Who'd have wanted to hurt her? Think about it."

Variety called the show an embarrassment and said that Bancroft was versatile to the point of being a caricature of the jaded superstar. John J. O'Connor in the *New York Times* wrote that the show sank slowly in a swamp of mediocrity.

In late 1974, industry publications reported that Brooks and Bancroft were considering teaming on camera for a remake of *To Be or Not to Be*, director Ernst Lubitsch's 1942 war comedy. This project would have to wait until the fall of 1982. On the talk show *Dinah!* (March 21, 1975), the actress was introduced by host Dinah Shore as America's finest actress and her friend. She laughed when she said she didn't want to talk about Brooks. Shore told the actress that when Brooks appeared on her show, he didn't talk about Bancroft. To this, the actress responded, "He's a dirty rat." Shore corrected herself and said that Brooks had said that his wife was wonderful. Bancroft commented that she wasn't working steadily but she had had time to work on her tennis and that after one whole year she finally had a good backhand. Shore reminder Bancroft of a tennis match they had played against Brooks and Burt Reynolds, Shore's romantic partner. They remembered that Bancroft and Shore won the match, which Bancroft said was due to the fact that Shore was a better player than Reynolds and she a better player than Brooks.

Talking about *The Prisoner of Second Avenue*, the actress commented that she had not seen the finished film. She said that Melvin Frank was a wonderful guy and that she had the nicest time in her life working with Jack Lemmon.

On September 14, 1975, the *New York Times* reported that the actress would next be seen on screen in the spectacle *The Hindenburg*, a film about the events leading up to the explosion of the giant German zeppelin in Lakehurst, New Jersey, in 1937. It was filmed on location in Munich, Milwaukee, Lake Forest, California, and at Universal. The screenplay was by Nelson Gidding with a screen story by Richard Levinson and William Link, based on the novel by Michael H. Mooney.

Bancroft played Ursula, the countess, a wealthy widow whose historical counterpart was Margaret Mather. Her last name is said to be von Reugen though this is never stated in the film. She is considered one of the persons to watch after a bomb scare is received to destroy the hydrogen-fueled-airship LZ129 that leaves Frankfurt on May 3, 1937, and is due to land in Lakehurst on May 6. The zeppelin's Gestapo special security officer is German Colonel Franz Ritter (George C. Scott) who knows Ursula (he and her deceased husband used to be members of the same flying club). Ursula is from a distinguished Baltic family and lives on the island of Peenemünde, where the Nazis have confiscated her house and land and where they are developing rockets. Ritter fears that if the Nazis knew that Ursula knows about the rockets, they would not let her leave the country. She has caught the airship to go to Boston to see her deaf daughter Trudy (Deanna Martin) and visit friends—and she intends *not* to go back. The idea of Bancroft playing a mother of a deaf daughter is a variation of her role in *The Miracle Worker*.

Ursula is bitter toward the Nazis for what they have taken from her and she tells Ritter that her new game is to break rules, which makes her more suspicious. The countess demonstrates her rule-breaking by seducing the ship's radio operator (Shep Houghton) to get a cigarette lighter, which is a danger to the ship's safety. She also uses a tactic to stop being cheated at a card game by fellow passengers and professional gamblers Emilio Pajetta (Burgess Meredith) and Major Napier (Rene Auberjonois), stamping her feet to confuse their cane-tapping signals. The men don't seem to have lingering bad feelings toward the Countess since they assist her in escaping the ship when it crashes at Lakehurst. As the ship prepared to land, she had learned that her passport had been confiscated, which meant that she was not able to enter the U.S. Ritter tells her he will escort out of the ship, but he is killed in the crash. The countess survives and joins Trudi at the airport. During the crash, we see that The Countess has a bag of jewels, which she drops, and only manages to save some of them. Ursula is a romantic interest for Ritter, although their romance is more that of old friends than lovers. Her character becomes subsidiary after it is revealed that the bomber is rigger Carl Boerth (William Atherton).

The film is a reunion for Bancroft with Scott, who had appeared with her on Broadway in *The Little Foxes*. Bancroft is seen both in color and in black and white, since director Robert Wise uses black and white for the climactic crash sequence to match the real-life newsreel footage he intercuts. Bancroft's hair is by Lorraine Robertson and is worn in a wavy long style that falls halfway down her back, worn tied up and in a bun, and she has a side part. Her costumes are by Dorothy Jeakins. Although she plays a European, she does not have an accent. The only memorable line Bancroft has is when Ursula is annoyed by the Frankfurt airfield workers going through her luggage, and says, "I'd expect more courtesy on a cattle boat." The actress has little to do and her scenes with Scott, where Ursula tells Ritter about her trip and that she is not going back, are brief moments. In the crash scenes Bancroft looks only slightly disheveled and we never seriously fear for her safety. Wise gives her a potentially tragic moment after Ursula walks away from the burning ship, as if she is looking for Ritter. The camera pulls away from Bancroft in long shot but the moment isn't concluded because we don't see her realize that Ritter has not survived.

The film was released on December 25, 1975, with the taglines "The truth at last? What really happened to The Hindenburg?" and "Of 97 aboard, eight had a motive for sabotage. One

Portrait for *The Hindenburg* (1975).

had a plot." It was lambasted by *Variety*, Vincent Canby in the *New York Times*. Pauline Kael asked if Bancroft took this *Ship of Fools*–Simone Signoret spinoff role, what could the roles she *rejected* be? Roger Ebert said Bancroft camped it up. A box office success, the film won an Academy Award Special Achievement for visual and sound effects. It was also nominated for Best Cinematography, Best Art Direction–Set Decoration and Best Sound.

On November 30, 1975, the *New York Times* published an article about actress Louise Fletcher that mentioned that Bancroft had turned down the role of Nurse Ratched in the 1975 film *One Flew Over the Cuckoo's Nest* and Fletcher took it. It was said that Bancroft was one of a number of actresses (Ellen Burstyn, Collen Dewhurst, Jane Fonda, Angela Lansbury, Geraldine Page) who declined, most of them because they thought the character was too grotesque a monster. Fletcher won the Best Actress Academy Award.

Bancroft made a cameo in *Silent Movie* (1976), written by Mel Brooks, Ron Clark, Rudy DeLuca, and Barry Levinson, based on a story by Clark, and directed by Brooks. In this 20th Century–Fox production, film director Mel Funn (Brooks) attempts to make a comeback and has a deal with the Big Pictures studio to make the first silent movie in 40 years if he can cast big stars. Bancroft played herself though at this time in her career she was not the big office attraction that the others approached by Funn (Burt Reynolds, James Caan, Liza Minnelli, Paul Newman). Neither is Marcel Marceau, though he is wanted for his mime skills. Bancroft was obviously involved only because she was Brooks' wife.

Bancroft appears at the Rio Bomba Club with four young men as suitors. She gives the waiter a bracelet as a tip and uses a long cigarette holder to smoke, although the cigarette burns out when the four men all light it simultaneously. Funn and his associates Marty Eggs (Marty Feldman) and Dom Bell (Dom DeLuise) pretend to be the club's attraction, The Flamencos, although she recognizes them immediately and is aware that they want her for their movie. Funn accidentally brings her to him when his whip lashes her champagne glass and they tango together. He hits her head on a table when he dips her, then twirls her into the kitchen where she crashes into a waiter holding plates. Bancroft returns dancing with Marty and crosses her eyes imitating him, then she dances with Dom who places her on a table where she dances alone. After Bancroft agrees to do the movie, she jumps into the arms of the three men and lands lying across their arms. When they retreat offstage, they bump her head against a wall and knock her unconscious, then carry her out. Bancroft returns to take a bow and drags the men off-stage as they stand on her boa. We later see a *Variety* headline, "Anne Bancroft for Silent Flick." In the end credits, Bancroft repeats her eye crossing to camera.

Bancroft's hair (by Mary Keats) is worn in a medium-length style with a touch of gray at the sides, and her one outfit is a Patricia Norris flame-red satin dress with a silver lining and a long white feather boa. Released on June 16, 1976, it was praised by *Variety* who called Bancroft's tango wonderful. In the *New York Times*, Vincent Canby wrote that Bancroft was very funny. A box office hit, it was reissued in 1978 as *Silent Movie Plus* with added additional scenes.

According to Carl Reiner's book *My Anecdotal Life*, he taught Bancroft how to cross her eyes one at a time, but Brooks said that his wife knew how to do it independently. In a 1978 interview for Danish television, Brooks reported that the actress had a headache for two days after having her head bumped against the wall.

On February 8, 1976, the *New York Times*' Judy Klemesrud wondered if Bancroft would receive a Best Actress Oscar nomination for *The Prisoner of Second Avenue*. She did not. The actress next appeared in the Paramount/Dino De Laurentiis thriller *Lipstick* (1976), scripted by David Rayfiel and directed by Lamont Johnson. Los Angeles fashion model Chrissy McCormick (Margaux Hemingway) is raped by the music school teacher and avant-garde composer Gordon Stuart (Chris Sarandon) of her younger sister Kathy (Mariel Hemingway). Bancroft played District Attorney Carla Bondi, who prosecutes Gordon. She loses the case but later defends Chris (charged with murder after she kills Gordon), and this time Carla wins.

Bancroft is billed fourth with an "and," with her name underlined. Her hair by Kathryn Blondell is an unmanaged style and its color has gray speckles, which seems to suggest that Carla is a no-nonsense woman not overly concerned about her appearance. Bancroft's wardrobe by Jodie Lynn Tillen is a series of blouses and skirts of muted color, the exception being the orange blouse with a big tie and a black skirt she wears in her office. Carla wearing no makeup in court is perhaps another suggestion that she is a no-nonsense woman, which director Johnson seems to reinforce with a series of unglamorous close-ups of Bancroft as reaction shots. The actress makes Carla's anger funny when being mean to Chris in court and yelling objection. She is also funny when speaking over the playing of his music in the trial and elongates the word "furious" when Carla asks him, "Were you furious that she ran out on you?" Bancroft expresses concern for her client by stroking her hair after the faux-defense questions and placing her hand on Chris' shoulder when asking her questions in the court witness box to calm her. The actress' best scene is perhaps Carla's six-minute questioning of Gordon, where she changes from smiling niceness to coldness.

The film was released on April 2, 1976, with the taglines "It isn't always an invitation to a kiss" and "She believed she was the weaker sex until the day she was violated. The story of a woman's outrage and a woman's revenge." It was lambasted by *Variety* and Roger Ebert in the *Chicago Sun-Times*. In her memoir, *Out Came the Sun: Overcoming the Legacy of Mental Illness, Addiction, and Suicide in My Family*, Mariel Hemingway commented on the film and reported that Bancroft was nice and supportive.

She next guest-starred in the six-hour TV miniseries *Jesus of Nazareth* (1977), filmed on location in Morocco and Tunisia from September 1975 to May 1976. It had a teleplay by Anthony Burgess, Suso Cecchi D'Amico and Franco Zeffirelli and was directed by Zeffirelli. The series told the life of the prophet Christ (played by Robert Powell as an adult) who was crucified in Jerusalem for treason for proclaiming himself to be King of the Jews, and then rose from the dead. Bancroft played Mary Magdalene, a Galilee whore who finds faith, is forgiven her sins by Jesus, sees his rise from the dead, and tells the disciples about it. Mary's change of life comes easily since she is insightful enough to be affected when someone says that God curses her for being a prostitute and says that she does not value her profession since we see her throw away her payment. She is a witness to Jesus' miracle of the loaves and fishes and she goes to see him when he is at the house of Jewish leaders, and washes his feet with her tears. We also see Mary voting to save him when the rabble is given the choice of whether to have Jesus or Barabbas (Stacy Keach) freed from their death sentences. She attends the crucifixion where the Virgin Mary (Olivia Hussey) accepts her as "family." Mary kissing his feet is an action repeated when she does the same to the dead Jesus after he is taken down from the cross.

Bancroft's hair by Giancarlo Marin and Ennio Cascioli is a wavy long style and she has two period costumes by Marcel Escoffier and Enrico Sabbatini. She wears a red dress and a black shawl as the prostitute, and then a green dress with the black shawl (and no makeup) after she has faith. The actress speaks with an American accent, but since other actors use similar foreign accents for the context, this is an acceptable contrivance. She yells at youths her torment her outside her house and screams to save Jesus in the vote, and gets her face slapped for not voting to free Barabbas. Bancroft sobs when Mary sees the miracle of the loaves and fishes, and cries when she kisses Jesus' feet. She is funny when misleading the youths who torment her with a smile and then a slap when they approach. The actress' best scene is when Mary tells the disciples that Jesus has arisen. Bancroft uses over-gesturing with outstretched hands and self-conscious touches like placing her hand on her forehead.

The series premiered on the Italian television channel RAI, where it was seen in five weekly episodes from March 27 to April 25, 1977. The *New York Times* reported on March 16, 1977, that NBC was to broadcast the series in April in the United States despite a campaign by various evangelical religious groups. NBC said that the protests had been based on erroneous information about the series, promulgated by people who had not seen it, and more in response to a statement made by Zeffirelli in an interview. The director had said he saw Jesus as an ordinary man—gentle, fragile, simple—and that he knew that the public was going to be annoyed that he destroyed their myths. The protestors called the comment and the series by implication wicked and a blasphemy, although religious consultants to the series included the Archbishop of Canterbury and representatives of the Vatican. They urged a boycott of the products of the General Motors Corporation which had been one of the financial backers of the series and was to sponsor the two-night presentation on Palm Sunday (April 3, 1977) and Easter Sunday (April 10). General Motors withdrew, saying that commercial sponsorship could be regarded as inappropriate for a program about the life of Jesus. This was despite the fact that company officials had screened the miniseries in rough form a week prior and considered it artistically excellent. NBC planned to counter the protest campaign by holding screenings for religious leaders and the religious press, with the first scheduled for March 17, 1977.

On April 1, 1977, John J. O'Connor in the *New York Times* reported that the broadcast was to proceed with sponsorship picked up by Procter & Gamble and the series endorsed by Catholic, Protestant, Jewish and Mormon officials. O'Connor had presumably already seen it since he said it ranked among the best and most impressive efforts to tackle a subject that was delicate and monumental. It was telecast in two three-hour installments with limited commercial breaks.

The *New York Times* of April 3, 1977, printed a review by O'Connor, who again praised it, though he wrote that Bancroft sometimes strayed close to a poor imitation of Anna Magnani. Additional footage was reportedly added for a 1979 rerun and the show broadcast in four two-hour installments. One source reports that Bancroft was first shown when Mary gets out of bed with the client, whereas in the viewed print we first see her alone and opening the door to her house. The series was nominated for the Outstanding Special Emmy and Best Supporting Actor Emmy for James Farentino, who played Simon Peter. It is considered part of a TV miniseries trilogy which began with *Moses the Lawgiver* (1974) and ended with *A.D.* (1985), which was set just after the death of Jesus Christ and chronicled the life and adventures of his disciples. The character of Mary Magdalene does not appear in either the prequel or the sequel.

In his book *Jesus: A Spiritual Diary*, Zeffirelli wrote that during the casting process he said that Bancroft would be the ideal Mary Magdalene but he realized he was asking the impossible because he had heard that she seldom worked by choice. She didn't like to be away from her husband and child and demanded prohibitive fees mainly to discourage requests and remain at peace. But three days later, he was told that she had accepted the part. The actress told Zeffirelli that she had always been fascinated by the figure of Mary Magdalene. She said also the offer came from a director she respected so she couldn't refuse. To Bancroft it was a project that gave her every guarantee and surrounded her with companions she admired. There was little money but the actress did not mind because she could earn more in other, less exciting projects, and she would have the satisfaction of playing the role. Later Zeffirelli reported that Elizabeth Taylor was originally to play Mary Magdalene but she fell ill.

In his book *Born Again: My Journey from Fundamentalism to Freedom*, Tom Harpur reported that he spent time with the company in Morocco. He said Bancroft and the other stars were eager to discuss Jesus with a former teacher of New Testament in the long breaks between takes. Harpur said that one day there was a sudden downpour and he found himself in a doorway with Zeffirelli and Bancroft and the three had a lively 30-minute discussion. He said Bancroft was surprisingly well informed about the Gospels and she had some challenging questions such as why no actual description of Jesus' appearance or mannerisms seemed to exist.

On June 12, 1976, Alan Ladd, Jr., senior vice-president of 20th Century–Fox, announced that the Bancroft was to co-star with Shirley MacLaine in *The Turning Point*. The film was to be produced and directed by Herbert Ross with shooting to begin August 9 in New York. Arthur Laurents' original screenplay dealt with the rivalry between longtime friends whose lives took separate paths. Laurents was said to have based the story on the friendship between ballerinas Isabel Mirrow Brown and Nora Kaye, the wife of Herbert Ross and the executive producer of the film. The film would also have a similarity to the John Van Druten play *Old Acquaintance*, which had been made into a 1943 Warner Bros. film and a 1958 British made-for-TV movie.

On August 6, 1976, the *New York Times* interviewed Ross and reported that Bancroft was to play an aging ballerina in the backstage dance drama. An article dated August 9, 1976, reported that filming had begun on location the previous week and that it would take a month. After that, the company would move to the West Coast with location shooting in Century City and interiors at the Fox Studio. Location shooting would also take place in Oklahoma.

MacLaine is Deedee Rodgers, a teacher at the Rodgers School of the Ballet in Oklahoma City and former member of New York's American Dance Company. When the company tours Oklahoma, she reunites with her 37-year-old former friend Emma Jacklin (Bancroft), their prima ballerina. Twenty years prior, Deedee left the company when the two younger women were rehearsing *Anna Karenina*. She got pregnant by fellow dancer Wayne (Tom Skerritt), who also left the company and married her. Emma has remained single. She has had some kind of relationship with the choreographer and artistic director Michael Cooke (James Mitchell) though it is suggested that he is actually gay. She has also had an affair with Carter (Marshall Thompson), a married man who had told her he would leave his wife for her if she gave up her career. She lives alone in a New York apartment and she has three little dogs. Both Deedee and Emma are envious of the other's life, where Emma has remained the "artist" and Deedee has become a housewife. Although Deedee is said to be a dance teacher, we never see her dance. Deedee asks Michael, who choreographed *Anna Karenina*, whether he would have chosen her over Emma for the part, but he tells her that he honestly cannot remember. Deedee comments that Emma covers up her anger with "ice" although the ice melts when Deedee begins an argument at the gala party and Emma expresses her anger verbally and then physically, throwing a drink in Deedee's face and then slapping her.

Emma is generous toward Deedee's daughter Emilia (Leslie Browne), who is also a dancer and Emma's godchild. She invites the girl to join a class at the company and speaks well of her to Michael and the company head Adelaide (Martha Scott). Emma suggests to choreographer Arnold Berger (Daniel Levans) that Emilia be cast in the new ballet, "Ellingtonia," based on the music of Duke Ellington, whereas Emma herself is not wanted by Arnold. Michael asks Arnold that the new ballet for the season be for Emma and he choreographs a solo for her, but Emma rejects it when he shows it to her. She tells him that she cannot just dance without feeling as he asks, and he says that his choreography should be the star of the ballet and not a dancer. Emma also recommends a masseur to Savilla Haslam (Antoinette Sibley) who has replaced her in the role of Giselle, and helps Emilia get over a hangover and perform. She listens to Emilia's concerns over the choice of a career versus her relationship with fellow dancer Yuri Kopeikine (Mikhail Baryshnikov), and lets her sleep over at her apartment. She also ensures that Emilia is invited to the gala party and sends her a dress for it. Emma bows to Emilia after her gala dance in front of the press, though Deedee will accuse her of doing so as a manipulation.

Emma suffers from being an aged dancer, whom Deedee calls "over the hill." Emma is replaced by Savilla, but she agrees to coach Emilia in the new ballet. She also offers to help Deedee get a teaching job in the company when she takes Emilia to New York, since Deedee tells her that Adelaide is not offering her one. For the company's 25th anniversary gala performance, Emma dances the suicide scene from *Anna Karenina*, although Michael refuses to watch it because he feels that she is too old for it. Deedee also refuses to watch the dance, which she tells Michael is beautiful, because it hurts her and reminds her of what she gave up. Adelaide asks Emma to coach Emilia in the company's upcoming production of *Sleeping Beauty*, a ballet that Emma once performed. She doesn't answer the question and we don't see her doing so before the ballet is performed.

The climax is the extended argument between Deedee and Emma, which begins at a bar at the gala party and continues in the theater foyer and outside the building. Deedee releases her resentment of Emma as "little toads." Emma says that Deedee telling her twice before the gala that she shouldn't have bought Emilia a dress actually motivated Emma to dance better than she had in years. Another little toad is

Portrait for *The Turning Point* (1977).

when Deedee says that she didn't see the performance. Deedee feels Emma made her doubt herself and Wayne and claims she had told her 20 years ago that she had better have the baby or Deedee would never hold onto him. Emma denies this, claiming she said that if Deedee had an abortion she might lose Wayne. Deedee also remembers Emma telling her to forget about Michael's ballet because there would be others. But she realized that a ballet like his only came along once in a career and Deedee wanted it. Emma says Deedee is wrong to blame her because the choice was Deedee's and it was now too late to regret it. Deedee accuses Emma of trying to become a mother to Emilia, but Emma denies it and only claims to want to be the girl's friend. It is Deedee calling Emma "a killer" that begins the physical action, where Emma throws a drink in her face. Deedee flees but Emma chases her, with Emma calling her second-rate and that she had Wayne's child to prove that he was straight in a world where a male ballet dancer was assumed to be gay. Emma says Emilia came to her for advice because Deedee had been off having an affair with married man "Rosie" Rosenberg (Anthony Zerbe), a former conductor of the company. Deedee calls her a bitch and the women begin physically fighting, slapping each other with hands, hitting with their purses, hair pulling, slapping each other's bottoms, and then laughing at what they are doing. It is after this that Emma confesses that she doesn't remember exactly what she had said to Deedee, but that she would have said anything to make sure that she got the ballet. Emma admits that Deedee was a good dancer and a threat to her. This is a great relief for Deedee, who later tells Wayne that the choice she made was what she wanted.

Bancroft appears in 35 scenes, some of them continuous, and plays a supporting role to MacLaine who is in 48 scenes. Her hair by Kathy Blondell is worn in a shoulder-length style, loose with a side part, as well as up in a sculptured style in a bun and off her forehead, and in a ponytail. She also has red sparkly pins in it for a performance. Bancroft's costumes are by Albert Wolsky. Unlike MacLaine who is first shown facing the camera, Bancroft is first seen in a long shot with her back to the camera. She looks physically thinner to present herself as a disciplined and experienced dancer, and it actually makes Bancroft look older than we had previously seen her. Emma is shown in classes doing movements. Her performance in *Anna Karenina* is more stylized movement than dance. Ross' cutting away from the performance to Deedee outside the stage is rationalized by the drama of her not being able to watch Emma, but perhaps it is also done to avoid showing Bancroft's lack of dancing ability. He also gives the actress two long close-ups: one after Arnold rejects her and the other when she reacts to Adelaide's request for Emma to coach Emilia in *Sleeping Beauty*. Bancroft is funny when glaring at Arnold when he shows her his ballet solo. Bancroft has a moment of hiccups which seems to come from her being upset over Arnold's rejection of her, which initially appears to be a laughing-into-crying moment, and we see her crying as Emma watches Sevilla perform. While the climactic argument between Deedee and Emma is a lot of fun and the cat fight borders on camp, Bancroft's best scene is perhaps the one where she tells Deedee of her love of dancing: "All I'm doing offstage is waiting to get back on."

The film was released on November 14, 1977, with the tagline "The generations change. But the choices remain the same." *Variety* called Bancroft magnificent and said that *The Turning Point* was one of her career highlights. Vincent Canby in the *New York Times* said that the actress gave a powerhouse performance. *The New Yorker*'s Pauline Kael wrote that Bancroft overdid her sacrificial-artist laceration and had the worst case of nobility in the eyebrows since Greer Garson. Bancroft and MacLaine were nominated for Best Actress Oscars. The film received nominations for Best Picture, Best Supporting Actor for Mikhail Baryshnikov, Best Supporting Actress for Leslie Browne, Best Director, Best Original Screenplay, Best Cinematography, Best Art Direction–Set Decoration, Best Sound and Best Editing. It won none of the awards. There was talk of a sequel but it didn't happen.

In preparation for the part, Bancroft was said to have taken ballet training from Sono Osato and Nora Kaye. The actress commented that she identified with Emma because she too made a choice in her life to have a career, and no matter what, she wanted that career and pay for the price for it. And Bancroft felt she had paid the price for it.

MacLaine said that Bancroft was a little aloof, but with Ross as director, that was the way to go. She also claimed that he and Bancroft did not tell her that she would throw the drink in her face for the scene in the bar. One source says that the take used in the film is the one where the drink was thrown, and in rehearsal Ross had not asked Bancroft to do so. This supposedly allowed for MacLaine's honest shock to be captured. However, MacLaine supposedly felt the action was an insult, which took away her chance to act her reaction rather than being shocked. Ross advised that for the fight, MacLaine was worried that she might hurt Bancroft since she was bigger and stronger. However Bancroft told her that she could take it, perhaps because she had had the experience of fighting in *The Miracle Worker*. MacLaine said that her co-star did take care her of herself and that she was stronger than she looked.

Footage of Bancroft in *The Miracle Worker* and *The Graduate* were used in the American Film Institute documentary *America at the Movies* (1976), a two-hour compilation of scenes from 83 films. Directed by George Stevens, Jr., it was broadcast on PBS on September 22, 1976.

In 1976, Bancroft attended classes at the Actors Studio. An actor said that her "lady-like airs" caused snickers from fellow students and friends. This was thought to be a Bancroft that they couldn't readily relate to and her airs were laughable. The actress behaved as though she had just condescendingly come over from a Park Avenue penthouse with all the breeding of a Vanderbilt. In the '50s and '60s, some of the world's most glamorous women had come to study dressed casually, usually without makeup, and completely their private selves. Although Bancroft had professional charm, her attitude turned off some who still recalled with a degree of fondness the down-to-earth actress of the past. It was thought that perhaps her Method actress training might have been partially responsible for the unwelcome posture since in recent times she had played grand ladies. One had to wonder whether this new Bancroft might have been her rehearsing a performance, testing it on fellow students and even friends. Others wondered whether the actress was becoming the part.

A *New York Times* article dated March 30, 1977, was devoted to women directing in Hollywood and mentioned Bancroft. Robert Lindsey wrote that she had participated in the American Film Institute Rockefeller-funded workshop and Bancroft had made a short film on videotape. This was done as a kind of an apprenticeship before taking on major directing posts. Bancroft made two black and white shorts. She also wrote both, and said that she had more interest in writing than directing. One was called *The August* and it starred Salome Jens and Hope Lange. The other was *Fatso*, which she would later develop into a feature. In his 1978 Danish TV interview, Brooks reported that the *Fatso* short was 20 minutes long, and said that she also hoped to develop *The August* into a feature (this is something that Bancroft never managed). She confessed that she hadn't wanted to direct but she had been asked to in the group the year it started (1976). At that time, Bancroft declined because she wanted to be taken care of, having someone else direct her. But by the second year, when her son was growing up and had started school, she had some empty hours. Bancroft said that during Max's early years she had done one project a year, and before he went to school she took him wherever she went. Once he went to school, she worked around his schedule so that she could be available for him. Bancroft felt that she had to make those kinds of compromises though other people might not have done so. Asked if she had sought the advice of her husband about the films she directed, the actress said no because she didn't want to make a Mel Brooks film. She wanted to make an Anne Bancroft film. She said it was a matter of identity and that Brooks agreed with her.

The April 15, 1977, *New York Times* reported that Bancroft had been signed to star in *Golda*, a play by William Gibson based on *My Life*, the 1975 autobiography of Golda Meir, under the direction of Arthur Penn. The play would cover Meir's life from a child in Russia, a girl in Milwaukee, a young woman in Palestine, and prime minister of Israel. Meir had collaborated with Gibson and Penn in Israel and had been given the right to approve the script. The Theatre Guild production was scheduled to open out of town in the summer and go to Broadway in October. The journey of the play began after Guild producer Philip Lagner secured the rights to the book which had been published after protracted negotiations with Meir. In the spring of 1976, he called Gibson to ask if he wanted to write the play. Gibson met with Meir while she was getting an honorary degree at Wellesley College in Massachusetts. He then traveled to Israel where he stayed for three months and started to write. Gibson returned to the U.S. to write more and then returned to Israel with Penn. After two months there, the play was finished.

On June 23, 1977, the *New York Times* featured an Associated Press photograph of Bancroft with Meir in Tel Aviv. On August 14, 1977, Margaret Croyden reported from Tel Aviv for the *New York Times* about another meeting between Bancroft at Meir's home. The article said that the play was now scheduled to open at New York's Morosco Theater in November after previews in Baltimore and Boston. Bancroft would be on stage throughout. To prepare for the part, the actress had come to Israel with Margaret Gibson, the wife of the playwright, to spend a week with Meir and learn about the state. Bancroft had never been there and was not Jewish. She said that at first she was scared to meet such a powerful and legendary figure in a foreign country and she was also apprehensive about conditions in Israel. Bancroft found the place not as frightening or unsafe as the media had led her to believe. The two women had an instant rapport and all her anxiety was gone. They planned the week's schedule for the actress which included joining Meir for at a wedding, a bar mitzvah, a diplomat's dinner, a poetry reading, a party given by Israel's national theater and a Friday night dinner at the kibbutz where Meir lived in an apartment with her daughter Sara. Meir would also take Bancroft to see the Golan Heights, the Galilee, and the "Good Fence" near the Lebanese border.

Bancroft said that Gibson attracted her to the project because anything he wrote was of interest to her. When she read the parts about Meir's personal life, she cried, and when the she read the military parts, she got angry. She wanted to do the play because it involved her on a purely personal level. Bancroft said she had come to Meir to watch her move and learn her mannerisms and listen to her talk. She also needed to find a passion in her own life that matched Meir's, something that would give her a clue to playing the role. She questioned Meir about her personal habits, the Yom Kippur War and her emotional life. When the group went to the kibbutz in Revivum, the coffee and fruit and home-baked cake served reminded the actress of her own experience in the Bronx, and she spent the night in Meir's bedroom. Bancroft said that one of the difficulties of the role was trying to reconcile the Meir who was a world-renowned figure and prime minister with the Meir who was a mother and wife and woman. She felt that Meir never dreamed of being prime minister but when it happened, she was prepared. But the cost was high.

The personal connection that Bancroft sought was found when she realized both women shared the same temperament and the actress identified with Meir's view of life and the plight of Israel. The most moving and telling event came with the actress' attendance at the bar mitzvah of an American boy, the grandson of a dying friend and colleague of Meir's. Everyone was crying and when they said "Israel" in the ceremony, the word jumped out and hit Bancroft with a special force. In that moment, she looked at Meir crying (Meir had told her that she never cried). Croyden noticed that Bancroft changed after the meeting to suggest Meir's influence. She now seemed to gesture in a different manner and spoke in a more authoritative tone. The writer felt that the actress conveyed some of Meir's tough spirit and plain style.

Bancroft found rehearsals difficult. One night she came home exhausted and wailed at Brooks that he didn't know how hard acting was. In response he picked up a blank piece of paper and put it in front of her with a pencil, and said, "That's how hard writing is." Bancroft looked at the piece of paper for a long time and she realized she had nothing to say. She went to her job the next day full of pep and never complained about acting again.

On September 19, 1977, the show opened in Baltimore. One-fifth of the budget was spent on large-scale visuals—maps, charts and photographs covering the Yom Kippur war—but then these were cut because it was felt they were ineffective. During previews at the Wilbur Theater in Boston, an early morning fire destroyed the set. The show was moved across the street to the Shubert Theater and was presented on a bare stage with a desk from the carpenters' room, some chairs, lights and black backdrop. Audiences loved the show.

The play began previews on Broadway from November 2, 1977, with the scenery rebuilt. Meir visited New York and was photographed with Bancroft for the *New York Times* on November 4, 1977. The *Times* reported that on November 6, Meir saw the show at a special benefit preview, and afterwards went backstage to embrace Bancroft and tell her she was terrific. After 16 previews, the play opened on November 14 and ran until February 16, 1978. Bancroft was photographed with Meir on opening night.

Richard Eder of the *New York Times* praised Bancroft's whole-hearted and remarkable interpretation of the title character. She had transformed herself physically for the role, with a bulbous nose, a half-twisted mouth, and her head jutted forward from round shoulders. The resemblance to Meir was striking. But Eder wrote that Bancroft's real accomplishment was the recreation of the woman's mind and spirit. Walter Kerr, also writing about the play in the *Times*, said that Bancroft for the most part kept a tight, quiet, curt rein on the role. If her performance was really confined to a single key it was because Gibson's play offered no emotional progression.

On Sunday, December 4, 1977, Bancroft participated in an afternoon and evening of food and fun on behalf of the widows and orphans of New York City policemen. She joined Broadway's best at 7:30 p.m. at a show at the Shubert Theater with WCBS-TV anchorman Jim Jensen and radio disk jockey Ted Brown. Proceeds would help the police department's Honor Legion start a sixty-eighth year of sending $150 checks and clothing to survivors of fellow officers as a Christmas gift.

On February 1, 1978, the *New York Times* reported that performances of *Golda* were suspended for a week because Bancroft was ill. She was said to have the flu complicated by a secondary infection, and was given doctor's orders to rest. The illness was later described as influenza aggravated by bronchitis. Tresa Hughes, Bancroft's understudy, had substituted in the role on January 31, 1978. Bancroft returned to the play on February 11, 1978; it was only scheduled to run for ten more performances. It was scheduled to go to Los Angeles in the fall.

On February 18, 1978, the *New York Times* reported that Bancroft had been unable to do the last three performances of the season due to illness. Nominated for the Best Actress in a Play Tony Award, she lost to Jessica Tandy for *The Gin Game*. She did not attend the ceremony held on June 4, 1978, at the Shubert Theatre.

On March 1, 1978, the *New York Times* published an article by Mel Gussow entitled "How and Why *Golda* Sank." It had been a predicted winner, reuniting the successful team of Gibson, Penn and Bancroft, and it had a large advance sale. Despite mixed reviews, business was close to capacity but the show closed after 93 performances. The investment was thought to be lost unless the property was sold to films or TV. Philip Langner said there *was* a film offer and talk of a ten-hour television special. In July 1978 an entertainment headline said that Fox hoped a rewritten *Golda* would be golden on the silver screen for Bancroft. But these projects did not eventuate. A revised version of the play—a one-woman show entitled *Golda's Balcony*—was a success, setting the record as the longest running one-woman play in Broadway history. It starred Tovah Feldshuh, was directed by Scott Schwartz, and ran at the Helen Hayes Theatre from October 15, 2003, to January 2, 2005. Gibson said that he had made the text of *Golda* vanish and it never would be performed again.

Bancroft still praised the play but said she was discouraged by the demands of working the show eight times a week, and she had no plans to return to Broadway. She would think very deeply before she did another show as the cost was extremely high and this often made Bancroft wonder if it was worth it. She quipped that she would only do so when Brooks went to China and Max went to college, since her husband had no intention of going to China and her son was only five.

Although Bancroft's absence was thought to be the reason for the show's failure, Gussow claimed that things went deeper than that. Although the play was based on Meir's autobiography, Gibson had said from the beginning that he was more interested in the State of Israel than her life. She had been given veto power over the outline of the play but not the actual script, and Meir wanted the only romantic involvement mentioned to be her marriage. Bancroft said that Meir also didn't want any jokes in the play, but some were left in. Meir became such a large influence that Gibson and Meir were co-authors and they split the royalties. She was unhappy with how the character was portrayed, particularly how Bancroft presented her as an elderly woman. Meir said if that was how she looked and sounded, she would not have been elected. Bancroft said Meir wanted a dignified portrait: She wanted to look perfect while making powerful decisions. The actress was told that she kept her head down too much, though this was something Bancroft had copied from life. Meir never was able to lift her head and she walked with a limp, but these were things that Meir did not recognize. Bancroft thought that it was difficult for Meir to see herself on stage, particularly as she was a woman with a certain amount of vanity. When the actress visited Israel, Meir commented on how fat she was, and while this was not in the script, Bancroft wanted to act it. However, the actress decided to accede to Meir's request and she altered her performance. The limp was modified, the downed head was raised, and she walked a little faster. When Meir saw the show, she was pleased with the changes. Gibson was not: He felt the performance lost variation, nuance and texture. But he did not feel that this is what led to the failure of the show. The problem was cigarettes.

Bancroft did not smoke but Meir did so this was included in the play. The actress never intended to inhale but she was no nervous that she inhaled 17 cigarettes in the two hours of the performance. Meir had gotten chronic bronchitis from her habit and Bancroft got acute bronchitis followed by influenza. The producer said that the actress had tremendous grit and determination but she became very rundown. A doctor waited in the wings for two or three nights in a row and Bancroft was described as the walking wounded. She was forced to leave the show in February due to the illness and the box office receipts dropped to zero. Gibson blamed himself for the failure but Bancroft did not agree. She said there were mistakes and she found the show debilitating but that is was still a sensational evening. The audience was extremely moved and gave standing ovations.

Bancroft did not attend the 50th Academy Awards on April 3, 1978, where she was nominated for Best Actress for *The Turning Point*. The winner of the Oscar was Diane Keaton for *Annie Hall*. In her acceptance speech, Keaton said that naturally she was very honored to have been nominated with actresses like Bancroft.

Bancroft participated in the ABC-TV special *The Stars Salute Israel at 30!* which was shot on May 7, 1978, and broadcast on May 8. The two-hour gala birthday part was organized by the American Committee to Celebrate Israel's 30th Anniversary with Vice-President Walter F. Mondale as chairman. The event had proceeds going to benefit cultural and arts projects in Israel. The show was written by Buz Kohan and Bob Arnot and directed by Marty Pasetta.

Bancroft was awarded the *Ladies Home Journal* 1978 Woman of the Year award in the category of the New Performing Arts (Stage and Dance). The ceremony was held on June 13, 1978, at Washington's L'Enfant Plaza Hotel. It was reported that the actress was unable to attend, but she was photographed there.

Bancroft joined Mel Brooks on the Danish Danmarks Radio family talk show *Lørdagshjørnet* aka *The Saturday Corner* in the episode broadcast on September 2, 1978. Interviewed by Henrik Iversen, Brooks promoted *High Anxiety* (1977) and spoke about how *Silent Movie* was going to be re-released. Bancroft joined her husband in the last minutes of the show and she spoke in a soft voice. She reported that this was the first time that the couple had appeared to be interviewed together. Brooks kissed his wife so sloppily that she had to wipe her mouth, and together they say excerpts from the songs "When You Wore a Tulip (And I Wore a Big Red Rose)" and "For Me and My Gal." The couple also danced a little as they left the stage.

The actress was reportedly offered the part of Julia Tate Moon in Paramount's comic western *Goin' South* (1978). Other actresses under considered were Jane Fonda, Meryl Streep, Jessica Lange and Candice Bergen. The part was given to Mary Steenburgen.

Bancroft appeared on the 90-minute Walt Disney family documentary *Mickey's 50* (1978), broadcast on NBC on November 19, 1978. The show, written by Phil May and directed by May and Mike Jittlov, was made to commemorate the 50th birthday of Mickey Mouse and highlighted many moments in his career.

8

Fatso

The *New York Times* of May 1, 1979, reported that Mel Brooks' Crossbow Productions was making the feature version of *Fatso*, which the actress was writing and directing. The same article revealed that Brooks was to finance a film about the hideously deformed Englishman known as the Elephant Man, John Merrick. This was following the success of the Broadway play by Bernard Pomerance, although the Brooks film was not to be an adaptation. The play *The Elephant Man* was produced in London by Foco Novo Productions and The Hampstead Theatre and then in New York by the American National Theatre and Academy at St. Peter's Church. The Broadway production, directed by Jack Hofsiss, had opened at the Booth Theatre on April 19, 1979. Brooks' film went into production at Elstree Studios in London in September 1981. Brooks said that the original screenplay by Christopher DeVore and Eric Bergren had been written months before Pomerance's play appeared. They had based it on the journals of Frederick Treves, the British surgeon who took care of the Elephant Man. In the film, Bancroft played actress Mrs. Kendal, the first high-society figure to befriend the Elephant Man.

She also appeared in her own *Fatso* (1980). Shot at 20th Century–Fox, it told the story of 40-year-old Italian-American "Dom" Anthony DiNapoli (Dom DeLuise) who works in New York's DiNapoli's Card Shoppe and is a compulsive eater. Bancroft played his married sister Antoinette, who shares a house with her brother and works in the same store. Upset by the premature death of their fat cousin Salvador (Manny Medina), Antoinette makes an appointment for Dom to see a diet doctor. A female customer of the store tells him about the support group Chubby Checkers. But it is Dom's romance with the Polish antique gift shop worker Lydia (Candice Azzara) that helps him stop over-eating, although wedding photographs of the couple under the film's end credits show that Dom continues to be fat after his marriage and that Lydia has children.

The film's title may suggest that Bancroft took an insensitive approach to the subject but this is not the case. One of the teachings of Chubby Checkers is that the participants must declare their fatness so as to rid themselves of shame so this makes the title seem less offensive. This idea is demonstrated when Dom acknowledges that his mother feeding him when he was upset as a child may have started his addictive behavior. He comes to learn that he has to be accepted by his family and Lydia as a fat man, to avoid internalizing his shame as self-hatred. Antoinette judges her brother harshly for his behavior but Lydia never comments on it. This is perhaps why it is not an obstacle for them to be together and also why he unknowingly loses weight when he is with her. We see them eating together once in a telling way when they share a sandwich. It appears that Lydia sees beyond Dom's physical appearance and recognizes that he is a sweet, emotional man who cares for her. Her attraction to him is because he reminds her of her beloved father, and her not eating sweets because they make her nauseous and her fear that she is diabetic would seem to establish a way for Dom to also not eat sweets.

Lydia and Dom are both Catholic, both of their parents are dead, both had Italian mothers, and both have younger brothers named Frankie. Before he meets Lydia, Dom may behave poorly by taking food from other people's plates, but he is also shown to clean up garbage on the street, help an old man cross and clean Lydia's shoe. Dom is also sensitive because he has a fear of asking Lydia on a date and initially chooses to eat rather than to approach her. But when she comes to his store to buy wrapping paper, he sees that she has an interest in him. The plot point of removing Lydia under unexplained circumstances is a test of Dom's dependence on her, which is heightened by the fact of his intention to propose. She eventually contacts him to tell him that she has been called to Boston for a family emergency and he goes to her. The impact of her absence is interesting in terms of Dom's reaction to it where he goes from falling back into eating excess and then resignation to his condition before the narrative reconciliation and happy ending. He doesn't even fight back against Antoinette's beating with the assumption that he believes he deserves the punishment, though he does tell his family his realization that he doesn't have the self-control to stop over-eating and they have to accept him as he is.

Unlike Lydia, Antoinette reacts violently against Dom. This is perhaps not a surprise since she is family and presumably has lived with his problem all her life. But another reason for her behavior is that she is shown to be an emotionally violent woman. When he is out of breath after dancing with her, she demonstrates tenderness by stroking his head and face. However Antoinette's beating Dom with a cane in the climax is hard to forgive, particularly since she hugs him afterwards but does not apologize. Her anger can be rationalized as a reaction to his excess, as when he eats the family's entire meal and goes missing all night and takes their car when he believes that Lydia has abandoned him. Antoinette's feelings of concern for him are conflicted.

Bancroft perhaps attempts to counter-balance the tone of addictive behavior and scorn for the subject by providing humor in the narrative and treatment. She presents the grieving Italians at Salvador's funeral as comic grotesques and she provides close-ups of cakes in a bakery in contrast to close-ups of people eating. Bancroft also supplies farcical moments. Antoinette returns from the store's back room just when Dom is kissing Lydia's cross; when his smile drops in reaction to Lydia pointing out two early American cocks in her store; the TV commercials for food that Dom sees which also includes a scene of Charles Laughton eating a chicken from *The Private Life of Henry VIII* (1933); and Dom brandishing a gun and then a kitchen knife at Frankie (Ron Carey) to get back the keys to the locked kitchen cupboards and the fridge. Frankie takes the knife and threatens Dom with it, and then puts it down which allows Dom to pick it up again. The scene where the Chubby Checkers interveners Sonny (Richard Karron) and Oscar (Paul Zegler) come to assist Dom when he is tempted to eat results in the inevitable conclusion. Their talk of food results in them breaking open the cupboards so that they all eat to excess. Bancroft supplies one shot that nearly redeems the scene: the men's bulging stomachs advancing on Frankie.

The use of DiNapoli as Dom's surname is an apparent tribute to Bancroft's mother's maiden name. Bancroft delivers some funny lines, as when Antoinette tells Dom that she had made an appointment for Salvador to see the diet doctor but he didn't go because

Still for *Fatso* (1980).

he went and had a pizza instead. After Frankie realizes that the gun Dom has threatened him with is a toy, he says, "That ain't real"; Dom replies, "You're right. But this is!" referring to the kitchen knife. Dom is funny when he cries when a nurse (Madeleine Taylor Holmes) lists all the foods he can no longer eat, and when he lets go of a balloon he is blowing up when Antoinette attacks him with a knife for his eating some of the birthday cake of Anthony (David Comfort). There is also a subtle gay joke, when Lydia tells Dom that some wrapping paper is too gay and a gay-looking man that Antoinette is serving overhears and thinks she is referring to him.

The director appears to extend the running time of scenes for longer than necessary although the performances never come across as indulgent, which is often the mark of an actor-turned-director. The film is noteworthy for having some Italian dialogue without the use of subtitles, for a number of montages (including one of Dom and Lydia kissing in different locations) and hand-held camerawork. The first kiss between Dom and Lydia is unconventionally shown in an extreme long shot and Bancroft adds to the surprise with the kissing montage that otherwise would be considered too much.

Bancroft's hair is by Vivian McAteer and worn in a shoulder-length graying style pulled back from her forehead, and she is repeatedly seen with her hair in curlers. Costumes are by Patricia Norris and favors nondescript dresses with work and kitchen smocks. Her hysterical screaming at Salvador's corpse and her later screaming at Dom in the climax is both funny and scary, since the actress swears and cries, expressing Antoinette's mix of hurt and anger. We also see her dancing with DeLuise as he hums

"Sweet Georgia Brown," which prefigures the use of the song in Brooks' *To Be or Not to Be*, and later dancing at the St. Anthony Church Bazaar.

Jim Haspiel visited the set for an article on Bancroft that appeared in the January 1980 *Films in Review*. He saw her emote behind the camera as she watched a take, emulating the performance she observed, down to the detail of licking her lips when the actor licked his. Haspiel saw Bancroft dissatisfied with the results of a scene where a derelict walked into camera view and sat down so that on subsequent takes she physically spun the actor around in circles a dozen times before pointing him towards the camera to get the effect of a naturally dizzy drunk. Haspeil also witnessed Bancroft direct and act in another scene, and then pause between shots to watch her performance on a television monitor with videotape-playback. She made Haspiel an extra, putting him in the background in one of her close-ups.

Director of photography Brianne Murphy attested to the influence Mel Brooks had on the shoot. She was never allowed to go to dailies, only Bancroft and he did. This was despite it being the usual practice that the D.P. would go to see dailies with the director and the editor, and the director would say what they did and didn't like. On the set, everybody loved Bancroft and she and Murphy had a wonderful camaraderie. Around four or five in the afternoon, Brooks came to pick his wife up. This seemed to be at his convenience and not hers, because often when he appeared, Bancroft would want to complete a shot. One day he came onto the set without saying hello to anyone and went over to the video monitor. In the middle of the shot Brooks said "Cut!" and "That's no good." The camera operator reportedly looked at him and then Murphy and asked "who the fuck this little guy was," and all hell broke loose. Bancroft was so upset that she left the set despite the fact that the crew knew that no one except the director ever ordered cut. The next day on the set, Murphy was all ready to start but Bancroft was missing. After an hour, the assistant director told Murphy that Bancroft wanted to see her in her dressing room. Bancroft said that she had been crying all night. She said what had happened the day before was just terrible and Brooks had recommended that the camera operator be fired because he felt he was potentially dangerous. There was a battle of wills over whether the operator would be kept or not and finally the matter was dropped altogether. Murphy summed up the experience saying that Bancroft was a very talented person and the D.P. always thought she could have been a great director.

Bancroft thought that to be a director, you had to have a certain kind of personality, which she didn't have. She didn't like manipulating people and her greatest philosophy was to let everybody be who they wanted to be, but it wasn't workable. Somebody had to have a dominant hand and Bancroft said she didn't have that kind of hand. She told TV interviewer Charlie Rose (April 25, 2000) that after *Fatso*, she vowed she would never direct again. In the May 1987 *Films and Filming* she said that *Fatso* was a film she would prefer to forget and that she hated it. Bancroft said that the writing of the script was really wonderful and as soon as she gave it to Fox, everything changed. Fifty million people had something to say about it. When she was writing, it was just her and the people in her head. Bancroft confessed that she was happy that she never had to direct again.

Fatso was released on February 1, 1980, with the tagline "Starving for a great movie?" It was lambasted by Janet Maslin in the *New York Times* and Roger Ebert in the *Chicago Sun-Times*. When the film was screened at the East Hampton Library in October 2010, it was introduced by Bancroft's younger sister Phyllis Italiano. She said that the short *Fatso* was about their family where their older sister was 5'4" and 250 pounds; the other inspiration was DeLuise, who was beginning to have a weight problem. After the short was finished, people thought it was great and asked Bancroft to turn it into a movie but she didn't know how to do that. Brooks told Phyllis that it was either Bill Gibson or Arthur Penn who encouraged by her saying to just start with the words "Fade in." So Bancroft sat down at her desk and wrote for two straight weeks and produced the film, which Phyllis claimed was riddled with stuff about her upbringing and family. Phyllis said she worked on the film with her sister from the beginning to the end, and that he also had a little part in it. She is billed as Phyllis Wetzel playing Lucy.

Bancroft appeared on the CBS-TV special *The Muppets Go Hollywood* on May 16, 1979. The show was written by Jerry Juhl and Don Hinkley and directed by Stan Harris. It was a party hosted by Dick Van Dyke and Rita Moreno and filmed at the Cocoanut Grove in Los Angeles. Bancroft is seen arriving at the Grove in the same car as Brooks and Dom DeLuise and Carl Reiner.

According to Marilyn Beck's June 12, 1979, column, Bancroft had agreed the previous year to take on the role of Joan Crawford in the Paramount biographical drama *Mommie Dearest,* based on Christina Crawford's 1978 memoir-exposé about her mother. Bancroft had reportedly been unsatisfied with the screenplay adaptation and had asked for rewrites. She was said to have director approval and had promised to keep herself available until producer Frank Yablans could work things out to her satisfaction. Reportedly other actresses had been considered; one was Sigourney Weaver, but apparently the role was a hard sell because the character was so unsympathetic. Bancroft was announced for the part with Franco Zeffirelli as the director, reuniting with the actress after *Jesus of Nazareth*. However she reportedly withdrew from the production after being still dissatisfied with numerous versions of the screenplay. The *New York Times* reported on December 11, 1979, that the adaptation proved to be very difficult to manage, with James Kirkwood the latest to give up, after efforts by Christina Crawford and Robert Getchell. Getchell got a screenplay credit on the film with producer Frank Yablans, director Frank Perry and Tracy Hotchner. Bancroft said that she found the screenplays offered to be hatchet jobs on Crawford's character and had asked for Arthur Miller to do a rewrite. Zeffirelli also withdrew and was replaced by Frank Perry. Although he reportedly did not want Bancroft, thinking her wrong for the part, Perry was prepared to go with her and was willing to make changes if she could say what she wanted changed. However the actress could not suggest what to change so he told her since that was the case, he would do the film without her. Bancroft reportedly responded with "Terrific" and Perry went to Faye Dunaway. Dunaway wrote in her autobiography *Looking for Gatsby* of another reason she heard for Bancroft's withdrawal. The general sentiment in Hollywood was that the actress who played Christina's version of Crawford would pay a price for taking on such a legend. This would become true for Dunaway since the film proved to be a career disaster for her. The film was released on September 18, 1981, and was generally lambasted. However it proved to be a surprising box office hit, and despite the fact that Dunaway's performance was praised, she also won the Worst Actress Razzie Award for it.

Bancroft described her *Mommie Dearest* experience as a saga and a half in her 1987 *Films and Filming* interview. She said they had the opportunity to write a brilliant script because Crawford was the epitome of stardom, of power and of losing that power. "It could have been such a statement, such an indictment, and it wound up being some silly … it wasn't even silly. It just didn't make sense." Bancroft said they should not have made it.

She was next in Brooksfilms' *The Elephant Man* (1980). The biographical black-and-white drama was shot from October 13, 1979, to May 1, 1980, on locations in London and at the Lee International Studios in London. It was based on the book *The Elephant Man and Other Reminiscences* by Sir Frederick Treves and in part on the book *The Elephant Man: A Study in Human Dignity* by Ashley Montagu. Directed by David Lynch, it told the true story of John Merrick (John Hurt), a seriously deformed 21-year-old in Victorian London who is rescued from a freak show by London Hospital surgeon and anatomy lecturer Frederick Treves (Anthony Hopkins). Bancroft played Mrs. Kendal, a London stage actress who is the first society person to visit Merrick in his hospital room. As a person who is said to always be at the forefront of fashion and form, her visit creates the precedent that leads to other society people to visit him. Mrs. Kendal's decision to visit Merrick came after she read about him in the newspaper; her visit shows bravery despite the paper's contention that Merrick has the manners of a gentleman. Mrs. Kendal presumably arranges for him to attend the pantomime, where she thanks him on stage in front of the crowd after the show, and we are told that she supplies his nurse Nora (Lesley Dunlop) with a gown to wear at the show. However we also hear that Mrs. Kendal knows that Merrick is dying. We do not see her visit him again.

The actress appears in just three scenes. Her hair is by Stephanie Kaye and Paula Gillespie and worn in a long style which is loose in her first scene and worn up in the other two. Period costumes are by Patricia Norris. Bancroft uses a British accent and her best scene is perhaps when Mrs. Kendal visits Merrick. We see her smiling performance in reaction to his hideousness, dropped when he looks away from her. The character may reveal her narcissism in bringing Merrick an autographed photograph of herself but her also bringing a copy of *Romeo and Juliet* is paid off when the couple enact a scene from the play. Mrs. Kendal speaks Juliet to his Romeo that he reads to her, and her kissing of his cheek may be the climax of the performance or an expression of the woman being touched by Merrick's sensitivity. Bancroft also gets two good lines in the scene, when Mrs. Kendal says "The theater is romance" and "You are not the Elephant Man. You're Romeo."

The film premiered in New York on October 3, 1980, and then was given a wide release on October 10, with the tagline "I am not an animal! I am a human being! I ... am ... a man!" Vincent Canby in the *New York Times* wrote that Bancroft played in her best grand-lady style in scenes that were surprisingly affecting. Pauline Kael in *The New Yorker* wrote that although Bancroft was

Portrait for *The Elephant Man* (1980).

more toned down than in other recent appearances, she seemed to have dropped in from another era. A box office success, it was Oscar-nominated for Best Picture, Best Director, Best Actor, Best Adapted Screenplay, Best Art Direction–Set Decoration, Best Costumes, Best Editing and Best Music. Two stills exist which appear to show Bancroft in deleted scenes. One has her wearing a white feathered hat, and the other has her in all black including a veil, standing in front of what looks like a church. This latter still may represent the scene of Merrick's funeral. The Broadway play was filmed and aired as a made-for-TV movie in 1982 with Penny Fuller playing Mrs. Kendal. Fuller won the Best Supporting Actress Emmy Award for her performance.

The September 6, 1979, *New York Times* featured an interview with Mayor Ed Koch where he recalled two meetings with Bancroft and Brooks. He said he ran into the couple at Maxim's in Paris and Brooks reminded Koch of the first time they had met. In 1962, Koch was trying to get signatures on petitions for a race he was making for the Assembly. When Koch knocked on the Brookses' Village brownstone door, a monster dog rushed by, pursued by Brooks and Bancroft. Koch also joined in the chase and that's when Brooks says the couple signed his petition. Koch corrected him, claiming that Brooks had signed but she had not.

In 1979, Bancroft and Brooks bought the Crest Theatre in Fresno. The couple were said to have owned movie theaters up and down California. On July 10, 1980, producer Robert Stigwood said in the *New York Times* that Bancroft had wanted the female role in the film *The Fan*, based on the novel by Bob Randall. The part of Sally Ross, a celebrated actress appearing in her first Broadway musical and terrorized by a besotted fan, was played by Lauren Bacall. The actress was one of the winners of the 1st Annual Actors Studio Awards held on November 5, 1980, at the Waldorf-Astoria Hotel. The award was a bronze mask of Eleanora Duse presented to the Actors Studio members by Lee Strasberg, the artistic director.

Bancroft was cast in NBC's eight-hour miniseries *Marco Polo* as the mother of the adventurer who traveled to China with his father and uncle in the 13th century. The title character was played by Alexander Picolo as a child and by Ken Marshall as an adult. The narrative was structured around flashbacks about Marco, as stories he had told writer Rustichello (David Warner) in a Genoa prison, and which in 1298 Rustichello retold to monks of the order of St. Dominic. Marco's merchant father Niccolo (Denholm Elliott) and Uncle Matteo (Tony Vogel) left Venice before the boy was born in 1254 to make their fortune in the Orient. His mother suffers from an unspecified illness and Marco is cared for by his Aunt Flora (Sada Thompson) and Uncle Zane (Richard Cucciolla), who runs a cloth stall in the market. Marco's mother will receive pagan objects as gifts but only one letter from her husband that she has read so many times that she can recite it. It is said that her illness uses up her money so that she has no inheritance to give to her son or sister and this necessitates Marco working for his uncle. In 1269, Niccolo returns to Venice, and Marco joins him in 1271 to travel to various countries, including China, till 1292.

Guest star Bancroft has hair by Renata Magnanti and Elda Magnanti which is long and black and worn off her forehead. She has one outfit by Enrico Sabbatini, a white nightgown under a brown throw. The actress does not employ an Italian accent, and provides tears and operatic sobbing for her dying scene. Director Guiliano Montaldo undermines the focus on Bancroft with a moving camera that goes around a pillar in the room and framing that has our view of her blocked by the back of Picolo's head.

The miniseries was broadcast over four evenings, May 16 to May 19, 1982. John J. O'Connor in the *New York Times* wrote that Bancroft had perhaps the cushiest role in the entire production since she didn't have to get out of bed to die.

The actress supplied narration for *Shogun* (1980), the edited version of the TV miniseries *James Clavell's Shogun*. The original series, based on the novel by James Clavell, told the story of Pilot-Major John Blackthorne (Richard Chamberlain), an English navigator who had transforming experiences in feudal Japan in the early 17th century. Shot on location in Japan and at Japanese studios as well at Paramount, it had a running time of 547 minutes and narration by Orson Welles. Broadcast on NBC over five nights between September 15 and September 19, 1980, the show was a ratings success and won several Emmys. It was later recut into a new version. Some sources say a 150-minute version was broadcast on December 31, 1980; other sources claim a 125-minute version with Bancroft narration was released in 1980 to European theatrical film markets.

Bancroft was mentioned in a January 11, 1981, *New York Times* article about the struggles of women film directors. Bancroft was said to be one of the actresses who were interested in directing for whom the prospect was most promising. On January 19, 1981, it was reported that she was being promoted as a candidate for an Academy Award nomination for her *Elephant Man* performance. She did not receive a nomination.

The *New York Times* of July 31, 1981, reported that the actress had signed to return to Broadway to star in Tom Kempinski's drama *Duet for One*. She was to play a violinist stricken by a crippling disease in the two-character British play, which was due to open on January 7, 1982. The story was thought to have been inspired by the medical and musical history of Jacqueline DuPre, the English cellist whose career was cut short by multiple sclerosis. Ellen Burstyn had been originally announced for the role but had dropped out, citing artistic differences. These were related to the fact that she wanted Lee Strasberg to co-star with her, but director William Friedkin did not want him. The play had originally been staged at the Duke of York Theater in London with Frances de La Tour.

Ironically, Burstyn was in contention to take on a role that Bancroft had presumably passed on: Annie Sullivan in William Gibson's *Miracle Worker* sequel *Monday After the Miracle*. The new play was to open on Broadway shortly after the first of the year, with Arthur Penn directing. Taking place 20 years after the events of *The Miracle Worker*, the new play was the story of Sullivan's marriage to critic John Macy, and Helen Keller's place in their household. Penn directed the production at the Actors Studio, and it would be seen at the Spoleto U.S.A. Festival in May 1982. Its Broadway run was delayed until 1982, where Jane Alexander played Sullivan. This production ran from December 14 to 18, 1982 at the Eugene O'Neill Theatre. Bancroft was also not cast in CBS's November 15, 1998, production of the play which starred Roma Downey as Annie.

On August 30, 1981, it was announced that Max von Sydow would co-star in *Duet for One* as Bancroft's psychiatrist. The production was to run at the Royale Theatre. On September 11, it was reported that the play would now open on December 17, 1981. According to an October 2, 1981, news item, the advanced opening was due to the fact that the Royale's previous show, the musical comedy *A Day in Hollywood/A Night in the Ukraine* had closed on September 27, which was earlier than expected.

Michael Palin wrote in his memoir *Halfway to Hollywood: Diaries 1980–1988 (Volume Two)* that on December 2, 1981, the actress had been suggested for the part of Lady Isabel Ames in the British HandMade Films comedy *The Missionary* (1982). The screenplay

Still for *Duet for One* (December 17, 1981–January 2, 1982).

was by Palin and the director was Richard Loncraine. On December 9, Palin attended a private screening of *The Elephant Man* to see Bancroft's most recent performance. He wrote that he felt the actress was too old for the part of Isabel, and maybe too strongly dramatic for a character that had to have a skittishness and a light, naughty side. Palin decided he preferred Maggie Smith.

After 11 previews from December 7, 1981, *Duet for One* opened on December 17 but only ran until January 2, 1982. Frank Rich of the *New York Times* considered Bancroft as Stephanie Abrahams miscast and misdirected. He wrote that it was unfair to ask for her to be accepted as a woman of 38 since Bancroft was 50. Rich praised her anger, bitterness, pugnacity and willful, self-deceiving air of gaiety. However he wrote that she was also pinched and shrill and seemed too controlled and fierce. The softness that must have existed somewhere in the soul of a great, sensitive musician was never seen, and the audience did not experience the frailty and the full terror of a woman in the throes of a degenerative disease. In the February 28, 1982, *Times,* Walter Kerr described Bancroft as "permitted or persuaded to give a monotonously shrill performance." In a January 8, 1982, article, Mel Gussow commented that she operated a motorized chair with aplomb.

In the book *Hurricane Billy*, Nat Segaloff wrote that Burstyn had bought the rights to the play after it had opened in London and she approached William Friedkin. The director cast von Sydow, who was to come to New York from Sweden, but then Burstyn wanted Strasberg instead. When Friedkin disagreed, the actress withdrew and Bancroft replaced her. He commented that he thought Bancroft was occasionally brilliant in the role but that Burstyn would have been consistently unpredictable and fantastic.

Back in Los Angeles with Mel Brooks, the actress enjoyed spending time with Max. She said that the best time of the day was when the family came together at about seven o'clock to have dinner and talk. Bancroft felt that coming together as a family was one of the greatest rewards of life and of having a family. For recreation, the Brookses played tennis and occasionally the couple would have a night out on the town. They liked going to the Tail o' the Clock restaurant in Studio City to hear Johnny Guarnieri play the piano.

Footage of the actress in *The Prisoner of Second Avenue* appeared in ABC's three-hour comedy documentary *Hollywood: The Gift of Laughter* (1982), a retrospective look at 60 years of great moments in film comedy. It was broadcast on May 16, 1982.

Starting in the fall of 1982, she and Brooks finally made *To Be or Not to Be* (1983). The Brooksfilm–20th Century–Fox comedy was directed by Alan Johnson from a screenplay by Thomas Meehan and Ronny Graham. Meehan had previously written for Brooks and Bancroft on the television specials *Annie, the Women in the Life of a Man* and *Annie and the Hoods*. The original film had a screenplay by Edwin Justus Mayer based on a story by Melchor Lengyel. This starred Carole Lombard and Jack Benny as Joseph and Maria Tura.

The film was set in 1939 at Warsaw, Poland's Bronski Theatre, which is headed by actors Frederick Bronksi (Brooks) and his wife Anna (Bancroft). She has the actress affectation of a pet dog, Mutke (Scamp), although this also suggests a lack of intimacy between Anna and Frederick who we don't see as a romantic pair. This distance may also be influenced by their competing egos, which is highlighted when he has her name in smaller print under the title and in parentheses on a poster, which she objects to. This joke is carried over into the film's end credits where Bancroft's name is in parenthesis. The emotional distance allows Anna to feel justified in accepting the romantic advances of bomber pilot Andrei Sobinsky (Tim Matheson). He proclaims that love should be monogamous whereas she tells him, "True love should never stand in the way of having a good time." Anna is prepared to leave Frederick for Andrei but not immediately and she tears up the letter the pilot writes telling of their love. The affair shows that she is an unfaithful wife, as does the repetition of the gag at the end of the narrative where another man leaves during Frederick's recital of the speech from *Hamlet* so he too can have a rendezvous with Anna. She is also a morally duplicitous character since she lies to Professor Siletski (Jose Ferrer) and Colonel Erhardt (Charles Durning) in pretending she has a romantic interest in them. But since the narrative presents these Gestapo agents as bad guys and the Bronksis as the good guys, Anna's behavior can be forgiven. We can also forgive her the affairs since Frederick is presented as a self-centered buffoon. The Bronskis may be against the Nazis more because they close their theater than to help Andrei to stop Silestski from murdering resistance fighters, but they also help to hide Jews and take them to England when the company escapes from Germany. Frederick's aid to the hidden Jews is shown to be of arbitrary interest to him, although he agrees to the idea. However, Anna's effort to save her homosexual dresser, Sacha Kinski (James Haake), from being sent to a concentration camp is more direct, and helped by Frederick to help Anna. This effort continues when she has Sacha play her in the "Ladies" number at the theater and when she physically tries to stop a soldier from taking him. Anna's infidelity becomes a weakened plot point once Andrei comes to Warsaw and lives with the Bronskis since the narrative becomes more interested in Frederick's efforts to deceive Siletski and Erhardt.

She is put in danger a few times; for example, she is held captive in the office of Siletski when he goes to see Frederick as Erhardt but then is saved when Frederick impersonates Siletski to have her released.

Anna gets some funny lines which helps to make her likable. When Andrei writes the letter to Frederick, he says it's the decent thing to do and it's the honorable thing to do, and Anna adds, "It's the stupid thing to do." After the Bronskis' house is appropriated by the Gestapo, she is told not to sit in a chair that now belongs to Erhardt. Anna responds, "Forgive me. I have such a rotten memory. Ten minutes ago it was my chair."

Bancroft's hair is by Cheri Ruff and worn in a medium length brunette style with the suggestion of gray roots. Her costumes are by Albert Wolsky. One white evening gown with diamond-shaped appliques recalls a satin evening gown with a diamond waist piece designed by Irene and worn by Lombard in the Lubitsch film. Wolsky also has an oddly uncoordinated outfit of a blue suit with a brown neck scarf and a red hat. Bancroft sings "Sweet Georgia Brown" in Polish and initially speaks dialogue in Polish until the contrivance is announced that from then on English will be spoken. She then speaks with her American accent, like the other actors playing Poles, except for the actors playing Nazis who use German accents. We also hear Bancroft sing pieces of "You and the Night and the Music," "Sweetheart" and "Heart and Soul." It's good to see her play comedy which includes some farce and slapstick when she falls to the floor after being kissed by Andrei. Her two scenes with Jose Ferrer work better because he comes across as a believable threat as opposed to the clown that is Charles Durning's Erhardt. The soft-focus photography of the actress is disappointing but worse is the "Sweet Georgia Brown" number where she sings and dances with Brooks, given that the couple have relatively little to do on screen together in the film. In the number Brooks attempts to upstage Bancroft, which may have some context for the Frederick character. However director Johnson has cutaways to the audience, and there is an obvious use of a body double for Bancroft in long shots and when Anna tumbles over Frederick's back in the dance.

The film was released on December 16, 1983, with the tagline "That is the movie!" *Variety* wrote that the mainstay of the film was a superbly sustained comic performance by Bancroft. The film was praised by the *New York Times*' Vincent Canby, who said that the revelation for film audiences was that she was such a wildly gifted comedienne. Durning was nominated for the Best Supporting Actor Academy Award but lost to Jack Nicholson for *Terms of Endearment* (1983). Reportedly the film was not a box office hit.

Bancroft, profiled on the DVD featurette, commented that learning Polish for the film was difficult and she almost gave up on the first day. The actress said that so much of film work was drudgery—getting up early, sitting around and getting made up and getting your hair done, trying on costumes, learning lines and sitting around waiting to be told that they were ready for you.

In her 2000 Charlie Rose television interview, Bancroft said *To Be or Not to Be* was great fun and that it was the easiest movie she ever did. She said that she and Brooks hadn't tried to find a new project since and their hesitance was perhaps based on the fact that the film didn't make money at the time. She also said being in the film with her husband was a lot like being pregnant because some days were good and some days she felt like throwing up. Brooks commented that he and Bancroft had great concerns about working together in such a major capacity. They wondered if they would get on each other's nerves, but they actually became closer. Normally when Brooks was working on a film he would eat lunch alone and go over his lines in his trailer but this time he found himself knocking on her door and asking what she was doing. He said Bancroft was more than a good friend—she was his ultimate filmmaking consultant. If his wife was not moved by a project, he would not do it and he trusted her judgment about emotions more than anybody else on Earth.

The film is also notable for having Max Brooks appear in it as the son of Rifka (Marley Sims), one of the hidden Jewish families. Bancroft commented that he had been begging them for a part so they gave him one line because they thought Max should know what it was like. After about three days he decided that he would wait until he was older to be an actor, and Bancroft didn't blame him. She knew there was so much work to it that her son hadn't expected, like just being there when you were needed. You couldn't be off reading a book or playing and this was something Bancroft said that made Max very disenchanted by the whole thing.

Brooks and Bancroft went abroad to promote the film. In London he appeared in the 55-minute Brooksfilms comedy television show *An Audience with Mel Brooks*, written by Ronny Graham and directed by Brooks. Bancroft was in the audience and came up on stage to recreate with him their Polish duet of "Sweet Georgia Brown." In the wake of the film, Brooks was asked if he and Bancroft would consider working together again and he quipped that they were not the Lunts. He said if they could find something that they really wanted to do together, maybe they would.

Bancroft's next film *Garbo Talks*, a comedy directed by Sidney Lumet, was shot on location in New York and at the Silvercup Studios in Astoria, New York. Chartered public accountant Gilbert Rolfe's (Ron Silver) mother Estelle (Bancroft) is dying of a brain tumor. She asks him to fulfill her last wish: to meet Greta Garbo. Estelle is a political activist who confronts construction workers who wolf-whistle at a woman in the street, and who encourages her New York Hospital Puerto Rican nurse (Antonia Rey) to ask for a higher wage. Her behavior has cost her her marriage: Her ex Walter (Steven Hill) tells Gilbert that he tired of her outrage and only wanted a quiet home life. We also learn that Estelle had not attended Gilbert's wedding because she had refused to cross a bartenders' picket line.

Bancroft received above-the-title billing but the narrative has her play a supporting role to Silver. Her hair is by Bob Grimaldi and worn in a medium length style with a side part with the color graying, since she admits to dyeing it. Her clothes (by Anne Hill Johnstone) include a memorable long red coat and white woolen cap. She occasionally overgestures to show Estelle's passionate anger. She is funny when confronting the construction workers, and when she replies to the idea that her request to see Garbo is a last wish. To the latter Estelle says, "It's not a last wish. I have a lot more. Just short on time." Bancroft is reserved in her pivotal scenes, when she asks to meet Garbo (Betty Comden), and in the climax when she meets her. Director Lumet gives Bancroft a long close-up as she reacts to the news that she has six months to live. In the meeting with Garbo, which incorporates a six-and-a-half minute monologue by the actress, Lumet only uses a slow pan into her that ends on a medium shot. He finally gives Bancroft the close-up we had wanted in the previous scene when in the next, Estelle tells Gilbert what Garbo had said to her.

Released on October 12, 1984, the film received a mixed reaction from *Variety* who described her performance as spirited, and was praised by the *New York Times*' Vincent Canby who wrote that Bancroft played with great verve and was so good that she almost managed to make her big last moment work.

When Lumet was casting the role of Estelle, he called Bancroft and told her that part was right for her except that she wasn't old enough. This could have proved to be a problem since Ron Silver, who was to play her son, was only 15 years younger than her. Bancroft assured Lumet that she was old enough and when they had a meeting, he peered at her face and agreed she really was old enough. Bancroft wanted to do the part because she felt that the character was very much like her mother and her youngest sister, whom she considered extremely political. Bancroft guessed that if she weren't an actress, she would be like that, too.

Interviewed by the *New York Times'* Leslie Bennetts (October 15, 1984), Bancroft was asked how director Lumet differed in his approach from Mel Brooks. Bancroft said if Lumet saw a take that wasn't that good, he would say, "Why don't we try it this way now" and he'd give you a suggestion. Brooks would say, "Now, that stunk!" Bancroft's *Garbo Talks* character was dying and Bancroft wanted to show other people and herself that she had a lack of vanity. She didn't care about being pretty or young. Bancroft said it was the hardest thing to put herself in front of a camera without makeup and have rings under her eyes and wear padding. When she played Golda Meir she wore a nose, a chin, jowls and glasses, and people could have looked at her and said, "What a great makeup job." But for this film it wasn't a great makeup job. It was how she looked in real life.

At the time, Bancroft lived in Santa Monica and she worked infrequently. This was partly because the roles available to older women were limited and partly because she didn't like to be separated from Brooks and her 12-year-old son. Bancroft didn't like to go away for any length of time, not because her family needed her that much, but more because she needed them. She had a good life and it was very hard to find something she really wanted to work in. The actress said most writers were men and they didn't write wonderful parts for women because they felt that women led the kind of lives they didn't want to write about. Long lay-offs didn't bother her any more. When she was younger, at the end of every job Bancroft thought she would never work again, and she would feel depressed and lonely. But as she aged, that feeling changed because she knew she would work again.

Bancroft wanted to work for different reasons. It used to be because she was afraid to face life, and it was a perfect excuse because work was a wonderful safe place to be. Now the actress needed to work for the work, to express certain things and get back to the discipline. Bancroft would say that she retired after every job but really she only retired until the next good part came up.

One good part that had come up was Aurora Greenway in the film of the Larry McMurtry novel *Terms of Endearment*. Jennifer Jones had coveted it and Janet Leigh and Louise Fletcher were also considered. Director James L. Brooks chose Shirley MacLaine, who would win the Best Actress Oscar for her performance.

9

Agnes of God

Bancroft's next film, shot in the fall of 1984, was the mystery *Agnes of God*, an adaptation of the Broadway play by John Pielmeier (March 30, 1982–September 4, 1983). Directed by Norman Jewison, the film was shot on location at the former Rockwood Academy in Rockwood, Ontario, and in other sites in Ontario and Quebec.

Mysterious circumstances surround the death of an infant secretly born to Sister Agnes (Meg Tilly), a young nun in a remote Quebec convent, Les Petites Soers de Marie Madeleine. Agnes is charged with manslaughter and Dr. Martha "Marty" Louise Livingstone (Jane Fonda) is the court-appointed psychiatrist asked to determine whether the girl is fit to stand trial. Bancroft plays Mother Superior Miriam Ruth, a role originated on stage by Geraldine Page. Page was nominated for a Tony for her performance.

In Mother Superior's past life she was a smoker, which resonates since Martha is a chain smoker, and she will smoke a cigarette that Martha gives her. This behavior marks Mother as a nun with a sense of humor. Mother jokes with Martha about what saints would have smoked, and has many funny lines. After Martha first speaks with Agnes, Mother asks her, "Is she totally bananas, or just slightly off-center?" She tells Martha, "No one knew about Agnes' pregnancy. No one. Not even Agnes." When Agnes refuses to eat except for the host, Mother comments, "I don't think a communion wafer has the recommended daily allowance of anything," and she confesses to Martha about her estranged children, "I think they tell their friends that I've passed on." Mother tells Martha that she can smell an ex-Catholic a mile away, and when she forces her way into Martha's office, she announces to the receptionist (Laurel Lyle) that she is General MacArthur.

She has come to the church after a failed marriage that produced children and grandchildren. Agnes is revealed to be Mother's niece and she tells Martha that she only knew her sister was an alcoholic after Agnes was taken into the convent. Mother claims she didn't know that the girl was molested by her mother. She calls Martha "dear" in patronization and tells the doctor that she doesn't approve of psychiatry, warning that she doesn't want Agnes' mind "cut open." Her fear that Martha will take the nun away from God comes from what Agnes means to her, since Mother says that Agnes' singing has removed her own religious uncertainty. Agnes' voice reminds her of the voice of a guardian angel she used to hear when she was a child. Her fear of losing the girl is also a fear of losing the angel again. Mother is envious of Agnes' closeness to God and suggests that perhaps this closeness may mean Agnes is a saint. Mother recognizes Martha's religious prejudice against the Catholic Church, since Martha had a bad experience being raised by nuns and her own sister died in a convent. Mother agrees to help Martha find a way to have

Agnes escape prison or the asylum, and then Martha can have her declared legally innocent. To this end, Mother approves of Martha hypnotizing Agnes, but only if she is present. Mother's involvement in the baby's birth is revealed as her having known she was pregnant and having left a wastepaper basket in Agnes' room, something the other nuns don't have. She planned to take the baby to a hospital and left Agnes to go to get help. This is something that is questionable since when we first see Mother going to Agnes' room, she appears to be dressed in sleep attire. She tells Martha that leaving Agnes alone with the baby was because she panicked, but she wasn't to know that the nun would decide to kill the baby. The narrative concludes with the girl being found not responsible for her actions and being returned to live at the convent, so that Mother will remain with her.

Bancroft's clothes are by Renee April. She speaks French and also sings prayers. The actress presents the emotional transitions of her character

Still for *Agnes of God* (1985).

where Mother can change from anger at Martha to calm or humor, and also a tenderness and mothering attitude toward Agnes. Director Jewison has Bancroft covering her face during the first hypnotism scene, afraid of Agnes's physical re-enactment of her labor, and also a close-up where she responds to Agnes' look at her with fury. The actress has many scenes of banter with Fonda that are enjoyable. The screenplay has one line that has an unfortunate link to one of the actress' previous films: Agnes tells Mother that God blew up the Hindenburg.

The film premiered in Canada on August 21, 1985, and was released in the U.S. on September 27 with the tagline "What unspeakable crime took place behind the third floor window? Only Agnes knows. And Dr. Martha Livingston is the one person who can unravel the mystery." Janet Maslin in the *New York Times* said that Bancroft was shrewd and forceful, and Roger Ebert wrote that she used her craft to give the illusion that she knew where she stood. There were Academy Awards nominations for Best Actress (Bancroft), Best Supporting Actress (Meg Tilly) and Best Original Score.

Norman Jewison wrote in his autobiography *This Terrible Business Has Been Good to Me* that he received a telephone call from Bancroft when the word got out that he was casting the film. She told him she wanted to play the Mother Superior part. When Jewison told Bancroft that he would get back to her, he said she persisted. She told him that she was married to a director and she knew that directors didn't know how to make up their minds so she was going to help Jewison with his decision. He advised her that he felt she was too young and too beautiful for the part. To him, Bancroft would always be Mrs. Robinson, sexy and sensual. The actress told Jewison that she was coming over to his office right that minute. He said when Bancroft swept in, she pulled up a chair, sat down, leaned across, looked him in the eye and said, "So this is Mrs. Robinson? Look at these lines. Look at me." Bancroft wore no makeup, she was pale, and Jewison said there were dark half-moons under her eyes. He happened to have a nun's habit costume in his office and asked her to put it on. When Jewison saw her in costume, he realized she would be superb. Jewison said then he had to tell Geraldine Page that he would not be casting her. Ironically she would end up winning the Best Actress Oscar in 1986 for her performance in the drama *The Trip to Bountiful* (1985). Jewison wrote that Bancroft as a Catholic identified with the role of Mother and that the story was particularly meaningful for her. He said there was a scene shot with Bancroft and Fonda, after the courtroom scene, where Martha came back to the convent. It was meant to provide a better ending for the film but it ultimately wasn't used.

To prepare for her role, Bancroft reportedly spent time with a Mother Superior of a convent in Los Angeles and attended vespers at a convent in Quebec. The actress commented that after seeing the film, she wanted people who believed in God to think again and people who didn't believe to think again, as well.

In *The Private Life of a Public Woman*, Patricia Bosworth wrote that Jane Fonda felt challenged by working with Bancroft (Fonda had been in awe of ever since they had met at the Actors Studio in the 1960s).

Bancroft was the co-host with David Frost of the 60-minute ABC-TV special *That Was The Week That Was* (April 21, 1985). The show offered satirical reviews of current affairs and cultural developments. Bancroft sang about the inevitable extinction of trees.

Bancroft's next film, the indie *'night, Mother*, was an adaptation of the Broadway play by Marsha Norman (March 31, 1983–February 26, 1984). The play won the Pulitzer Prize for Drama and received Tony nominations for Best Play, Best Director (Tom Moore) and Best Actress for stars Kathy Bates and Anne Pitoniak. (The latter appeared in the film *Agnes of God* as the mother of Jane Fonda.) The film, scripted by Norman and directed by Moore, was shot at Universal.

Jessie (Sissy Spacek), a depressed middle-aged epileptic, shares a farmhouse on the outskirts of a small Middle Western town. She has moved back to live at her mother Thelma's (Bancroft) house after she has divorced from (unseen) carpenter Cecil and with her (unseen) son Ricky. Jessie announces that she intends to commit suicide on the Saturday night when the women are home alone together, after she has had a talk with Thelma. The woman is not looking to be talked out of the act, but rather tells her mother so that she can explain and so that Thelma does not blame herself. The talk involves Jessie preparing her mother to live alone again, advising her about housekeeping matters, but she also has Thelma make her hot chocolate, offers to give her a manicure and gets to ask questions that she has always wanted to ask. Jessie has assumed the role of housekeeper for Thelma, partly because she has become housebound while her mother still goes out to visit her friend Agnes Fletcher (Sari Walker) and to see her son Dawson (Ed Berke), his wife Loretta (Carol Robbins) and their children, Melodie (Jennifer Roosendahl) and Kenny (Michael Kenworthy). Thelma says that when Dawson and his family come to her house, Jessie leaves the room. Jessie admits that she knows that her mother has allowed her to look after her in order to give her daughter something to do. This is suggested when we see Thelma sloppily leaving behind things as she walks around the house and Jessie picking up after her. But this assumed role is not enough for Jessie to keep on living: She says she is tired, hurt, sad, feels used, and is not having a good time and sees no reason for it get any better. After her daughter's announcement, Thelma goes through a series of reactions to the news—disbelief, shock, anger, trying to get her help by telephoning Dawson and a doctor, disapproval, reasoning, sarcasm, panic, provocation, sorrow and finally acceptance.

The epic conversation between the two women has Thelma reveal she has lied to Jessie about Agnes burning down houses and having a house full of birds and eating ocher twice a day, all to amuse her daughter. Thelma reveals that Agnes is scared of Jessie because of her corpse-like cold hands, although she does come to the house when the daughter is in the hospital. Thelma advises that she never loved her deceased farmer husband (Jessie's father) who always made insulting remarks. Thelma feels that Jessie understood the man better than she, since they used to have private talks together, though he called his daughter a runt and felt she never had a chance. Thelma realizes that Jessie would not be killing herself if her father were still alive and reveals that Cecil had a girlfriend. The biggest revelation is that Thelma has never told her daughter how she used to have fits when she was a child, and that she didn't tell her husband because then she would also have to tell him that he too had fits.

Thelma is given a sense of humor and some funny lines. These include telling Jessie "You're as normal as they come, for the most part"; to the news of Jess is going to shoot herself, "How am I supposed to act? Okay by me, sugar. Might try it myself"; to the idea that Ricky may now try killing: "Killing's okay. Mum did it." When she comments about the epileptics: "Oh that was some swell time sitting here with the two of you turning off and on like light bulbs some nights."

Bancroft's hair is by Marina Pedraza in a short wavy style colored a lighter shade of brown and with gray strands, and with it worn off her forehead sometimes in a side part. Her wardrobe by Bob Blackman consists of a colored dress with a pink cardigan, a slip, a white patterned nightgown and an apron. Bancroft also wears glasses. Some may consider the actress miscast as a simple, Southern-accented country woman, since she comes across as being too urban and sophisticated. Bancroft occasionally is too broad in her rural impression and her technique shows in moments like when she swallows a piece of candy as emphasis on a line, when she

Still for *'night, Mother* (1986).

reaches for the shoe box she thinks Jessie has the gun in, and to find it empty, or when she imitates Spacek's dropping three marshmallows into her hot chocolate. Bancroft is convincing expressing the mother's protective attitude toward her daughter, and she is touching when she begs her not to go. This is particularly impressive in the way the actress underplays. Bancroft's true nature seems to come across when she plays Thelma's anger, when she provokes Jessie or is being sarcastic. She is funny when describing how Thelma would watch her husband staring off into the sea.

Her best scene is perhaps at the climax. Bancroft is heartbreaking when Thelma bangs on Jessie's closed bedroom door, telling her how she never knew how unhappy she was and howls her daughter's name before the gun is heard to fire which signals her death.

The film premiered on September 5, 1986, at the Toronto International Film Festival and received a limited release on September 12. The tagline was "It happened in 1983. It was a rare and remarkable theatrical experience. Controversial. Provocative. And shocking. Now, two Academy Award-winning actresses make the Pulitzer Prize–winning play the motion picture event of the year." Janet Maslin in the *New York Times* wrote that Bancroft initially seemed much too broad. Also in the *Times*, Vincent Canby later lambasted it and wrote that Bancroft's performance was busy. When asked by a Hollywood columnist if she was upset she didn't receive an Oscar nomination for *'night, Mother*, Bancroft quipped that she should have gotten one just for memorizing all those lines.

Interviewed by the *Times* (August 10, 1986), Bancroft revealed that she earned a third of her usual fee for *'night, Mother* and said it was so low-budget that she reused her paper towels twice and paid for her own speech teacher. The actress also said that she couldn't shake her character. She never got out of her costume between scenes and could hardly drop the accent. Bancroft related her character in *'night, Mother* to her husband's mother who was in the hospital for an operation at the age of 68 and called out "Mama, Mama" under the anesthetic. The actress said she bonded with Spacek doing the film, with Spacek saying that her favorite movie of all time was *The Miracle Worker*. Spacek described Bancroft as a powerhouse. For the film, Bancroft wore only the minimum makeup required by the camera and was willing and eager for the plainness of her character to show through. The actress was said to be very different from the frail, aging stage Thelma of Anne Pitoniak, who was nine years older than her film replacement. Bancroft said that she herself had a very strong face and had to make it softer for the part. She wanted to make herself fade so she cut and bleached her hair and tweezed and bleached her eyebrows.

Writer Marsha Norman said that Pitoniak's age gave the audience a concern for her physical health. With Bancroft playing the part, Thelma was still a vibrant and vigorous woman and the audience had a new awareness that what happened to her could happen to someone at the peak of their life, as opposed to someone who was nearer the end of it. Norman advised that it was harder for Bancroft to become her character than it was for Spacek. She felt that Bancroft was a smart person and she would ask questions as to how Thelma could make the mistake of saying what she should know to be a dangerous thing given the situation. Norman also advised that as soon as the actors left the set, Sissy would come out of Jessie, but Bancroft "lived further away."

In the May 1987 *Films and Filming*, interviewee Bancroft said she was proud to have done *'night, Mother* regardless of the fact that it didn't make a penny. She felt it was a great film and lamented that if a film didn't make money, it was seen to have no value in the U.S. Bancroft said the part was the most exhausting of her recent roles. There were more lines for herself and Spacek than Hamlet and they were on screen every minute. She said she and Spacek spoke from the beginning of the day until the end, and it was worse than being a telephone operator.

Bancroft, Oscar-nominated for Best Actress for *Agnes of God*, attended the 58th Annual Academy Awards on March 24, 1986. Just before presenter F. Murray Abraham announced the winner, he said that he "considered this woman the greatest actress in the English language." The camera showed Bancroft rolling her eyes in reaction to this comment, before Abraham announced the name of Geraldine Page.

Bancroft's next film *84 Charing Cross Road* (1987) was directed by David Jones from a screenplay by Hugh Whitemore, based on the play by James Roose-Evans which was based on the book by Helene Hanff. The book had already been adapted by Whitemore into a 75-minute drama for the BBC-TV series *Play for Today* (November 4, 1975), with American actress Anne Jackson playing Hanff. The play was staged on Broadway by Roose-Evans and ran at Nederlander Theatre from December 7, 1982, to February 27, 1983. The part of Hanff was played by Ellen Burstyn. One source claims that one day when the Brookses were relaxing at the beach on Fire Island, a man came up to the actress and gave her a copy of the Hanff book. She fell in love with it and it was claimed that Brooks bought the screen rights for Bancroft as an anniversary present. The actress called this claim "lies" in her BBC talk show interview with Terry Wogan. Burstyn said she learned soon after the play closed that Brooks had bought the rights for his wife as a birthday present. The film was shot from on location in England, including the Lee International Studios and the Shepperton Studios, and in New York.

The story centered on Hanff, a New York script-reader and television writer who lives in a one-room apartment. She has a transatlantic business correspondence with Frank Doel (Anthony Hopkins), the bookseller who works at Marks & Co., 84 Charing Cross Road in London. This correspondence takes place from 1949 to approximately 1968, when Frank dies. Helene receives a letter from the new company's secretary on January 8, 1969, telling her of Frank's death. The narrative has Helene attempt to travel to London to see Frank and his company for Queen Elizabeth's coronation, but her plans are thwarted when the writer has to have her teeth capped instead which absorbs her budget. When she is finally able to get there, the shop appears to have been abandoned, since there is no staff, just remnants of their files.

Bancroft and Hopkins previously appeared in *The Elephant Man*. The top-billed actress has two hairstyles by Jean-Paul, one a shoulder-length straight style with bangs, the other a short-cropped wavy style worn off her forehead. Her costumes are by Jane Greenwood and she wears glasses in both time periods. Director Jones occasionally uses the device of her talking directly to camera, either for letter recitals or as if she is speaking to Frank directly, which helps to establish an intimacy with the audience. This device and Helene's generosity of spirit help to make her likable, as does the actress when she is funny. She has a moment when Helene calls the dog in the park where she switches from a sweet voice saying "Come on" to her hard voice, saying, "Let's go home." Bancroft's reciting a John Donne sermon from a book is a bit too actressy for a character who is a writer, and Jones doesn't provide a satisfying comic payoff when Helene is mistaken for a demonstrator at the Columbia University student sit-in. The scene in which Helene makes the decision to go to London is perhaps Bancroft's finest in the film, and we see her transition from sorrow to determination.

The film was released on February 13, 1987, with the tagline "A big love affair that began in a little bookstore." *Variety* wrote that Bancroft gave a fantastic performance, bringing Helene alive in all her dimensions and in the process creating one of her most memorable characterizations. Vincent Canby in the *New York Times* said that the actress performed bluntly.

Bancroft, interviewed by *Good Morning America* about the film, said that what appealed to her about it was that Helene was such a rare human being to be able to get so much from books (Bancroft loved books too). The actress reported that David Jones and she made a silent agreement where he would be allowed what he wanted to do and she would be allowed what she wanted to do. They rarely questioned each other and had complete faith and trust in each other.

The actress' interview on *Wogan* may be one of interviewer Terry Wogan's most awkward. This was said to have been caused by the fact that Bancroft was only told that the show was being broadcast live moments before she left the green room. In his autobiography, *Terry Wogan—Is It Me*, he wrote that he first met her in makeup. Bancroft was weeping and shaking and stammering through tears, and told him that she didn't want to be there. The actress didn't do live interviews. In an interview, Wogan claims he suggested she count to ten before walking onto the set. His autobiography denies he made this suggestion, though he does confirm that Bancroft did count as she descended the set steps and went to her seat, perhaps like a mantra. Wogan wrote he had managed after ten minutes in the dressing room with her to stop her crying, but she had become more catatonic than calm. Whatever Bancroft had done to prepare herself had proven ineffective. She reportedly went on to answer only yes and no to all Wogan's questions. He wrote an article for *The Telegraph* (June 12, 2005) in which he said he couldn't get a word out of her. However, in an article in *The Sun* (February 1, 2016), Wogan recalled that Bancroft did speak. An excerpt on YouTube.com shows the actress looking terrified as she enters the set, and Wogan counts as he escorts her to her seat. Bancroft does give more than just yes and no answers to his questions, commenting that she doesn't find interviews easy. However you can understand Wogan's predicament since, although the actress speaks, her answers aren't conducive to a conversation. She really makes the interviewer work.

Elsewhere, Bancroft commented that she was initially skeptical that the play could be made into a film. It didn't seem right, certainly not at the time that people would send letters back and forward. Bancroft was concerned that she had no scenes where she talked to those she wrote to or those that wrote to her. She thought it needed more action, like someone pulling out a gun or having a car crash. But her doubts were dispelled and the actress became a wholehearted supporter of the project. Bancroft only had two weeks in between the making of her last two films. This violated one of the actress' professional rules that she would have a lengthy break between assignments. However the financing for *84 Charing Cross Road* proved to be troublesome and the final schedule was partly dictated by the availability of Anthony Hopkins.

The actress was offered a play in Britain, which she declined because she preferred to have a summer with Max. She went to Fire Island with her 14-year-old, her husband and her two sisters and their children. Max Brooks reported that it was Bancroft's idea to buy a beach shack on the island and the one next to it so that her sisters and their children could spend the summers together. They spent three months out of every year there. No cars were allowed in the area and their television didn't work very well.

Bancroft appeared at the 44th Golden Globe Awards, held on January 31, 1987 at the Beverly Hilton Hotel. She was nominated for Best Actress in a Motion Picture Drama for her performance in 'night, mother. The award was given to Marlee Matlin for the romance *Children of a Lesser God* (1986).

In her *Good Morning America* interview, Bancroft said that she had always chosen to be in the position where she could pick her scripts. She would not do anything that she didn't love, even if that meant that she didn't eat for a year because she would just wait until the right thing came along. She said there was also a price to be paid for it, being out of work a lot. Although Bancroft had directed and produced, she didn't agree that she had power in Hollywood. She said this was because she didn't speak her mind in public. The actress only spoke her mind in her house, the only place where she felt she had complete control, but not in every room. Asked again about Mel Brooks at home, Bancroft said he was wondrously funny and there was a side of him that the public never got to see. He could make her laugh at times when she didn't expect it, like when they were in the middle of an argument. The couple didn't get involved with each other's work. They made a pact not to work when the other was working so that they could be available to hug and kiss each other during those times.

In 1987, the Brookses moved to a new address in Los Angeles, a 12,000 square foot Spanish-style house in La Mesa Drive in Pacific Palisades. It towered over the others in the exclusive neighborhood and had an indoor swimming pool. The Brookses also had a getaway home in Malibu as well as a co-op apartment on Manhattan's East 89th Street, beachfront condos on Fisher Island off Miami, and various residences in Southampton, Long Island.

The *New York Times* reported on April 8, 1988, that she was to appear in the Mel Brooks film *The Fortune Teller*, to be produced by Merv Griffin. It was never made. Bancroft next appeared in the romantic comedy *Torch Song Trilogy* (1988). The screenplay was by Harvey Fierstein, based on his play, and it was directed by Paul Bogart. Jewish drag queen Arnold Beckoff (Fierstein) works at New York's Club East 4th as Virginia Hamn and lives in Brooklyn. The narrative covers his life from 1952 to 1980. The play came from three short plays entitled *The International Stud, Fugue in a Nursery* and *Widows and Children First!* Together they made a four-hour evening which was edited down to two hours for the film version. Fierstein originally wanted Amy Heckerling to direct, partly because she had gone to the same high school as he did, but decided against her because he didn't want to be able to boss her around which he feared he might. He said he needed someone who was able to slap him around and make sure he did what was needed to be done, and that was Bogart.

Bancroft played Arnold's mother, Ma Beckoff, a teacher who moved to Florida after she was widowed. Ma disapproves of Arnold being gay. Her reaction to the Young Arnold (Benji Schulman) caught in her closet wearing her clothes and lipstick changes from amusement to concern. Although she claims not to judge Arnold's lifestyle, she actually does. Consequently, he does not confide in her about the murder of his 27-year-old lover, model Alan Simon (Matthew Broderick), and how he has adopted a 15-year-old gay boy named David (Eddie Castrodad). Ma cannot accept the comparison Arnold makes between his loss of Alan and the death of his father Jacob (Edgar Small), to whom Ma had been married for 35 years. In an argument, Ma tells Arnold, "You cheated me out of your life and then blamed me for not being there." Because she cannot accept any of her son's relationships, it is doubtful that Arnold had another choice except to exclude her.

This is apparent at the conclusion, when she leaves when she hears that David has the radio play the Ella Fitzgerald song "This Time the Dream's on Me" as a tribute to Arnold's love for Alan and a love message from a son to his father.

Despite's Ma's intolerance, she is still funny when being sarcastic, when calling Arnold "Some big shot," and when she tells the men on the bus who wouldn't give her a seat, "Thanks to you gentlemen, I now have varicose veins." The play describes Ma as a woman who is 60-ish and "a fighter."

Bancroft is top-billed, even above Fierstein who plays the leading role. Her hair by Morey Greenberg is in a shoulder-length brunette style in the opening scene (a flashback to Arnold's childhood). After that, her hair has gray temples or gray strands at the front. Her clothes are by Colleen Atwood and include hair ribbons, a flower-patterned orange robe and pastel-colored dresses. She sometimes wears glasses. The actress over-gestures which is acceptable in the context of her playing a Jewish woman, and she makes Ma likable despite her often offensive behavior. Bancroft is especially funny when glaring at Arnold at Jacob's funeral service over him bringing Alan and in the scene in the hired car when she and Arnold argue when they go the cemetery. Perhaps her best scene is the extended one where Ma and Arnold have a long argument in his apartment. Bancroft is particularly good in showing Ma's transition from yelling in anger to crying in regret over doing so and she is teary when she assumes that Arnold is "throwing her out" because she cannot give him the respect he demands of her.

The film was released on December 14, 1988. Janet Maslin in the *New York Times* wrote that Bancroft played in a manner that might seem scenery-chewing in another context. Roger Ebert (*Chicago Sun-Times*) wrote that he had had reservations about Bancroft in some of her recent performances, because she tended to go over the top, but he believed her in this role.

Fierstein said that he received Hollywood offers for just the last act of the play. Herbert Ross who wanted to direct it with Richard Dreyfuss in the Arnold role. Fierstein decided to hold out for someone who wanted to do the whole piece. He reported that Bancroft got annoyed by Broderick sitting behind her and slurping a popsicle at a rehearsal for the scene in the funeral parlor after the death of Jacob. He was doing so because it was a very hot day but it so disturbed her that she demanded the actor not be allowed on the set when she was shooting after that. Her demand was met. Feirstein interpreted her response as the actress taking out Ma's emotions in the scene on the younger actor. He also reported that Bancroft got paid nothing to do the low-budget film. Fierstein had met the actress on *Garbo Talks*. Lumet rehearsed the screenplay like a play. Bancroft had seen Fierstein do the play on stage and during rehearsals they hung out and laughed a lot. He told her if he did the film version of *Torch Song Trilogy*, he wanted her to play Ma, and she agreed. Estelle Getty had played the part on stage. There was a discussion about casting her in the film, since she had attained fame after starring in the television comedy series *The Golden Girls*, but New Line Cinema preferred Bancroft. Another source claims that Fierstein told Getty when they were doing the stage play that if he could sell the movie rights, he wanted Bancroft to play Ma and she understood. Fierstein commented that he thought Getty would have been wonderful in the film and that her performance would have been very different from Bancroft's. Fierstein reported he would tease Bancroft and bite her legs in the makeup trailer and that this horseplay helped the actors cope with their job of presenting an ugly family relationship. He said they really liked each other and she always stayed emotionally available for their scenes, though Fierstein said she was perhaps a more Italian than Jewish mother. He reported that in the cemetery scene, Bancroft preferred to a wear a headscarf rather than a doily that his mother wore on her head, and that in the climactic apartment scenes she got so angry at him she nearly killed him 30 times. He said that this was evidence that she was an intense actress.

Bancroft's next film, writer-director Carl Reiner's *Bert Rigby, You're a Fool* (1989), starred Robert Lindsay, the British actor who got raves on both sides of the Atlantic for his performance as the Cockney turned heir in the musical *Me and My Girl*. Making his American film debut, Lindsay played a British coal miner song-and-dance man who wins an amateur-night contest and winds up in Hollywood.

The musical was filmed at the Lee International Studios in Shepperton and on location in England, and around Los Angeles. Lindsay goes to Hollywood to make a L.A. Gear shoe commercial and ends up as a gardener, handyman and butler for the millionaire film producer Captain I.I. Perlestein (Jackie Gayle). Bancroft played his wife Meredith, a former film dancer. She tells Bert that she appeared with Fred Astaire in *Royal Wedding* (1951) and *Silk Stockings* (1957). She is a flirtatious woman who we are told is having an affair with actor Jim Shirley (Corbin Bernsen) while he prepares to make a film for her husband. She wants to be unfaithful with Bert, but he declines because he has a girlfriend back home in Langmore. Meredith's neglected existence is also suggested by her having a toy dog which she carries around, with her husband either oblivious or unconcerned about her flirting with Bert in front of him. It is her association that allows Bert to be hired as the accent coach for Shirley, who is to play an Englishman in the new Perlestein film. However, the promised secondary role of a bartender in the film does not eventuate when his association with the Perlesteins ends.

Bancroft, seventh-billed, gets a "Special Appearance By" credit. She wears her hair in a puffy style with a white ribbon holding it back. Her clothes are by Ruth Myers. The actress sings two songs with Lindsay, "I'll See You Again" and "All of You" although it is apparent that her vocals are dubbed. We hear what appears to be Bancroft's real singing voice when Meredith reprises "All of You." She also dances with Lindsay to "All of You" although director Reiner has her movement upstaged by Bert's pratfalls. Bancroft uses a Brooklyn baby-voice for Meredith, pronouncing her "r" as "w," though the woman drops what is an apparent affectation when she flirts with Bert. Her reverse pretension, where she calls Bert "Bertram," may be a strategy that she has used to ensnare her husband or perhaps it is to suggest that she is a dumb aging chorus girl. There is a disconnect between the character and Bancroft, since she is not believable playing such a woman. She was nominated for the 1990 Worst Supporting Actress Razzie Award and was beaten by Brooke Shields for the action comedy *Cannonball Fever* (1989).

Released on February 24, 1989, *Bert Rigby* was not a box office success. On the February 23, 1989, *Good Morning, America*, Bancroft said she could tell from reading the script that the extent of her part was not anything that would be terribly good for her career. It was just something she wanted to do from somewhere in her insides that made her bubble and start dancing. The actress loved creating the part, taking what the author gave her and flying with it. She knew Reiner would allow her to do what she envisioned and then mold it for her a little bit so Bancroft had great fun with it. She said she and Lindsay had wonderful chemistry though she joked that on the outside they couldn't stand each other.

At this time there had been plans for Bancroft and Brooks to reunite for the crime comedy *I Love You to Death* (1990) with him directing her and Kevin Kline. Ultimately Lawrence Kasdan made the film and Tracey Ullman was be Kline's co-star. From November 16 to December 17, 1989, Bancroft appeared in the Manuel Puig play *Mystery of the Rose Bouquet* at Los Angeles' Mark Taper Forum. She portrayed an old, rich, autocratic patient in an Argentine psychiatric hospital. She suffers from depression after the death of her grandson in a car accident and is attended by a middle-aged nurse (Jane Alexander). Dan Sullivan in the *Los Angeles Times* wrote that Bancroft was too sharp and too involved with life to appear convincing as a depressed personality. He said there was also a slight problem with her Bronx accent, which the actress hadn't taken any trouble to modify. However the old lady's shrewdness was wonderfully conveyed and it was a sharp and entertaining performance. There was a plan to bring the production to Broadway in 1990 and Bancroft reportedly optioned it as a film.

The actress next appeared in the fantasy-romantic comedy *Love Potion No. 9* (1992), written by Dale Launer (inspired by the Jerry Leiber–Mike Stoller song) and directed by Launer. Paul Matthews (Tate Donovan), a nerdy biochemist, visits a gypsy palm reader, Madame Ruth (Bancroft) who sees that he does very badly with women and predicts he will have none in his life. To help him, Ruth gives Paul a sachet with a drop of potion no. 8, which she says will make women find him fascinating. She is shown to be unorthodox in her treatment of Paul, since to read his palm she first spits in it, and she also takes a Polaroid of it to show her sister.

Paul has no faith in the potion and throws the sachet away. Ruth's assessment of Paul's luck with women appears to be demonstrated when we see him rejected by Cheryl (Rebecca Staab), who doesn't like his clothes or car. Even when his friends get him a prostitute, Marisa (Mary Mara), he just talks with her. Paul seems better suited to his equally nerdy co-worker, comparative psycho-biologist Diane Farrow (Sandra Bullock), since they have the same apartment interior decorations and taste in music and literature. Diane has a ten-year sex-buddy, Gary Logan (Dale Midkiff), but no romantic partner and no real date in four years. She and Paul had had a lunch date four years previously but Diane put him off thinking she still had a chance with Gary.

The effectiveness of Ruth's potion becomes apparent when Paul's cat finds the sachet, licks it and is swamped by other cats after it meows. Paul tells Diane about the potion, which he describes as condensed liquid salt, and she tests it on two chimps. Paul and Diane learn that it will only work for four hours at a time. Needing to test it on humans, they volunteer themselves, and divide up the remainder of the potion as a throat spray. Both Paul and Diane find it effective with various strangers and their new experiences help to raise their self-confidence. Paul comes to realize that the woman he really wants is her. She seems to come to the same conclusion but then suddenly announces she is engaged to Gary. Paul learns that Ruth had given Gary a large container of undiluted potion no. 8 and he has used it on Diane. He obtains a vial of love potion no. 9, but she warns him that it will only work if she was once ever in love with him. Paul has to drink from the same cup in which he has placed the potion and then kiss her. Paul enlists Diane's friend Sally (Hillary Bailey-Smith) to give Diane a glass of champagne with the potion in it, but Gary intercepts it and drinks it. After trying to disrupt the wedding, Paul finally kisses Diane after she has married Gary. He thinks he has lost her, but Diane comes to Paul so that they can be together.

Bancroft is billed tenth and her gypsy clothes are by Timothy D'Arcy. She wears glasses, moves with a walking stick and speaks with a European accent. The film was released on November 13, 1992, with the taglines "Imagine if sex appeal came in a bottle" and "If you've got it—You get it!" Vincent Canby in the *New York Times* wrote that Bancroft supplied the only laugh.

In the early 1990s when Max left home, the actress suffered from empty-nest syndrome and wondered what she would do instead. She missed him terribly and her house became a different place without Max and his gang of guys coming over and jumping in the pool. There was a big void and later she would admit that she wouldn't ever overcome it. She thought she better try a couple of things and she let her agent know that she was available. This led to her appearance on the comedy TV series *Freddie & Max,* shot in London. The title characters were a researcher for Neptune television, Freddie Latham (Charlotte Coleman), and aging American movie and theater actress Maxine "Max" Chandler (Bancroft). Max, ensconced in a Savoy Hotel suite, is being paid to write her memoirs and she hires Freddie as her live-in personal assistant. Max has a white little dog called Ralphie which is both a stereotype of an actress' affectation and also an emotional support for a woman who has no husband. We are told that she had been married three times and that she is rich but also "spoiled, pampered and indolent." Since Max tells Freddie that the girl reminds her of herself, this sets up the dynamic to be both combative and sympathetic, with Max repeatedly firing and rehiring her. Freddie's efforts to write Max's memoirs are aided by visits by the actress' agent, a director, a former husband and her son. We also see Max act in a radio play of *The Importance of Being Earnest* as Lady Bracknell, make an appearance on the breakfast TV show *Good Morning Britain,* do a reading for a TV dog food commercial and a eulogy for a fellow actress.

The material is regrettably slight though there is an occasional funny line. Max tells Freddie that she was cast in her first Broadway show after the director mistook her for Kim Stanley. By the time she admitted the truth, she was already sleeping with him so it didn't matter. Another has her comment on the rumor about her bisexual actor husband being found in bed with his stunt double, which she believed because she thought he would have loved the idea of screwing himself. Referring to the commercial she is offered, she tells her agent that when one has done 23 movies and has a couple of Tonys, "you don't expect to screen test for soup mix."

In all but one episode, Bancroft's role is more of a supporting one. Max comments that she had played Mother Courage and that she has a couple of Tonys. Bancroft wears a shoulder-length hair style with gray strands at the front with the dark color at the back, and she alternates wearing it tied back and loose. Her

Portrait for *Freddie & Max* (November 12, 1990–?).

clothes by Jennie Tate suggest wealth and an actress' mild flamboyance. Over the end credits, we hear Bancroft sing "Let's Call the Whole Thing Off" with Coleman. Given that she plays an actress, her grand manner and large gestures have context and is in contrast with Coleman's bland ordinariness. However, Bancroft's smiling delivery of conceited charm becomes monotonous. The show lasted six episodes. After she had finished it, Bancroft made up her mind that it was not for her because it wasn't something she could pour herself into. It was something she could do off the top of her head and therefore she was not interested.

Bancroft had a cameo in writer-director Andrew Bergman's romantic comedy *Honeymoon in Vegas* (1992). This was filmed from August 19 to November 8, 1991, on location in Las Vegas and Hawaii and at Columbia Pictures in Hollywood. The story: New York private detective Jack Singer (Nicolas Cage) takes his schoolteacher girlfriend Betsy Nolan (Sarah Jessica Parker) to Las Vegas to get married but loses her in a poker game to professional gambler Tommy Korman (James Caan). Bancroft is not listed in the film's opening credits and is fifth-billed in the end credits. She played Jack's mother Bea, who is only in one scene. Dying in a hospital in 1987, she has her son promise her that he will never marry. Although this promise seems to validate the claims that Bea is "crazy" and "strange," it is perhaps Jack's breaking it that leads to his troubles in the following five years. Bancroft wears a hospital gown and has gray hair, and widens her eyes to indicate her death. Bea is also mentioned later in the narrative as Jack says he has dreams about her being naked.

The film was released on August 28, 1992. It was praised by Joseph McBride in *Variety*, Vincent Canby in the *New York Times* and Roger Ebert in the *Chicago Sun-Times*. A box office success, it was later made into a Broadway musical with a book by Andrew Bergman and lyrics by Jason Robert Brown. The Bea character even had her own song, "Never Get Married." Bancroft described her role as a one-page part, but said it was a very funny situation.

She next appeared in the romantic drama *Mr. Jones* (1993), filmed from November 11, 1991, to February 21, 1992, on location in San Diego and at the Sony Pictures Studios. The title character (Richard Gere), a bipolar manic depressive 35-year-old former pianist and carpenter, is treated at the California Marvista Institute mental hospital by psychiatrist Elizabeth "Libbie" Bowen (Lena Olin) who falls in love with him. Bancroft, third-billed, plays the head of the institute, Dr. Catherine Holland. Her hair (by Laura Connolly) is a gray color at the front and brown at the back in a medium-length style. Bancroft's wardrobe is by Rita Ryack. The actress has little to do in the film. In one scene, Catherine addresses a group of visitors to the institute's psychiatric emergency room and speaks about the unofficial policy being medicate, vacate. She then asks if that sounds cold-blooded and answers, it *is*.

The film was released on October 8, 1993, with the tagline "Everything That Makes Him Dangerous Makes Her Love Him Even More." Janet Maslin (the *New York Times*) wrote that Bancroft was predictably crisp. The film was not a box office hit.

Bancroft was inducted into the Theater Hall of Fame in a ceremony that took place at the Gershwin Theater on January 27, 1992. Movie-wise, she next appeared in a remake of the French-Italian action thriller *Nikita* (1990). This new action crime drama, titled *The Assassin* (aka *Point of No Return*), was filmed from March 30 to June 22, 1992, on location in New Orleans, Los Angeles and Washington. Bridget Fonda starred as 23-year-old Maggie Hayward, a feral drug addict sentenced to death for murder but given a

Still for *Mr. Jones* (1993).

second chance by the government in Washington. She is recruited to be a female operative. Part of her training is done by Amanda (Bancroft; the role was played by Jeanne Moreau in the original film). Amanda gives lessons in speaking, walking and dining etiquette and these are presumably done to help Maggie fit into society so that she can fulfill assignments. One strategy offered is that when she gets angry, Maggie should smile and make an offhand comment like "I never did mind about the little things." This line gets a payoff at the end. Maggie is employed to impersonate Angela (Olivia D'Abo), the girlfriend of Fahd Bahktiar (Richard Romanus); he has been peddling nuclear information to the Arabs and is to be eliminated. When Angela is being handled by Maggie and her assistant Beth (Lorraine Toussaint), the job is bungled, and Victor the Cleaner (Harvey Keitel) is brought in to clean up. When he kills Beth, Maggie smiles and says the line to repress her feelings. Maggie seeks the advice of Amanda, the only person she says has been nice to her in her training, about how to get out of her position as an operative. Amanda tells her that the idea of leaving is a possibility that has never entered her mind, so Maggie turns to her superior, Bob (Gabriel Byrne), to help her achieve this goal.

Bancroft's hair, by Vivian McAteer, is worn gray in a straight neck-length style and with a side part, though it is also seen tied back. Her wardrobe is by Marlene Stewart. Bancroft speaks French in the film, and she gives a great look of disgust when Maggie swears at her.

The film was released on March 19, 1993, with the tagline "The Government gave her a choice. Death. Or life as an assassin. Now, there's no turning back." It was praised by Todd McCarthy in *Variety*, Janet Maslin in the *New York Times*, and Roger Ebert. According to Maslin, Bancroft was very well cast and combined a maternal smile with her best Mrs. Robinson whip-cracking mode. The film was lambasted by Peter Travers in *Rolling Stone*.

The actress advised that it was not a great but a very nice part. In his book *I'll Be in My Trailer*, director John Badham wrote that Bancroft approached her roles from an emotional level and then was methodical about what she prepared. She was invited to view the dailies but declined, saying she no longer liked to look at herself on screen. Badham wrote that the actress' beauty was one of great soul and depth. Reassuring and complimenting her could not defeat the sadness that enveloped her.

She next appeared in the comic drama *Mrs. Cage* for the PBS series *American Playhouse*. The show was originally planned for the fall of 1991 but the schedule was pushed back to accommodate Bancroft's schedule. It was an adaptation of a two-character play by Nancy Barr, which (directed by Barr) had run in September 1990 at the Two Lights Studio in Santa Monica. From February 5 to 23, 1997, it ran on Broadway at the Kaufman Theatre. For the TV version, Bancroft enacted the title role, a housewife who committed a spur-of-the-moment murder in a supermarket parking lot. Hector Elizondo played a policeman to whom she confessed. The teleplay was by Barr and it was directed by Robert Allan Ackerman.

Lillian Cage (Bancroft) is a housewife in her late 50s with a secret crush on Billy (Jack Noseworthy), the teenager who bags her groceries. When the boy is shot by Phyllis Dean (Tracy Brooks Swope) at the supermarket, she takes the gun and shoots the woman, then goes to the police station. As Mrs. Cage is questioned about the shocking killing, the drama reveals her rage and sense of emptiness which makes the murder seem tragically logical. She is a bewildered woman who has seen the world change dramatically in her 36 years of marriage to a successful lawyer. She has spent her days taking care of a home, meticulously starching and ironing her husband's shirts, and raising a daughter. Her ambitious daughter is now contemptuous of her, and her husband is indifferent. The person she kills in the parking lot is an abrasive career woman. Mrs. Cage is at a dead end in her life, with few options, and her life, she feels, is irrelevant.

Broadcast on May 20, 1992, it was praised by Tony Scott in *Variety*, who wrote that Bancroft gave a stunning performance and artful delineation of the character. John J. O'Connor of the *New York Times* said she gave a sharply etched yet delicately shaded performance that was utterly convincing.

Interviewed by Susan King (*The Los Angeles Times*, May 17, 1992), Bancroft said that the rage of Mrs. Cage didn't have to do with women or age or upbringing. People had more rage than they knew and she was one of them. Sometimes in life there were episodes that got you in touch with it and she just happened to be more in touch with it than other people. Bancroft also said that it was difficult to find good parts these days. She said they were making movies for children because it was children who went to the movies. The actress confessed that it had been tough for her to juggle all her careers, being married to Brooks for 28 years and being the mother to Max, now a college sophomore. Her life and career had now changed since she realized it was time for Max to learn how to lead his own life. One thing she said she would never do again was direct a movie, which she admitted to being one of the worst experiences of her life. The actress thought you should try everything because that is how you learn. She had no plans to return to the stage. To *New York Times* interviewer Bernard Weintraub, she said in an article published on May 18, 1992, that she understood Lillian Cage, and the tale of a woman in the grip of turmoil seemed to resonate personally with her as well as professionally. The character's cry that she thought herself irrelevant also resonated with the actress because she said people called her that all the time. They said her work was unimportant at the moment because what they wanted was Arnold Schwarzenegger. Bancroft acknowledged that while her career may have seemed impressive, her age had plainly diminished her choices. Film roles were relatively sparse. The actress laughed when asked if it was difficult for an actress in Hollywood not to be Julia Roberts' age of 24. She said it was very difficult in every field and in every part of life not to be Roberts' age any more. Bancroft admitted that she didn't care much if the work was in television or the movies, and that most of the scripts she saw were just not good.

10

Neil Simon's Broadway Bound

The actress returned to American television for *Neil Simon's Broadway Bound* (1992). This ABC Productions drama had a screenplay by Simon based on his play and was directed by Paul Bogart. The play had run at the Broadhurst Theatre from December 4, 1986, to September 25, 1988, and was directed by Gene Saks. Linda Lavin, who played Kate, won the Best Actress Tony Award, and the play was nominated for the 1987 Pulitzer Prize. The play was the third in Simon's trilogy about Eugene Morris Jerome, which had begun with *Brighton Beach Memoirs* and continued with *Biloxi Blues*. The character of Kate had been originated by Elizabeth Franz on stage in *Brighton Beach Memoirs* and was played by Blythe Danner in the 1986 film. The character did not appear in either the stage or screen versions of *Biloxi Blues*.

Broadway Bound is set in the Jerome household in Brighton Beach, New York, in February of 1948. Living in the house is 55-year-old ladies raincoat cutter Jack (Jerry Orbach) and Kate (Bancroft); their sons, 22-year-old stockroom worker Eugene (Cory Parker) and Gimbels boy clothing salesman Stanley (Jonathan Silverman); and Kate's father Ben (Hume Cronyn). Kate is around 50 years old and has been married to Jack for 34 years. Kate cares for her father and her sons, cooking and cleaning. Eugene will describe her as having a hard life with sentiment knocked out of her, but she shows pleasure in the success of her boys. He says that she will bask in their later success, and while she has an unhappy romantic life with Jack, she considers herself a lucky woman because she once danced with George Raft. Ben tells Eugene how Kate at 15 danced at the Primrose Ballroom, where she won cups and danced with Raft when he was known as the best ballroom dancer in New York and before he became a movie star. The possibility of her becoming a professional dancer was dashed when she burned her back in a shop fire, with the injury making her unable to walk for a year. Kate also met Jack at the Primrose. She tells him she knows he is unhappy and no longer loves his wife. Kate admits that she and Jack have not been together as a man and wife for a long time, and he confesses to having had an affair with Audrey, which is now over. Kate assumes that the qualities Jack attributes to this woman, of being refined and educated, do not apply to her, and this leads her to say, "You stay with me 'cause she won't have you. I got some bargain." She knows that he has lied about not seeing Audrey again and this leads Kate to warn him that if he sees the woman again, he can never come back to the family. This will prove to be prophetic as Jack does leave Kate and never returns, remarrying after two years. Kate says she can cope with Jack having a sexual affair but she cannot forgive him having feelings for another woman. He claims that his affair is non-sexual, that Audrey is just a friend. Later we learn that the woman has not long to live. Jack may leave Kate to be temporarily with Audrey, but he stays away for other reasons. Even before he leaves, his relationship with Kate is damaged: She refuses to speak directly to him and sends messages via her sons, although it appears she still shares a bed with him. Kate will tell Ben she expected Jack to leave. Her lack of emotional response when it finally happens suggests it is a relief for her and ends her suffering.

Kate's life is supported by Ben, since he predicts Jack leaving her. Ben decides for this reason that he must stay living with his daughter. He chooses to do so rather than accept the offer of his other daughter, Blanche (Michele Lee), to live in Florida. Kate also declines her sons' offer to move to Manhattan after they get writing jobs on *The Phil Silvers Show*. This success follows a 30-minute comedy radio sketch the boys wrote. In the sketch, comedian Chubby Waters (Jack Carter) visits the Pitkin family of Coney Island. Mrs. Pitkin (Marilyn Cooper) may sounds like a stereotypical Jewish woman, but Jack recognizes her as a parody of Kate. Kate says the character reminds her of someone but she can't think who, and perhaps blindly says she liked the sketch and is proud of her sons. Jack is angry and ashamed, feeling that they have made fun of their family.

Top-billed Bancroft's costumes are by Rita Riggs. Director Bogart has a one-take shot of Bancroft walking through the rooms of her house, filmed from the exterior windows, and he gives her a long shot as she smokes on the back porch. At the end, Kate retells the story of the night she danced with Raft. While Bancroft delivers the monologue well and underplays, the foxtrot she does with her son to "It Had to Be You" on the radio is a letdown. This is because Bogart photographs it badly, having a close-up of their feet, a shot where their legs are not seen, and then an odd aerial view of the couple.

The film was broadcast on March 23, 1992. It received a theatrical release in the United Kingdom, Australia, Germany and France. Jeremy Gerard in *Variety* said that Bancroft beautifully managed the crucial luminosity in the Raft monologue. Hume Cronyn won the Outstanding Supporting Actor in a Miniseries or Special Emmy Award, and the show was nominated for Outstanding Directing, Outstanding Individual Achievement in Writing, Outstanding Supporting Actor for Jerry Orbach and Outstanding Supporting Actress for Bancroft.

She next appeared in a supporting role in the mystery thriller *Malice* (1993). This had a screenplay by Aaron Sorkin and Scott Frank (based on a story by Sorkin and Jonas McCord) and was directed by Harold Becker. The film was a remake of the made-for-TV movie *The Operation* (1990). The new film was shot from October 3, 1992, to January 14, 1993, on locations in Massachusetts and at the Culver Studios in Hollywood. Massachusetts Westley College dean Andy Sapian (Bill Pullman) and his wife, art teacher and hospital volunteer Tracy (Nicole Kidman), are trying to have a baby but after a medical emergency, her fetus of four weeks is aborted by St. Agnes surgeon Dr. Jed Hill (Alec Baldwin) and her ovaries removed when he finds them damaged. Tracy sues and wins a settlement of $20 million, since it is reported that Jed had been drinking before operating. She leaves Andy, whom she blames for giving Jed permission to perform the surgery. Bancroft played Mrs. Kennsinger, whom Tracy had told Andy had died 12 years prior. He tracks her down and Mrs. Kennsinger, while shown to be a drunk, reveals that her daughter is a confidence trickster who has run an insurance scam. Mrs. Kennsinger reports that the family were all scammers, and shows him a card trick as evidence of her own ability. She also tells of Tracy's past. Andy discovers that Tracy and Jed are lovers. She turns against Jed, killing him when he learns that she has improvised the idea of being pregnant to their plan. Tracy is caught by Andy and Detective Dana Harris (Bebe Neuwirth) when she attempts to kill Billy (Michael Hall), a neighbor they've been told was a witness.

Fourth-billed Bancroft wears her hair (by Judy Cory) in a wavy fashion, colored a mix of brown and blonde and gray, and won in a bun. Her wardrobe by Michael Kaplan is a blue nightgown over what appears to be a white negligee and a blue cardigan. Bancroft uses a Boston accent and swears to show the character is drunk and bitter. She expresses anger and contempt at how gullible Andy has been. Her best moment is her response to Andy telling her that she is drunk: "You're stupid."

The film opened on October 1, 1993, with the taglines "Her doctor wasn't playing God. He thought he was God," "See it before someone tells you the secret!," "Deception. Betrayal. Murder. Some things you never see coming," and "A thriller from the Director of *Sea of Love*. Vincent Canby in the *New York Times* said she was super in a very small but vivid one-scene set-piece. Peter Travers in *Rolling Stone* wrote that she had an Oscar-begging cameo. It was a box office success.

At the 65th Annual Academy Awards, Bancroft and Dustin Hoffman presented the awards for Best Original Screenplay and Best Adapted Screenplay. They were broadcast live from New York in the Russian Tea Room. Bancroft scored applause from the audience after pronouncing the Italian names for the novel and film sources for *Scent of a Woman* (1992), which made her laugh. Hoffman gave her the envelope with the name of the winner but she handed it back to him, saying, "You were supposed to do this one." The award was given to Ruth Prawler Jhabvala for *Howards End* (1992), based on the E.M. Forster novel. Bancroft and Hoffman accepted the award on the writer's behalf since she was unable to appear at the ceremony. At one point, the couple stared at each other and Hoffman asked Bancroft if she was trying to seduce him, recalling the line from *The Graduate*. To this, she replied, "Not any more," which makes both the audience and themselves laugh. Hoffman hugged Bancroft, and she said, "Are we having fun."

Bancroft contributed to Michael F. Jacobson's book *Cooking with the Stars: Healthy, Delicious Recipes from Celebrities' Own Kitchens,* published by the Center for Science in the Public Interest in November 1993. Her recipes included Tomato Veggie-Sauce, Garbanzo Stew and Millie Italiano's Stuffed Peppers.

The actress next appeared in the made-for-TV war drama *Oldest Living Confederate Widow Tells All* (1994). This had a teleplay by Joyce Eliason based on the novel by Allan Gurganus, and was directed by Ken Cameron. The movie was shot on location in Madison and Milledgeville, Georgia. Lucy Honicut Marsden is played as a 99- and then a 100-year-old by Bancroft. Lucy tells her life story in flashbacks: Lucy (played in her younger years by Diane Lane) lives in Falls, North Carolina, and the narrative covers her childhood, marriage to Captain Marsden (Donald Sutherland), the birth of her six children, his death and her eventual residence in a retirement home. Lucy's life as an older woman has parallels with her younger self, where she befriends an unpopular person, Etta Pell (Gwen Verdon), and also has an unlikely romantic partner, Prof. Taw (E.G. Marshall). Unlike others in the home, Lucy retains a mental agility even when she is physically limited by being in a wheelchair. She still has an interest in sex while the professor states that he does not. When her birthday is celebrated with a town ceremony, Lucy gives a speech where she tells how her life was about her children. Although they are by then all deceased, she retains a positive attitude and hope.

Bancroft's hair by Darlene Brumfield is a white long wig, which she wears off her forehead and sometimes in a bun, and once in a plait. Her wardrobe (by Van Broughton Ramsey) is mostly pallid pastels, although she dresses more colorfully for her birthday. Bancroft uses a Southern accent and her hard voice when she is angry. Bancroft is successful when showing anger, for example when she is insulted by the professor, and she makes it equally funny. While the teleplay has the clichéd awakening from a nightmare scenario for the older Lucy, the actress adds anger to her memory which redeems it. Director Cameron uses cutaways of the attending audience at Lucy's birthday speech, which dilutes its effectiveness.

The show was broadcast on May 1 and 3, 1994, with a running time of 240 minutes. Patricia O'Connell in *Variety* wrote that Bancroft picked up effortlessly from where Lane left off. It won Emmy Awards for Cicely Tyson as Best Supporting Actress in a Miniseries or Special, and for Art Direction, Costume Design and Hairstyling. The show's other Emmy nominations included Outstanding Miniseries, Music and Bancroft for Supporting Actress in a Miniseries or a Special. The Allan Gurganus novel was later adapted into a one-woman play that ran on Broadway for only one night (November 17, 2003), at the Longacre Theatre, with Ellen Burstyn as Lucy.

She next appeared in a Great Performances/BBC-TV Production/Thirteen WNET drama, Paddy Chayefsky's *The Mother*. This was a remake of the April 4, 1954, *Philco Television Playhouse* broadcast which was directed by Delbert Mann and starred Cathleen Nesbitt in the title role. The remake was filmed at the Lifetime Studios on Astoria, New York, and the director was Simon Curtis. The mother of the title, Mrs. Fanning (Bancroft), is a recent widow who lives alone in a Bronx apartment in 1954. She wants to work but keeps being fired from sewing shop operator jobs. She goes for another one at Tiny Tots Sportswear though her daughter Annie (Joan Cusack) wants her to move into her apartment with her husband and children. Mrs. Fanning resists her daughter's offer because she believes that work is the meaning of her life. Now that her three children have grown up and are all married and her husband has died, she thinks it is even more important to keep busy. Mrs. Fanning is compared in the narrative with two other mature women who sit in the park all day. Despite her losing the new job, she will continue to try and find work, since she tells Annie that if she lives with her she will have nothing to do. Mrs. Fanning was a sewer before she married and she then spent 40 years helping her husband work in a grocery store. However, there was a period when he worked as a house painter and it seemed that was when she was a housewife and raised her children. There is also an inconsistency about her husband since Mrs. Fanning says he died one month ago but Annie says her mother has lived alone for eight years. Additionally the issue of the attacks Mrs. Fanning reportedly has, one of which cost her a job appointment, is something that would seem to mean she shouldn't be working, but the plot point is dropped.

Top-billed Bancroft wears her hair in a short gray style with white strands at the front and a hair clip. The actress' hair being gray is a plot point: Women who work in the sewing shop advise her to dye it to stay employable since women with gray hair are considered old and no longer useful. Bancroft's wardrobe by Jane Greenwood consists of only one outfit, a white lace-collared black dress with a gray overcoat and red hat. She speaks with an Irish accent and underplays for the first third, since the character is said to be depressed, except for when she yells on the telephone to the super to get heat in her apartment. The actress' best moments are perhaps when Mrs. Fanning has a series of telephone conversations with her children and she tries to choke back her emotion which suggests that she is lonely. Bancroft does the laughing-changing-to-crying trick, and her sobbing over parceling out her furniture to Annie creates empathy. Director Curtis gives the actress a lovely close-up when Mrs. Fanning travels on the bus home after having tried to sleep in Annie's apartment but realizing she would rather be in her own home.

The show premiered at the Museum of Television and Radio on October 5, 1994, then broadcast on October 24. John Leonard in *New York Magazine* wrote that Bancroft was splendid.

Bancroft next appeared in the romantic comedy *How to Make an American Quilt*, filmed from October 27, 1994, to February 6, 1995, on location in Ventura County and Redlands, Fillmore and Banning, California and at Universal. Twenty-six-year-old Berkeley student Finn (Winona Ryder) visits the home of her great aunt Gladiola "Glady" Joe (Bancroft) in Grasse, California, to write her thesis on women's handiwork in tribal cultures. Glady accommodates a group of women with a quilting bee, and they work on a new piece for Finn's wedding to Sam (Dermot Mulroney). The quilt presents the love stories of the women who make it and the narrative is a tapestry of their backstories, which include Glady's sister Hycianth aka Hy (Ellen Burstyn) who had an affair with Glady's husband Arthur (Rip Torn). Glady creates a wall sculpture in the laundry from the pieces of porcelain figurines she has smashed in her anger as a shrine to her unhappiness, which she later demolishes as a metaphor for her forgiveness of Hy. A storm is the catalyst for her act, since it damages some of the wall so that Glady must decide whether to mend it or take it down. Her forgiveness of her sister is not a surprise since she has already allowed Hy to live with her and join the bee. Glady is seen smoking pot and drinking with her sister, as well as accompanying her to the local swimming pool; this suggests that the character can easily forgive. We see Glady singing along to Neil Diamond's "Cherry, Cherry" in the car with Hy on their way to the pool. Additionally the narrative has a flashback to Glady and Hy as girls (played by Claire Danes and Alicia Gorenson) and Glady learning quilting from the young Anna (María Celedonio). The older Anna (Maya Angelou) is a member of the modern bee.

Bancroft's hair (by Candace Neal) is gray with white strands at the front and a side part in the modern period, and brownish-gray in a flashback scene. Costumes are by Ruth Meyers. Bancroft speaks with the hint of a Southern accent which is unexplained, and in her best scenes she expresses her rage at the discovery of the affair and her empathetic crying in sadness. Director Jocelyn Moorehouse gives the actress a long close-up for the expression of her realization of the affair when she is sitting in a room between Hy and Arthur. Bancroft also has a transitional moment in the hospital room of Hy's dying husband James (Denis Arndt) where she changes from a look of disdain to Hy to reasonableness when she gives her a spoon to feed him ice cream.

The film was released on October 6, 1995, with the tagline "There's beauty in the patterns of life." It was praised by Caryn James in the *New York Times* but lambasted by Leonard Klady in *Variety* and Roger Ebert in the *Chicago Sun-Times*. Bancroft said that she accepted the part because she liked the script. She responded to its female focus. Bancroft saw the previous films directed by Moorehouse and liked them. The actress told Karen Karbo in an *Entertainment Weekly* interview (October 13, 1995) that when she walked into the rehearsal for the film, it was the first time in her career where there no men in the room. Bancroft thought she had died and gone to Heaven. She was also impressed with Moorehouse's ability to take charge and with co-star Winona Ryder. The actress said that the hardest scene in the film was when she had to sing the Neil Diamond song in the car with Burstyn and Ryder. Bancroft said Diamond's kids went to school with her kid and they lived right down the way in Malibu. She didn't know the song and it was sprung on the cast suddenly. Less of a challenge was the ability to stitch a quilt, which was required for close-ups. Bancroft learned it easily and she finished her own white-on-white quilt between scenes on a work table set up in the corner of the sound stage. The actress said she learned from quilting how she had great patience; and to be a great actress, great patience was needed. When asked about the age-old actress' lament that there just weren't enough good roles for women in movies, Bancroft replied that it was tough for women to get good roles in life, let alone in Hollywood. She said to look at the president's cabinet, on the list of doctors at any hospital, and at the astronauts where they were far more men than women.

The actress was a special guest voice in "Fear of Flying," the December 18, 1994, episode of the animated series *The Simpsons*. When Homer (Dan Castellaneta) wins free plane tickets, it is revealed that his wife Marge (Julie Kavner) is afraid to fly. Marge sees Dr. Zweig (Bancroft), a psychiatrist at the Springfield Psychiatric Center, for therapy. Dr. Zweig is sympathetic and competent enough to prod her into recalling childhood traumas that Zweig claims pinpoint the precise moment when Marge developed her phobia. The doctor is revealed to be passionate in her defense of the Monkees, when Marge recalls how her Monkees lunchbox was ridiculed when she was a schoolgirl. In addition Zweig is funny. She comments how Marge infringes on any number of copyrights when she describes a dream of herself as the mother in the TV series *Lost in Space*. Zweig yells at her patient to "Get back here and tell me about your father" after Marge attempt to leave the session, refusing to talk about the man she describes as a pilot. After Marge calls her father a trailblazer and an American hero for actually being a male steward, the doctor says, "Let's not go nuts." However Zweig is a little dismissive after Marge recalls three more memories that may also have contributed to her phobia, when Zweig comments, "Yes, yes. It's all a rich tapestry." This dismissiveness may be a result of the doctor being peeved at how Marge's last check bounced. The doctor is also observant enough to see the "far more serious problem" of Homer upon Marge. In their first meeting, Marge apologizes for Homer who questions the doctor's qualifications. Marge says that he is just afraid that she will blame all her problems on him. Zweig replies that she is not there to blame anyone, but writes "Husband" on her writing pad and underlines it. Zweig will urge Marge to stay in therapy after her fear is supposedly cured, saying they have only scratched the surface. The doctor's therapy does allow Marge to get on a plane again, which is all Homer wants, though the plane proceeds to have an accident and crashes into a lake.

Executive producer and show runner David Mirkin would later work with Bancroft on the film *Heartbreakers*. He reported that when he phoned her about doing the part, she asked how he directed. Mirkin advised Bancroft that casting a person whom he thought had what he was looking for was the secret. She told him that was good because she didn't like that fancy stuff. Director Mark Kirkland reported that the character was redesigned after Bancroft did her recording. The changes that were made were making Zweig's glasses split and adding the silver streak to her hair, which were done to make her look more mature. Bancroft brought Mel Brooks with her to her recording and she told Mirkin, "I can't get rid of him." When Mirkin was directing the actress, Brooks sat next to him and whispered to him his own directions. Mirkin felt that Bancroft completely understood how to play the character. He said she could do the reality and the comedy, had amazing timing and cadence, and was a joy to work with.

In 1994 Bancroft announced that she had the perfect dream: to live four months of the year in Los Angeles, four in New York and four in the Caribbean or Miami. She said she would like her husband to go along but she had to wait until he decided what he was going to do with his life. Bancroft felt that Brooks wouldn't decide, but rather life would decide for him.

The actress was next cast in the romantic comedy *Home for the Holidays*, shot from February 15 to April 19, 1995, on location in Baltimore, Los Angeles and at Warner Brothers. The film had a screenplay by W.D. Richter based on a short story by Chris Radant, and was directed by Jodie Foster. Museum Renaissance painting art restorer Claudia Larson (Holly Hunter) loses her job in Chicago and goes home to spend Thanksgiving with her family in Baltimore. Bancroft played Claudia's mother, Adele, who is married to 64-year-old, recently retired airport maintenance worker Henry (Charles Durning). Also visiting are Claudia's brother Tommy (Robert Downey, Jr.) and his friend, cook Leo Fish (Dylan McDermott), sister Joanne Wedman (Cynthia Stevenson) with her banker husband Walter (Steve Guttenberg) and their children Brittany (Emily Ann Lloyd) and Walter Jr. (Zachary Duhame), and Adele's 61-year-old sister and former schoolteacher Aunt Glady (Geraldine Chaplin).

Adele has a minor impact on the narrative, since although it is a company ensemble it is really centered on Claudia. Adele copes with the restless Henry and calls him "Tubby" to scold him for his over-eating but she also enjoys his love of dancing. She accepts Joanne's patronizingly bringing her own turkey to the lunch and supportively applies baking soda to Joanne's dress when it is stained by the turkey which is dropped over her. Her interest in Dear Abby is shown from her clippings and reciting one letter from mem-

Still for *Home for the Holidays* (1995).

ory to Claudia. The reason for Adele wearing the red wig is not explained, apart from it being for her vanity. As a mother she is able to intuit that Claudia has been fired. She bemoans her daughter's choice of abandoning her original career as a painter, exemplified by the portrait that she did of Tommy that hangs in her parents' house. Adele presumably knows about Tommy being gay, but the news that he has married his boyfriend Jack (Sam Slovick) is news to her and the rest of the family. Adele and Henry have little apparent dramatic reaction to Tommy, with perhaps her only concern being that she wants him to be happy and that perhaps being gay and different will be an obstacle. She uses a charming and flirtatious smile when she speaks to Leo, as if guessing that he is straight, despite Claudia's wrong assumption that Leo is Tommy's new boyfriend. Adele has Claudia'a ex-boyfriend, Big Heat tradesman Russell Terziak (David Strathairn), come to the house on the pretense of looking at their furnace, although she really wants Claudia to see him again. She is tactless when she tells Claudia that she can see her roots, when she sits behind in the car, and is inappropriately intimate with Claudia by undressing down to bra and slip in front of her in her childhood bedroom. Adele is funny in her treatment of a telephone caller who has the wrong number, telling him, "I never heard of him. Consult your directory."

The film is a reunion for Bancroft with Charles Durning, with whom she appeared with in *To Be or Not to Be*. Bancroft's hair (by Frances Mathias) is worn in a short gray straight style, with a copper-red short wavy wig over it. Her wardrobe is by Susan Lyall. We hear her scream when she thinks Henry will drop her turkey before the lunch, Bancroft reusing the comic howl we heard in *'night, Mother*. It's fun to see her dance with Durning. Bancroft has a good moment in reaction to hearing how Glady and Henry once kissed, where her smile drops. Her best scene is perhaps the one in Claudia's childhood bedroom when Adele recites the remembered Dear Abby letter as she undresses, and then looks at her aged body in a mirror.

The film was released on November 3, 1995, with the taglines "When you go home, do you wonder: Who are these people?," "On the fourth Thursday in November, 84 million American families will gather together.... And wonder why" and "We'll do it every year ... until we get it right." It received a mixed reaction from Emanuel Levy in *Variety* wrote that Bancroft was over the top from the first scene, though some of the excesses were in the script. Janet Maslin in the *New York Times* said that the actress made an ingratiating busybody and incidentally showed the camera that she was in the shape she was in when *The Graduate* was made. Roger Ebert wrote that Bancroft and Charles Durning beautifully found just the right notes of acceptance, resignation, wounded but stubborn pride—and romance. Peter Travers in *Rolling Stone* said that Bancroft could not be better. The film was not a box office success.

The actress made a cameo appearance in the horror comedy *Dracula: Dead and Loving It* (1995). This was filmed from May to July 26, 1995, at the Culver Studios in Hollywood. Directed and co-written by Mel Brooks, it was the third and last time she appeared in one of her husband's films. The plot was a parody of the infamous story of Dracula where London solicitor Thomas Renfield (Peter MacNicol) sells Carfax Abbey to Dracula (Leslie Nielsen), enabling the vampire to go to England in search of new blood. Bancroft played psychic seer Madame Ouspenskaya, the character name a reference to actress Maria Ouspenskaya who played a gypsy in *The Wolf Man* (1941) and *Frankenstein Meets the Wolf Man* (1943).

Bancroft only appears in one scene: In the Transylvanian village, she warns Renfield about the danger. Her hair is covered by a headdress and her period layered clothes with jewelry are by Dodie Shepard. Bancroft uses an accent and is photographed in soft focus close-up. With her fingers she pulls the skin of her neck to make a vibrato sound with her voice box, which Brooks has us hear for her exit after she is no longer seen.

The film was released on December 22, 1995. Joe Leydon in *Variety* said that Bancroft earned big laughs for her scene. The film was not a box office success.

The actress, interviewed by Mal Vincent for the *Virginian-Pilot* (October 10, 1995), said she had no yen to go back to the stage. When she last did a show in Los Angeles it was six weeks of pure hell and the only time she was happy was when she was actually on stage. To do the job, the actress had no other life; she had to leave for the theater at 7 p.m. which was the time when her husband got home so she would never see him.

The February 4, 2004, *New York Times* reported that in 1995, Scott Louis Panetti had reportedly tried to subpoena the actress for his insanity trial defense. In 1992 he had shot the parents of his estranged wife to death, and had wanted to call Bancroft as well as Jesus Christ and John F. Kennedy, after having fired his lawyers. She presumably did not attend. The actress appeared at the 10th Annual American Comedy Awards, held on March 6, 1996, at the Shrine Auditorium in Los Angeles. The show honored the nation's outstanding comedic talents in TV, motion pictures and stand-up comedy, and Bancroft was given a Lifetime Achievement Award.

The actress next appeared in the action drama *G.I. Jane*, filmed from April 8 to August 6, 1996, on location in Washington, D.C., Florida, South Carolina, Virginia and California, and at Shepperton Studios in England. Demi Moore stars as topographic analyst Jordan O'Neill, the first female trainee in the U.S. Navy's Combined Reconnaissance Team selection program. Bancroft played Lillian DeHaven, a Texan senator and the senior member of the Senate Arms Committee. Jordan learns that she is set up to fail since the Senator has only led the test case to prevent military base closings in her home state and to secure votes in an upcoming election. Lillian also does a turnaround from supporting Jordan to endorsing her expulsion from the Navy for what she knows to be a dubious charge. Her hair by Dorothy Fox is gray, which makes a scene where she has foil pieces in it for presumed coloring seem odd. Costumes are by Marilyn Vance and mostly suits of business attire, though there is one white evening gown with a silver cape. Bancroft wears glasses which also attest to her age, and the Senator has a line where she calls herself an "old dame without much time left." The actress suggests the character's vanity by repeatedly having her primp and play with her hair, even in public at her Senate committee hearings. Bancroft has some memorable lines, including "Nearly every waking day I'm forced to make decisions that would have Solomon himself shitting golf balls." Her best scene is perhaps her confrontation with Jordan after she has learned how the Senator has double-crossed her with charges of lesbianism. Bancroft also has a good moment where she runs out of fear to close a door after Jordan threatens to expose her duplicity. Director Ridley Scott sometimes gives her extreme close-ups that are unflattering to a woman of Bancroft's age.

The film, released on August 22, 1997. Todd McCarthy in *Variety* wrote that the pleasure Bancroft took at portraying an old pro politician who excelled at backroom deals proved contagious. Janet Maslin in the *New York Times* described Bancroft as ever-glamorous and playing her role with splendid wiliness. In his book *Ridley Scott: A Critical Filmography*, William B. Parrill wrote that he found Lillian so harsh as to be unsympathetic, with over-the-top mannerisms, a weird accent and a voice so grating that it is unlike the reality of Texan politicians. Parrill agrees that Bancroft is photographed in an unflattering way but he adds that the character is also unnecessarily crude.

G.I. Jane was a box office hit. In an alternate ending that was shot, Bancroft gives a eulogy for Jordan on television after the soldier is killed in the climactic Libyan mission. Scott said that Bancroft was his first choice to play Lillian; he thought she was good at representing strength and intelligence and women's rights, and was capable of pulling off the tricky balance of being tough but sympathetic. He also wanted to make the character a sort of grande dame and the actress was personally like that, although Scott felt she may not have liked to hear it.

Scott reported that Mel Brooks came to watch the confrontation scene between Lillian and Jordan. The director is said to have initially modeled the character on Senator Ann Richards of Texas who came to national attention in 1988 when she delivered the keynote address at the Democratic National Convention. Bancroft, quoted in the film's pressbook, said that she took the role because she had been playing a lot of domestic women lately and Lillian was a career woman.

Bancroft did voice work on the animated comedy *Antz* (1998), in which an orange worker ant, Z (Woody Allen), toils as a soil relocation engineer in the underground construction mega-tunnel of the colony located in New York's Central Park. He meets Princess Bala (Sharon Stone) when she visits the worker ant bar Chug. She is the daughter of the queen ant (Bancroft) and is engaged to the red soldier ant General Mandible (Gene Hackman). Z impersonates a private soldier ant when the army is presented in a royal review so that he can see Bala again, before the platoon goes above ground to defend the colony against a termite army. Z, the only survivor of the battle, kidnaps Bala after the queen asks to meet him. The queen gives Mandible permission to battle the termites, as well as ordering the general to rescue her daughter. Mandible has a plan to create his own colony with the soldier ants and Bala as the new queen, since the tunnel has been built under a lake that will flood the existing colony and kill the queen and the worker ants. Z helps to rescue the colony by creating a ladder up to the ground and the queen is saved. Mandible seems to have the rule of the colony so it is unclear why he is unhappy with the queen, though presumably his greater desire for Bala is based on her youth. The queen's role as the mother of the colony is also suggested by her seen to be handling baby ants in her first scene. The directors (Eric Darnell and Tim Johnson) reported that originally the scene featured the queen grunting and groaning as she gave birth and the sound of babies crying but these elements were cut as they distracted from the dialogue.

To show her royal heritage the queen wears strands of beads across her forehead and a necklace, as opposed to Bala who only wears one strand. Bancroft uses a formal intonation to suggest the queen's heritage. The character is a minor one so Bancroft has little of consequence to contribute. The film premiered at the Toronto International Film Festival on September 19, 1998, and opened in the U.S. on October 2, 1998. Praised by Todd McCarthy in *Variety* and Peter Travers in *Rolling Stone*, it was a box office success.

Bancroft, interviewed about *Antz*, said that there was nothing that would get an actor quicker than a good script because they were not easy to find.

The actress returned to TV in the made-in-Canada drama *Homecoming* (1996). This had a teleplay by Christopher Carlson and Mark Jean based on the novel by Cynthia Voigt, and was directed by Mark Jean. The four children of Liza Hillerman (Anne Louise Richardson), who live in Provincetown, Massachusetts, are left by their unstable single mother in their car in a mall carpark in Peewauket, Connecticut. Dicey (Kimberlee

Peterson), James (Trevor O'Brien), Maybeth (Hanna Hall) and Sammy (William Greenblatt) head for the house of their Aunt Cilla Logan in Bridgeport, Connecticut. Learning that she has died and that her daughter Eunice (Bonnie Bedelia) won't take them in, the kids then go to see their grandmother, Abigail (Bancroft), who lives on a run-down farm in Crisfield, Maryland.

We are told that Abigail has a reputation in Crisfield. The grocer Milly (Jacque Lynn Colton) tells Dicey that her grandmother is "crazy as a coot" and has no telephone as she had thrown hers through the plate glass window of the phone company. (Abigail rationalizes this behavior as a response to the telephone news that her son Sammy had been killed in Vietnam.) Dicey goes first to see Abigail alone and finds her to be unfriendly. The woman has been expecting the children to arrive since she says that the police had told them they were coming. Abigail withholds this information as she toys with Dicey, attempting to frighten her by telling her how children might be good to eat, though she does give her food. The grandmother has a bad attitude, although she tells Dicey that she has been happy since having been a widow for four years. Abigail is reluctant to take in her grandchildren, and only allows them to sleep over. The children strategize that if they do chores, they will not be asked to leave, and Abigail does not tell them to leave until one meal when they give her backtalk. She explains to Dicey that she cannot afford to keep them and she fears failing the children after she felt she had failed her own. Eunice writes that Liza has been found and is a catatonic in a state hospital mental ward, and again proposes that the cousin will take in Dicey and Maybeth and she has found a private home for the boys. Abigail takes the children to get on a bus back to Bridgeport but then changes her mind and goes back home with them.

Although Bancroft's character doesn't appear until almost the halfway point, she is the one upon which the children's future is dependent. Bancroft's hair by Bruce Appleby is a short style with gray strands at the front, with a side part, and a browner color at the back. Her wardrobe is by Mary Patridge Raynor. Bancroft uses a regional Southern accent and seems to have fun with the aggressive character, who initially comes across as the opposite of the expected loving grandmother to her abandoned grandchildren. Abigail is both emotionally and physically withholding, with her tight lips re-enforcing this idea. However her unseen observation of the children as they work and her softening of attitude becomes inevitable, since Abigail's sensitivity is apparent. She never becomes the clichéd, open-armed grandma, since the best that Abigail offers when she decides to take in the children is a smile. Her scene explaining why she can't keep the children is shot with Bancroft in close-up. She is funny in her gruffness. In her best scene, she treats Maybeth's injury in the bathroom. It is Bancroft's credit that she doesn't try to upstage the child actress and reveals the tenderness that she otherwise conceals from the others.

Carol Horst (*Variety*) wrote that Bancroft delivered a borderline hammy performance but toned down her act as the telepic proceeded. John J. O'Connor in the *New York Times* said that the always skillful actress gave an incredibly good performance.

Bancroft next made a cameo appearance in the thriller *The Sunchaser* (1996), shot on location in Arizona, Utah and Colorado. UCLA Medical Plaza oncologist Dr. Michael Reynolds (Woody Harrelson) is kidnapped by a patient, 16-year-old "Blue" Monroe (John Seda), and driven to the Arizona Shiprock Reservation in the belief that the lake on top of a sacred Navajo mountain will heal his cancer. Bancroft played Renata Baumbauer, a doctor of philosophy who transports the men from the Yavapai Wilderness to Flagstaff in her trailer-truck. A New Age hippy in the area for the Harmonic Convergence, she believes in the power of the mind, astrology and birthstones. Renata empathizes with "Blue" because he is half-Navajo and because she rejects western medicine as symbolized by Michael. Her disdain does not express itself in rudeness. Rather she is over-polite after Michael laughs at her ideas and she says, "If I could continue with my point..."

Bancroft's hair by Melissa A. Yonkey is a long curly style with turquoise-colored hair clips. There isn't anything memorable about what she is called upon to do in the part, although she adds funny sarcasm when addressing Michael as "Doctor."

The film premiered at the Cannes Film Festival in May 1996 and opened on September 27, 1996, with the tagline "It began as a kidnapping. It became a journey of hope." *Variety*'s Todd McCarthy wrote that Bancroft was amusing in her brief role. The movie was lambasted by Stephen Holden in the *New York Times*, and he added that Bancroft's gave the film's oddest performance. The Michael Cimino film was not a box office success.

She next appeared in *Great Expectations* (1998), based on the novel by Charles Dickens. It was shot from July 8 to October 18, 1996, on location in Florida and New York. The story had been previously told in the British silent short *The Boy and the Convict* (1909) and then in a number of American, British and Swiss film and TV versions. This version modernized the Dickens story: A ten-year-old orphan in the Gulf of Florida, "Finn" Bell (Jeremy James Kessner), lives with handyman Joe Coleman (Chris Cooper) and Finn's sister Maggie (Kim Dickens). Joe is hired by Nova Driggers Dinsmoor (Bancroft) to work on her estate Paradiso Perduto. She is the modern version of Dickens' Miss Havisham. Dinsmoor is said to be the richest lady in the state and people say she lost her mind 30 years ago when her fiancé left her standing at the altar. Dinsmoor is now a recluse and her estate is unkempt with plants growing over the wedding tables which still have their settings. Seeing Finn with Joe, she asks that the boy come to entertain her and play with her ten-year-old niece Estella (Raquel Beaudene). Unable to dance for the old woman, Finn instead draws and dances with Estella. Dinsmoor warns that although the boy will fall in love with and pursue her niece, the girl will break his heart.

The children grow up to be played by Ethan Hawke and Gwyneth Paltrow. Seven years later, after Estella moves to New York and Finn becomes a fisherman, Dinsmoor becomes his secret benefactor to allow him to also go to New York. He paints portraits of Estella for a one-man show at the art gallery of Erica Thrall (Nell Campbell). Estella has a boyfriend, Walter Plane (Hank Azaria), and although she has an affair with Finn, she agrees to marry Walter. Dinsmoor comes to New York for Estella's wedding and tells Finn how she had used the boy to train her niece in manipulating men as revenge upon the sex. She reveals that she only sent him to New York to ensure that Estella would marry Walter. When Finn returns to Florida, he learns that Dinsmore has died alone in her mansion, her body undiscovered for a month, and her house is to be torn down for a housing tract.

Bancroft is third-billed. Her hair is by Angel Deangelis and revealed to be a gray wavy style worn with bangs and a bun on the neck. Dinsmoor covers her age with short wigs—three blonde and one red. She also wears heavy makeup, making her a grotesque figure, which director Alfonso Cuaron emphasizes in one scene by giving her a mirror which shows her wrinkled facial skin in extreme close-up. Even when she is without makeup in one scene, Bancroft still has additional wrinkles on her face. The actress has costumes by Judianna Makovsky (all green) and she smokes with a long cigarette holder. Bancroft is heard before she is seen, and first seen with her back to the camera, before she sings and dances to the song "Besame Mucho." She gets to scream "What have I

Still for *Great Expectations* (1998).

done?!" to Finn after Dinsmoor reveals her duplicity. The scream is perhaps Bancroft's most affecting moment in the film. Dinsmoor may have surface interest as a grotesque but the actress only really has any depth to play when she reveals her agenda, when she is without her grotesquerie.

It was released on January 30, 1998, with the tagline "Let desire be your destiny." Roger Ebert wrote that Bancroft's performance was interesting and that despite the weird eye makeup, the cigarettes and the flamboyant clothing, she was human, and not without humor. Todd McCarthy in *Variety* said that her theatrical turn was colorful but predictable. The film was a box office success.

In Bancroft's January 16, 1998, *New York Times* interview, she said the problem the *Great Expectations* director and she had was how to make extreme behavior real. Bancroft saw the external part of those kind of people all the time on the street but the interior part was something else. She felt it wasn't hard, it was scary. Bancroft had to use the unconscious mind and her own fantasies to root the part in very real feelings she had. She got in touch with the rejection and hurt that everyone had had in their lives, and it was tough stuff. Bancroft commented that the role was not the usual one offered to her since mostly she was offered the sensible, intelligent, in-control kind of woman.

The Bancroft-Brooks union remained solid. The media continued to be intrigued by the two seemingly unlikely companions. For Bancroft there was no mystery as to why they had stayed together so many years. She reported that there was just nobody sexier than Brooks because he had the most brilliant, unique mind. Bancroft said that he kept her excited from the moment she woke up in the morning till the moment they went to bed. Brooks commented that the secret to their union included not discussing each other's work. There was so much to discuss about life and so much to do that took up their time that he didn't think there was more than one sentence in a week that was about show business. Brooks' summarized his marriage by saying that they had made a crazy child together and they had a pretty happy life. They liked and appreciated each other and also liked Chinese food, foreign films and the beach. Brooks said it had really been a great thing being married to her.

The January 29, 1997, *New York Times* reported that Bancroft was wanted by director Charles Burnett for the comedy-drama *The Annihilation of Fish*, about two eccentrics. The other eccentric was to be played by Danny Glover. The film would be made as the romance *The Annihilation of Fish* (1999) with Lynn Redgrave and James Earl Jones.

Bancroft and Brooks appeared at the 49th Primetime Emmy Awards held on September 14, 1997. He was nominated for (and won) the Outstanding Guest Actor in a Comedy Series award for his appearance in the *Mad About You* episode "The Penis" (February 11, 1997). Brooks also co-presented (with Carl Reiner) the Outstanding Comedy Series award, which was won by *Frasier*.

The Italian biographical documentary *Marcello Mastroianni: I Remember, Yes I Remember* (1997) featured an interview with the Italian actor shot in September 1996 (he died on December 19 that year). Among the events he described were meeting Bancroft at the Actors Studio. He had been invited to visit by Lee Strasberg and sent as the guest of distributor Joseph Levine. Mastroianni found her sitting on the floor talking to the men of the Studio. Bancroft was a gorgeous brunette who looked like the daughter of Anna Magnani, one of those genuine beauties from southern Italy. Mastroianni approached her and quoted lines he had spoken in *La Dolce Vita* (1960): "Who are you? Are you my mother, sister, the earth, the moon? Who are you?" Bancroft answered in Italian, "And who are you?" He was surprised that she spoke Italian, and also that her real name was Italiano. Mastroianni suggested that Bancroft show him around New York since he didn't speak English. He said she was very kind in taking him to an Italian restaurant in the Village called Pompeii where they talked about the theater and cinema. Mastroianni had a lovely evening with her, which Bancroft presumably paid for since he had come to New York with no money.

Bancroft was next seen in the comedy *Critical Care* (1997), directed by Sidney Lumet. Shot in Toronto, Canada, it concerned resident doctor Werner Ernst (James Spader) and his experiences working at the Memorial Hospital and Medical Center Intensive Care Unit. Bancroft played a nun who was possibly from the hospital's pastoral care program or possibly a hallucination of Werner's. She appears in the hospital corridor and then at the bedside of his comatose patient Joseph F. Potter (Bruno Dressler). She appears in only two scenes, wearing a costume by Dona Granata: a white nun's outfit with a floor-length habit, long wide sleeves, and a cornette. As the hallucination, Bancroft is seen in front of a blue backdrop, with Mozart's Quintet K.516 in G Minor on the soundtrack. The nun has a narrative point in helping Werner with his dilemma over Potter, since he is conflicted about how Potter is being used by his warring daughter's in a lawsuit over his $10 million estate. The nun tells Werner that he should love Potter, and this coincides with the man thought to be using Morse code to finger tap out "If you love me."

The film was first screened at the Chicago International Film Festival on October 6, 1997, and received a wide release on October 31, with the tagline "At Memorial Hospital no one ever dies.... Until their insurance runs out." It was praised by Roger Ebert in the *Chicago Sun-Times* and lambasted by Todd McCarthy in *Variety*. The film was not a box office success.

Mel Brooks was interviewed by Geraldine Fabrikant for a *New York Times* article published on October 26, 1997. He spoke about his real estate holdings, which he presumably shared with Bancroft, which had an estimated market value of close to $20 million. These included two homes in Los Angeles, one an ultra-chic sprawl on one of the city's fanciest streets, estimated as worth $5 million. The other was a Malibu beach cottage valued at $4 million. Brooks also owned two homes on Fire Island as well as a Manhattan apartment in and an office building on Wilshire Boulevard in Beverly Hills, with an estimated value of $6 million. In addition, there were two beachfront condominiums on Fisher Island, the resort off Miami Beach, worth $400,000 each.

In 1997 Bancroft commented that she didn't think about being beautiful but rather devoted her time to being healthy. She put in 40 minutes a day on the treadmill and adhered to the Pritikin diet of fish and steamed and water-sautéed organically grown vegetables. Bancroft said she occasionally cheated on ossobuco or a great Chinese meal. Her medicine cabinet was stocked with holistic products. Bancroft said she had embraced everything: Astragalus, CoQ-10 and all the vitamins that build up the immune system. She meditated for peace of mind and took naps to rejuvenate. Bancroft took collagen injections around her mouth three times a year but otherwise she was a do-it-yourself woman, taking charge of her own hair and makeup for public events. When someone called her an icon, Bancroft guessed she had to come to terms with the word, though the actress felt that everyone in Hollywood after a certain age became one.

She attended the 70th Annual Academy Awards on March 23, 1998. In June she appeared in the romantic drama *Up at the Villa* (2000) which was shot on location in Florence and Sienna, Italy. Directed by Philip Haas, it was based on a novella by W. Somerset Maugham. The story concerned a group of Brits and Americans living in Florence, Italy, in 1938. Bancroft played Princess San Ferdinando, wealthy widowed American who is friendly with the protagonist Mary Panton (Kristin Scott Thomas), a British widow who has an affair with married American Rowley Flint (Sean Penn). The princess is arrogant and cynical, a gossip and a blackmailer when necessary. The latter aspect is given a plot payoff when documents she holds that incriminate the local policeman Deppino Leopardi (Massimo Ghini) are used by Mary to get Rowley out of jail. The princess gets a funny line when she tells Mary that her husband was so ugly that he'd frightened the horses, and she is funny in her displeasure at the playing of the violinist at the restaurant.

Bancroft's hair by Aldo Signoretti is gray and worn in a period style with a back roll. Costumer Paul Brown dresses the princess in a series of black outfits with matching black feathered hats, presumably to indicate her widowhood, although she also gets a gray evening gown and a black and white dress and white hat for her final scene. The character's wealth is indicated by her outfits including furs and fox pieces. Bancroft gets to sing opera when the princess is drunk. Director Haas presents her unflatteringly when the princess is drunk and seated on a divan with legs sprawled. Bancroft's best scene is perhaps when the princess speaks of a one-night stand she had when she was young, although the idea that she is a secret romantic is later extinguished when she tells Mary that she made up the story.

The film was released in the United Kingdom on April 14, 2000, and in the U.S. on May 5 with the tagline "Danger is the ultimate attraction." Derek Elley in *Variety* wrote that Bancroft ate up the role with one flamboyant gesture after another, with a touch of malice that added edge to the part. A.O. Scott in the *New York Times* wrote that it was tempting to say that Bancroft was miscast but one was grateful for the odd, inventive Actors Studio inflections she brought to the film, like a jolt of bourbon in a cup of weak tea. Roger Ebert (*Chicago Sun-Times*) described Bancroft's monologue about how the Princess married for security and took lovers for entertainment as virtuosic.

In her April 25, 2000, Charlie Rose interview, Bancroft said she loved the movie because it was about something, it was entertaining, and it had a wonderful story where unexpected things happened all throughout it. Also the language was beautiful. Bancroft said she loved Sean Penn and that he was wonderful in the film, almost like a 1930s matinee idol. They had a dining room in the garden where they would all meet. This lasted for three months and, because the people were willing to sit and talk and expose themselves, it made for a very nice experience.

Bancroft was interviewed by *The New York Daily News*' K.C. Baker about the film (May 2, 2000), describing how in the picnic scene, although shaded by from the Florentine sun by a tent, she was still roasting. The actress said by the time they did her close-up, it was something like 104 degrees. Bancroft had ice packs everywhere—under her seat, under her arms and down her back as she was calmly talking.

Bancroft appeared in the CBS special *AFI's 100 Years ... 100 Movies: America's Greatest Movies* (June 16, 1998), talking about the adventure romance *The African Queen* (1951) which was ranked at #65. She sat in an office which featured a poster for the Mel Brooks *To Be or Not to Be* behind her. Bancroft commented that *African Queen* was a great allegory for married life or any other relationship that one had in life.

The actress provided the narration for the Ogden Entertainment documentary *Mark Twain's America in 3D* (1998). It was lambasted by Lael Loewenstein in *Variety* and Lawrence Van Gelder in the *New York Times*. Bancroft also narrated the PBS documentary *Living with Cancer: A Message of Hope* (1998).

In 1998, Bancroft and Brooks were among those generously providing the funding for the sports documentary *The Life and Times of Hank Greenberg* (1998), the story of the Detroit Tigers first baseman who combatted bigotry in the major leagues and became baseball's first prominent Jewish star. The film premiered in October 1998 at the Hamptons International Film Festival before opening on January 12, 2000, with the tagline "When America Needed Heroes, a Jewish Slugger Stepped to the Plate."

Bancroft was reportedly sought by executive producer David Chase to play Livia Soprano on the HBO crime drama series *The Sopranos*. Nancy Marchand was cast in the part instead. Marchand was nominated for the Outstanding Supporting Actress in a Drama Series Emmy Award in 1999 and 2000. In 2016, Chase said in an interview that, before he made the series, he had wanted to do a film about a Mafioso guy and his mother, picturing Robert De Niro and Bancroft in the roles. However this idea never got anywhere.

The romance *At First Sight* (1999) starred Val Kilmer as a blind man and Nathan Lane as his visual therapist. When Kilmer's girlfriend Mira Sorvino expresses disappointment in Lane's methods, he wisecracks, "You were expecting Anne Bancroft. A dramatic breakthrough out by the water pump," a reference to *The Miracle Worker*.

ABC's *The American Film Institute Salute to Dustin Hoffman*, held in Los Angeles at the Beverly Hilton Hotel, featured two Hoffman-Bancroft clips from *The Graduate*. As part of the event, Bancroft approached Hoffman's table where he was sitting with his wife and children. She told him to kiss her, after he was reluctant to do so. They had a kiss on the mouth that lasted 12 seconds and then she gave him a key from her purse and told him, "Mel's out of town."

Bancroft next appeared in a supporting role in the made-for-TV drama *Deep in My Heart* (1999), filmed in Toronto. Inspired by actual events, it told the story of Barbara Ann Cummins (Gloria Reuben, played by Keenan MacWilliam as Young Barbara, Olivia Kassardardjian as five-year-old Barbara and Jessica Smith as 13-year-old Barbara). She was born to Geraldine "Gerry" Eileen Cummins (Cara Buono as young Gerry, Bancroft as older Gerry) after a rape by an African American in 1961 in Boston. Gerry gives up the child to a foster home managed by Corrine Burrell (Lyn Whitfield) and the girl is adopted by Paul (Albert Schultz) and Annalise Jurgenson (Alice Krige) of Milwaukee when she is eight. Gerry is the catalyst to Barbara's journey. She never tries to look for her, but she is lucky that 34 years later her daughter wants to know her birth mother and finds her in Orlando, Florida. Gerry gave away the baby because she believes that, the baby being mulatto, she will have an easier time if she is around other African Americans. She tells the grown Barbara that she had a dream that being with people of her own skin color would teach the girl pride and courage, which Gerry claimed were qualities that she lacked. She also has a self-serving reason not to keep the baby since she feels that her African American skin reminds her of the man who raped her.

Top-billed Bancroft's hair (by Kelly Brennan) is worn in a short style that has it dark at the back with gray strands at the front. In a scene where Gerry is meant to be slightly younger, she has a dark gray style with slighter white strands. Bancroft's wardrobe by Georgina Yarhi is mostly drab although she gets a nice black dress with a white-leaf pattern when Gerry has the dinner to welcome Barbara to her home. The actress uses a Boston-Irish accent. Bancroft gets burdened with a howler line when Gerry says to Barbara, "I was always thinking of you even though I spent all the time trying to pretend I'd never known you." Bancroft's best scene is when Gerry tells her twin brother Gerald (Peter MacNeil) about being raped and having Barbara: She provides surprising line readings and reactions to what could have otherwise been played for melodrama.

The film had a teleplay by Ronni Kern and was directed by Anita W. Addison. It was broadcast on CBS on February 14, 1999. Bancroft's performance won her the Best Supporting Actress in a Miniseries or a Movie Emmy Award.

11

Keeping the Faith

Bancroft next appeared in the romantic comedy *Keeping the Faith*, shot from May 24 to August 18, 1999, in New York and New Jersey. Three childhood friends, now adults—rabbi Jake Schram (Ben Stiller), priest Brian Kilkenny Finn (Edward Norton, who also directed) and business analyst Anna Riley (Jemma Elfman)—become a love triangle. Bancroft played Jake's widowed mother Ruth, a spunky woman who swears and sublimates her "victory engine" by taking classes in kabbalah, Tae-bo and Native American drumming. Ruth has stopped speaking to her other son Ethan (not seen in the movie); she disapproves of his having married a Catholic woman, though she will come to regret this decision. She is shown to be intuitive about how Jake is romancing Anna. Perhaps after learning the lesson from Ethan, she does not judge him for it or tell him how to live his life or what to do when Jake breaks it off with Anna. Ruth has an almost-stroke and is taken to a hospital where she is visited by Jake and Brian. The condition is not serious and she is released soon after.

There are photographs of a younger Bancroft in Ruth's apartment, including one of the famous post-marriage shot of her with Brooks (with another head substituted for Ruth's husband). Her hair by Jacqueline Payne is worn in a short dark style with the front strands gray. Wardrobe is by Michael Kaplan and favors dark colored suits with a splash of color. Bancroft sings when Ruth performs a Hebrew prayer to bless a meal. Her anger and sarcasm is funny, and the over-gesturing is acceptable as the behavior of a Jewish woman. Bancroft's best scene is perhaps when Ruth is in the hospital: The actress plays against the sentiment of the moment, telling Jake she has been wrong in her treatment of Ethan.

The film, released on April 14, 2000, was praised by Emanuel Levy (*Variety*), who wrote that Bancroft brought authority to her role. The DVD featured deleted scenes, including two with Bancroft. The actress is also seen in the DVD production gag reel where she laughs with Ben Stiller in the hospital room scene.

Always looking for challenges, Bancroft wanted to work with first-time director Norton, Stiller and Elfman. She said she had a lot to learn from the young people and she wanted to see how they worked. Bancroft felt it was very different from the way she was used to working. Trained on the stage where actors were required to keep to the playwright's exact words, she was surprised by the actors' ad-libbing. Bancroft was encouraged to ad-lib along with them and she found that fun. On the April 25, 2000, Charlie Rose show, the actress said she admired Norton as an actor so she wanted to see what he would do as a director. She agreed that he had a future as a director though she wasn't sure that he wanted to any more. A lot of actors think they want to direct and then discover that they didn't really want to; *this*, Bancroft said, is what happened to her after *Fatso*.

Norton cast Bancroft because he needed someone who was strong and intimidating enough for one to believe that Jake was afraid of her reaction to his affair with Anna and that he would break up with a girl he was in love with out of fear of his mother's reaction. The director said nobody was better than Bancroft for that, and as Jake was intimidated by his mother so was Norton a little intimidated by Bancroft. He noted that she was not Jewish but considered her an honorary Jew, being married to Mel Brooks for nearly 30 years. Norton reported that Bancroft learned the Hebrew prayer phonetically. Since Ruth was looking down as she sang it, the words were put on the table for the actress to see. Norton said the actress supplied photographs of herself with her real son for the photographs Ruth shows Anna. The production notes for the film included the fact that it reunited Bancroft and Eli Wallach, with whom she hadn't worked since they had their first screen test together.

On May 29, 1999, Bancroft was interviewed on the Savvy Traveler radio show about her love for Fire Island. A typical summer day on the island had her getting up early to eat breakfast with her son, either on the front or back deck according to where the breezes were and how hot the day was. Then Max usually had swimming or boating lessons or just ran around. Bancroft would clean the house and sometimes make lunch for him and his friends.

On the April 15, 2000, Charlie Rose show, she was interviewed about her long career, her personal life, *Keeping the Faith, Up at the Villa* and more. As Bancroft worked to build back the career, she also wrote. She optioned the Anne Roiphe book *Lovingkindness* and she had been writing a screenplay for that for about three years with a role for herself. She also admitted that she really wasn't that talented as a writer.

Asked about Max, Bancroft said she had him so late in life that she almost called him Nick for nick of time. The actress was devoured by the job of motherhood, though she denied loving it. Bancroft felt a lot of different ways, as she often did about things. She said she was almost always in conflict and her son kept her in conflict all the time because he was a guy you could love and hate in the same moment. She said she wished she'd had more children and it was the one thing she regretted in life. The actress had her boy at 41 and she had to spend three months in bed. Bancroft had had strange labor pains for seven months and it was thought that she was going to lose the baby. He was born via cesarean.

Rose asked about her relationship with Mel Brooks and she said she had nothing to compare it to. She had had other relationships but they were hardly based on the same things. She said that they worked very hard at keeping aware of each other. She really had to care and be interested and she thought she was very interested in him and the actress hoped he was very interested in her. Bancroft said when Brooks came into her life, he wanted to swallow her up and she said, "You bet, c'mon, absolutely," and for the first few years that's what it was. Then little by little the actress realized that was dangerous because she was truly losing herself and she had been fighting back for her own identity ever since. Rose asked Bancroft if she wanted to work with Brooks again and she said that she would love to. Asked what his best film was, Bancroft picked *The Producers*. She reported that Brooks was then making a musical out of it.

Bancroft claimed to be very happy just sitting in her organic vegetable garden or fishing and being with her husband and all the simple things. Asked if she wanted to go back on the stage Bancroft said she would love to if she could find the energy and stamina. She ended the interview doing a funny imitation of Rose where she showed his segue from laughing to being very serious which made her laugh.

Her next film, the comic crime romance *HeartBreakers*, was shot from April 24 to August 1, 2000, on location in Los Angeles and Florida under the title *Breakers*. Sigourney Weaver and Jennifer Love Hewitt star as Max Conners and 22-year-old Page Conners, mother-and-daughter scam artists. Their victims are random repossessions operator Dean Cumanno (Ray Liotta) and Palm Beach millionaire William B. Tensy (Gene Hackman). Bancroft plays Barbara, who is said to be Max's former scam partner. Barbara agrees to Max's idea to scam Page, so that her daughter will not leave her and work on her own. This scam has Barbara as Gloria Vogal who works for the IRS. She takes the $300,000 divorce settlement that Max gets from Dean and threatens criminal charges for felony tax evasion and fraud unless another $247,811 is paid. This allows Max to enlist Page in the scam on William whom she wants to marry and divorce as she had Dean. Barbara does her own scam on Max by taking the settlement she gets from William's estate, which makes Max do a payback scam on her former partner with Dean romancing Barbara as Max' accomplice. Max tells Page that Barbara helped her when she was pregnant with her daughter and alone, but we also see another con that Max has learned. She breaks a glass at a restaurant and claims the glass pieces were in her lunch in order to get a free meal. Later we see Barbara doing the same scam, although she brings her own supply of broken glass.

Bancroft's hair (by Jasen Sica) is worn in a shoulder-length style with gray front strands, dark brown at the back, and a side part. Her costumes are by Gary Jones. Bancroft's best scene is when she plays Gloria since her contempt for Max is funny. She gets a good line when she says, "Your latest divorce settlement arrived this morning. Thanks."

The film was released on March 23, 2001, with the tagline "They Will Love You for Richer. And Leave You for Poorer." business!" A.O. Scott of the *New York Times* wrote that Bancroft was good in a small role. The film was a box office success.

HeartBreakers director David Mirkin said that doing the *Simpsons* episode with Bancroft gave them a relationship because they had a great time doing it. He begged the actress to do the part in *HeartBreakers* and she did. Mirkin described Bancroft as amazing, legendary, really hilarious and with amazing power. Sigourney Weaver commented that Bancroft was an extraordinary actress and that it took a long time to get her.

In Bancroft's interview with K.C. Baker (*The New York Daily News*, May 2, 2000), she noted that even with her 40-year track record, finding complex, intelligent roles wasn't been easy for her. In recent years, in part because of her high standards and the dearth of parts for older women, the former leading lady had taken on supporting roles. Bancroft had just finished the screenplay for *Lovingkindness*, about a widow devastated when her daughter joins an extreme right-wing Orthodox Jewish group in Israel and seeks an arranged marriage. The actress stated that the book was so profound that she just had to do it. In the proposed film, she would play the widow.

The actress was a guest on the comedy-talk show *The Rosie O'Donnell Show* (May 5, 2000) to promote *Up at the Villa*. Reportedly she had asked that there be no audience for the show. O'Donnell described her as kind, loving, smart and beautiful. Bancroft returned to television for *Haven* (2001), a historical biography shot on location in Ontario, Canada. Natasha Richardson starred as Ruth Gruber, American special assistant to

Minister of the Interior Harold L. Ickes (Hal Holbrook) under President Roosevelt. Ruth in 1944 traveled to Italy to help escort 983 Jewish refugees back to the U.S. on the troop ship *Henry Gibbons* with 1000 wounded American soldiers. The refugees are housed at the Fort Ontario army base in Oswego, New York, for the duration of the war, but President Harry Truman (Kenneth Welsh) eventually makes them permanent citizens. Bancroft played Sara, Ruth's mother, who is also called Mama Gruber. She lives in Brooklyn with her husband David (Martin Landau). Sara travels to Oswego to visit Ruth and help arrange the marriage of refugees Manya (Tamara Gorski) and Ernst (Henry Czerny). She does not want her daughter to go to Europe, fearful that as a Jewess she will be a victim of the Nazis. However narrative flashbacks show that Ruth was a student in Germany in 1937 and survived as an outspoken Jew. Ruth does not go to Italy alone; she is protected by soldiers, despite her given the supposedly protective title of "general." Sara has insight into the armed forces, since she provides Ruth with food for her journey as opposed to the service food that the soldiers are given. Sara wants her daughter to find a husband, and is envious of the relationship Ruth has with David. After David dies, Ruth becomes closer to her daughter, admitting that is not easy for her to tell her that she loves her, though she does.

Wardrober Michael Harris has Bancroft wear one outfit twice—a gray suit with a matching feathered hat. Bancroft uses tight lips to show Sara's disapproval of her daughter's assignment and big gestures presumably to present herself as a Jewish mother. Her anger is funny and she gets two funny lines. She orders that Manya's hair has to be done two hours before the wedding. "One hour for the hair and one hour for her to get nervous and ask for another hairdo." Manya objects to her hairstyle and says she wants to look like herself and Sara replies, "You're the bride. You have nothing to say about this." However the actress has nothing of real substance to do and only has brief scenes where she confesses to her daughter.

CBS broadcast in two parts on February 11 and 14, 2001, with the tagline "Her courage saved a thousand lives. A girl from Brooklyn defied the Nazis, challenged the US Government ... and changed the world." Steven Oxman in *Variety* described Bancroft as ever-feisty. She was Emmy-nominated for the Outstanding Supporting Actress in a Miniseries or a Movie.

Bancroft remembered that when she was in Israel for three weeks with Golda Meir preparing to play *Golda* on Broadway, Meir introduced her to people who all had stories like the ones of the refugees. The actress was surprised when she read the story because she didn't know that any such thing had happened. Bancroft felt compelled to do it because she thought the story of Ruth Gruber and her heroism had to be told. Bancroft defined Sara as a woman who doesn't see how brilliant her daughter is to be picked for the job she takes; she's only afraid that she will lose her child. The actress wondered if Sara would have gone to the refugees if David had not died.

Natasha Richardson said Bancroft immediately brought elegance and weight and truth and beauty to her part. Martin Landau said that working with her was joyful. The real-life Ruth Gruber commented that the actress as her mother was wonderful.

After previews from March 21, 2001, Mel Brooks' musical version of *The Producers* opened on Broadway on April 19, 2001, and ran until April 22, 2007, at the St. James Theatre. Bancroft was photographed at the opening night party held at Roseland Ballroom. The show was produced by Brooks, with a book by Brooks and Thomas Meehan and songs with music and lyrics by Brooks. Bancroft said she was one of the first to suggest to her husband the idea of making a Broadway musical from his film. He initially resisted it. The actress knew all that was keeping him from doing it was fear, as well as depression over his declining career and how many of his long-time friends were seriously ill or dying. To overcome his anxieties about it, Bancroft sent him to an analyst. Once Brooks agreed to proceed with it, with the additional urging of music industry mogul David Geffen, he thereafter referred to his wife as his Obi-Wan Kenobi for her wise counsel.

Bancroft was witness to her husband's long and often painful struggle with the song numbers. She admired his courage and believed he was putting his heart and soul into the endeavor.

The actress supplied the voice of Golda Meir for the historical documentary *In Search of Peace—Part One: 1948-1967* (2001). Chronicling Israel's first two decades and the ensuing Arab-Israeli peace conflict, it was intended to be the first in a trilogy designed to conclude with the signing of a final peace agreement between Jews and Arabs. To date only one part of the trilogy has been made.

On December 7, 2001, the *New York Times* reported that Bancroft was to appear in a new Edward Albee Broadway play, *The Occupant*, a look at the life of Louise Nevelson, the sculptor and provocateur. The Manhattan artist was known for her severe look of chinchilla coat, raccoon eyes and scalp swathed in scarves and for her towering wood and metal sculptures. The production at the Signature Theater Company would mark Bancroft's first stage appearance in more than a decade (her last had been in 1989 in *Mystery of the Rose Bouquet*). Bancroft stated that the story was too much to resist. She described it as being about a woman fighting traditions and conventions in order to find her own path in life. "And that's not just a problem for her or even just women. It's a problem for everyone: how do you find your own path?"

It was announced in *Playbill* on February 5, 2002, that Bancroft's co-star in the two-hander was Neal Huff and that previews had begun at the off–Broadway Peter Norton Space. In the February 17, 2002, *New York Times*, its director Anthony Page said that when he read the play, Bancroft was the first person he thought of. He felt it needed a lot of power, and a peasant quality, along with the grandeur. She commented that the play was profound and extraordinary. Bancroft said that she thought she would never go back to the theater but this changed when she watched a rehearsal for the musical version of *The Producers*. She saw the vulnerability of the actors and their work live onstage and there was something very exciting about it. While watching Nathan Lane and Matthew Broderick in the Chicago out-of-town tryout, Bancroft began to think about returning to the stage herself.

She and Edward Albee had been acquaintances for years but he had not thought of her for Nevelson. His original thought had been to get a wonderful actress without any name at all. When the idea of Bancroft came up, his first reaction was that she wouldn't return to the stage. But the actress accepted the part immediately after reading it, despite her husband's misgivings about being in New York in February. Bancroft said that one of the challenges of the production was trying to keep her eyes open with the fake eyelashes she had to wear. Nevelson wore two pairs of sable lashes on each eye, and the actress had trouble getting used to them.

Bancroft, suffering from bronchitis, was replaced by her understudy Kathleen Butler for preview performances. On February 19, 2002, the *Times* reported that Bancroft's bronchitis had advanced to pneumonia. She had taken the previous week off and would also miss the next week.

Bancroft had been seen in the role in previews by Dan Callahan, who wrote in *Slant Magazine* (August 5, 2008) that He found the play to be minor Albee, too tied to biographical details, and that the audience was restless throughout. But when Bancroft entered, she was in total control. Toward the end, as she did a lengthy monologue, a woman in the audience got up to leave. Suddenly, Bancroft dropped her grand, declaiming character and looked out at the woman. "Darling, you're leaving?" she asked, in the purest Bronx accent. "Please, dear, please, I'm almost finished! Gimme a shot, would ya?" The woman continued out the door as the audience laughed, and Bancroft shrugged, then instantly went back into her speech, as focused as ever. At another performance a woman reportedly had a persistent cough. At one point it got so bad that she got up out of her seat, presumably to get some water. Bancroft stepped to the front of the stage, looked at the woman and said, "It's about time. Go get some water or something." The audience laughed in response.

On February 25, 2002, the *Times* reported that because of the actress' illness, previews had been put off until March 19 and the opening night postponed indefinitely. On March 19, Bancroft had announced plans to return to the show but Butler had appeared that night instead. According to a spokeswoman, the star had been rehearsing. Bancroft was said to be healthier and stronger and definitely wanted to go back. On March 29, the *Times* reported that April 7 would be the last performance—for now. The company had taken a big financial hit from the play's on-again, off-again run. With Bancroft promised as the play's lead, the show had a sold-out nine-week run but now it had been cancelled, forcing the company to refund thousands of tickets. The actress had returned to the show the previous week but much of the damage had already been done. The company hoped to bring the production back the next season for another run with Bancroft. The show was eventually restaged by the Signature Theater Company at the Peter Norton Space from June 5 to July 13, 2008, with Mercedes Ruehl playing the lead.

On June 24, 2002, Bancroft participated in a salute to Mel Brooks at Alice Tully Hall. The event "Springtime for Mel Brooks," presented by the Film Society of Lincoln Center with the Academy of Dance on Film, focused on his work as composer and lyricist, through numbers from his film comedies.

Max Brooks was interviewed by Carolyn White for the magazine *Only Child* in 2002. Max said that Bancroft was a good mom because she put aside her career, at a time when she was technically a bigger success than her husband, to give her son a good family life. However the actress was terrified about how her son was an only child and how comfortable he was being alone. She was worried that he would become a social misfit, but that didn't happen. Max reported that Bancroft had an even stronger work ethic than his father. She made acting look easy though she was the hardest working woman he had ever seen.

For Showtime, Helen Mirren and Bancroft starred in Tennessee Williams' *The Roman Spring of Mrs. Stone* (2003), shot on location in Ireland and in Italy. Mirren's title character, a middle-aged, retired American actress, settles in postwar Rome after the death of her producer husband Tom (Brian Dennehy). Bancroft plays the Contessa, a former noblewoman who is now poor and who pimps male marcettas to rich tourists. She introduces Karen to a series of gigolos but she begins a sexual affair with Conte Paolo di Lio (Oliver Martinez). The Contessa expects a percentage of the money that Paolo gets from Karen, but the American is not forthcoming with money. Karen's friend Christopher (Roger Allam) describes the Contessa as an old harpy who forces her card on people.

He also tells how it is rumored that her title was inherited from an ancestor who was a male whore noted for the length of his appendage. Paolo calls the Contessa an old witch, which leads her to hit him in the groin. Her dire financial situation has her say that she has no assets and her family heirlooms were lost in the war. She claims to be starving and repeatedly steals food from Karen and also asks to borrow money to pay her rent. Despite Karen's attraction to Paolo, the Contessa says that she has no real dignity or real pride. She taunts the American by speaking of Paolo's former patroness Mrs. Coogan. The Contessa's contempt for Karen in revealed in the climax when she describes her to American actress Angel Hunter (Tara Lynne O'Neill) as a harlot who has lost her looks; a mediocre actress who struck it rich; and someone who purchased her way into prominence. The Contessa adds that Karen has caused a scandal in Rome by throwing herself at a younger man who has no interest in her, and that no one in Italian society will receive her.

Bancroft's hair by Aldo Signoretti is in a gray, wavy, short style with a side part as well a shoulder-length wig that sometimes looks red and sometimes brown. The actress uses an Italian accent with a formal intonation to suggest the Contessa's breeding. At the climax, the Contessa asks Karen the following three questions: "Do you think you can cause noble people to go hungry and then tell us how to behave? Do you think you can help the traitors who hung Il Duce upside down and then tell us how to behave? Do you think you can bomb us and kill our children and then tell us how to behave?" Bancroft delivers these lines with the appropriate indignity but she also has tears in her eyes, which adds to their effectiveness. Her best scene may be the one where the Contessa asks Karen for a loan perhaps because it shows the actress' range. Karen of course is aware of being played by the old woman and the Contessa knows this, but Bancroft still expresses the woman's vulnerability and shame at doing the asking.

Broadcast on May 4, 2003, the show was praised by Laura Fries in *Variety*, who wrote that Bancroft clearly relished her role. The show, with teleplay by Martin Sherman and directed by Robert Allan Ackerman, received Emmy Award nominations: Bancroft as Best Supporting Actress in a Miniseries or Movie, Mirren as Best Lead Actress in a Miniseries or Movie, and more. Bancroft lost to Gena Rowlands who appeared in the drama *Hysterical Blindness*.

On July 21, 2003, "An Evening with Anne Bancroft and Mel Brooks" was presented at the Avram Theatre as part of Southampton College's annual writers conference.

For the CG-animated feature *Delgo* (2008), Bancroft was engaged to voice the character of Sedessa, an eccentric leader who was said to be as ambitious as she was charming. For Bancroft, it marked a return to working in the animated feature realm after she had lent her voice to *Antz*. The directors were Marc F. Adler and Jason F. Mauer.

The animated adventure's title character (voiced by Freddie Prinze, Jr.) was a Lockni teenage Stonesage apprentice in the land of Jhamora who sees a conflict between the Lockni and Nohrin people. Bancroft voiced Empress Sedessa Graleon, the younger sister of the Nohrin King Zahn (Louis Gossett, Jr.). When the Nohrin people go to Jhamora to seek a new land, the ambitious Sedessa uses the army to govern and control, and her attacks include murdering Delgo's parents. The Nohrin king feels his sister has disgraced the royal family and after she poisons the queen and attempts to also poison Princess Kyla, she is found guilty of murder and treason. Sedessa is condemned to spend the remainder of her life in exile in a castle on a barren rock and her wings are cut off. Fifteen years later, she plans to invade Jhamora and kill the tribal leaders who guard her, getting the support of the Ando army. She plots with the Nohrin Colonel Raius (Malcolm McDowell) who kidnaps the teenage Kyla (Jennifer Love Hewitt) in an effort to create a new war between the Nohrins and the Lockni. Sedessa hopes to be queen but Kyla is rescued by Delgo and General Bogardus (Val Kilmer), and Sedessa is killed in a fight with Kyla. Sedessa having lost her wings is paid off when she cannot save herself when she is pushed off a cliff in the collapsing palace of Zahn.

Sedessa has a few characteristic that redeem her from being a cartoon villain. She plays the harp and has a sense of humor. When her house pet Stone Angler Pookie farts, as if to defecate in the king's palace, she comments, "Not on the carpet." When he returns a lost weapon to Delgo during the climactic fight, she says, referring to Pookie, "I should had had him stuffed."

Sedessa's design is a winged creature with yellow skin, green eyes, red fly-away hair, black-dotted skin and an upside down sickle marked under her right eye. She wears a skin-tight red body suit with black sleeveless jacket, black gloves, gold belt and black boots as a soldier. After she is exiled, Sedessa wears a red long-sleeved floor-length dress with a red choker and makeshift detachable red wings, and she has white wings for the climax. Bancroft's casting is a surprise given that Sedessa is drawn as a young, sexualized woman. There are times when the actress' voice is unrecognizable, as when Sedessa calls for help when she hangs off a cliff in the climax. This is explained by the fact that Melissa McBride was a voice double for Bancroft in some sequences so that the film could be finished after Bancroft died. Her last scream as Sedessa falls to her death is effectively horrifying. The film's end credits has a dedication to Bancroft "In Memoriam."

Delgo was released in the U.S. on December 12, 2008. The film was not a box office success. The DVD features Bancroft voicing a scene that was deleted, "Sedessa Dictates." In the scene she feeds Pookie a creature, then dictates a letter for Raius to her assistant Spig (voiced by Eric Idle).

Footage of Bancroft recording her voice is included in the DVD's behind-the-scenes featurette. Mark Adler reported that she recorded her work in a New York studio in the Hamptons, where she was accompanied by Mel Brooks. The co-director commented that in the scene where Sedessa speaks to a crowd in the background as Kyla is rescued, he hurriedly wrote a speech for the actress. He said Bancroft stopped mid-sentence in her recording of what Adler admitted to being bad lines, looked up at him and proclaimed, "Are you kidding?!" Adler auditioned dozens of actresses to complete the recordings. Melissa McBride, who had also recorded the characters of Miss Sutley and Elder Pearo, wanted to audition. She asked to see videotapes of Bancroft recording rather than just hear the lines she had done. In the audition, Adler reported that McBride clamped on her neck and pointed her nose towards the ceiling and the voice sounded so similar that it didn't even require any post-modulation. The one scene that he identified as definitely having being recorded by McBride is the one where Sedessa speaks before killing the Ando Brute leaders.

On October 29, 2003, Bancroft attended a party at Elaine's to celebrate the publication of the book written by her son Max, *The Zombie Survival Guide: Complete Protection from the Living Dead*. Bancroft said she always knew when Max was growing up that he was a little nuts and reading his book clinched it for her.

Bancroft was set to co-star with Adam Sandler and Tea Leoni in *Spanglish*, a romantic comedy. The film began shooting at the end of 2003 with Bancroft as Leoni's mother Evelyn Wright. But the actress withdrew after four weeks and with only two weeks left to film. Writer-director James L. Brooks said that she left because she was taken ill and had to have an operation. Mike Szymanski on the website Zap2it.com reported on December 21, 2004, that the illness was pneumonia. The actress was replaced by Cloris Leachman. Brooks didn't rewrite the part, however—he re-directed and it became wilder. Brooks said to see two women captured on film as Evelyn was intense because they were so different and both brilliant.

The October 26, 2003, *Variety* article reported that Bancroft and Mel Brooks were to produce Ann Randolph's play *Squeeze Box* Off Broadway and had optioned the film rights. The actress had seen the one-woman show enacted by Randolph (about her experience working in a homeless shelter) at the Court Theater in Los Angeles in 2002 and was bowled over by it. In an interview, she said, "When can you get a night when you laugh and you cry and you think and you feel?"

The actress was credited as the producer of the show, which ran at the Acorn Theater from July 29 to September 12, 2004. Bancroft did not call it producing; she just said that she loved it. The actress denied that she was a producer proper because that was something far more complicated than anything Bancroft could do. In the June 30, 2004, *New York Times*, Bancroft explained her decision to produce the show, saying it was love at first sight, like when she first met Mel Brooks.

Bancroft attended on opening night. The actress said she had the idea to bring the production to New York after seeing the success Brooks had with *The Producers* on Broadway.

12

The End

Bancroft was diagnosed with uterine cancer and as her condition deteriorated she was admitted to Mount Sinai Hospital in Manhattan. She and Brooks did their best to keep the news out of the media so that they could deal privately with it. This resulted in him being on the set of the film version of the musical version of *The Producers* less than he had wanted. The film began shooting on February 8, 2005, at the Steiner Studios in New York. It features a reference to Bancroft, who died before it was completed. In the "Along Came Bialy" number, when Max Bialystock (Nathan Lane) visits the rich old lady investors in their Fifth Avenue apartment buildings, among the apartment call buttons he pushes is one listed for "A. Bancroft."

The actress made her last TV appearance in "Opening Night," the March 14, 2004, episode of the HBO comedy series *Curb Your Enthusiasm*. In it, Larry David is cast by Mel Brooks (playing himself) as Max Bialystock in a Broadway revival of *The Producers*, as Brooks hoped to end the show's successful run. After Larry forgets his lines and Brooks leaves the theater, he improvises about his Cousin Eddy (Richard Kind) in the audience which allows him to remember the lines. The hopes of Brooks and Bancroft, playing herself, are dashed: As they wait in a bar, they hear the audience come in at intermission and rave about Larry in the show. Bancroft's hair by Patricia Grande is a shoulder-length gray wavy style with a side part. She is dressed by Wendy Range-Rao in a white dress with long pink gloves and a silver fox fur piece. She sings "By the Light of the Silvery Moon" with Brooks and a bar drunk (Bill Buell). She is physically intimate with Brooks, naturally as they are a married couple. Bancroft's mood changes from pleasure to pain, presumably aided by being inebriated. The actress looks funny slumped over the rear railing of the St. James Theater as she and Brooks watch the audience applaud the show at the end.

Bancroft's sister, Phyllis Italiano, reported that when Brooks was in London with *The Producers* (the show opened at the Theatre Royal, Drury Lane, on November 9, 2004), the actress underwent chemotherapy. Bancroft lost her hair and her sister told her that she looked like their father. The actress asked her sister to take her to the ocean so she could swim.

On January 11, 2005, Bancroft attended the re-cast *Producers* opening night party held at the Angus McIndoe Restaurant in New York City. Bancroft's hair was shorn short which seems to confirm that she had lost it due to chemotherapy.

The actress lived long enough to see her grandchild, Henry Michael Brooks, who was born in March 2005. The boy was the son of Max Brooks and his wife, Michelle Kholos, who had married in 2003.

On June 8, 2005, the *New York Times* reported that Bancroft had died on Monday, June 6, at Mount Sinai. She was 73 and the cause was uterine cancer, said Mel Brooks' spokesman John Barlow. Arthur Penn said that more happened in her face in ten seconds than happened in most women's faces in ten years. Broadway lights were scheduled to be dimmed on June 8, 2005, in her honor. A flower wreath was laid out on her Hollywood Walk of Fame spot at 6368 Hollywood Blvd.

On June 9, 2005, the American Academy of Dramatic Arts put a paid death notice in the *New York Times*. It read that the company mourned the loss of its esteemed alumna, Class of 1950, and they extended their deepest condolences to her husband and son. Bancroft was interred at the Kensico Cemetery in Valhalla, New York, as Anne Bancroft Brooks. She was placed near the plots of her parents Michael Italiano, who died in 2001, and Mildred, who would die in April 2010. A white marble monument with a weeping angel adorned her grave. The inscription on the headstone read "Cherished Actress, Beloved Wife, Mother, Grandmother, Sister and Daughter."

In the June 11, 2005, *New York Daily News*, Michael Daly interviewed Bancroft's 97-year-old mother, Mildred Italiano. She spoke about she encouraged her daughter's passion and her childhood. The article also quoted Bancroft who commented near the end of her career that the role that was dearest to her heart was in *Two for the Seesaw*. The actress said that was the one she wanted to play again.

Bancroft was remembered on June 22, 2005, at a tribute held at the Academy of Motion Picture Arts and Science's Samuel Goldwyn Theater in Beverly Hills. The event was hosted by Carl Reiner. At the start of the evening, Mel Brooks requested that no one go up to him to express their sympathy. He said he didn't need their tears because he had more than enough of his own. A retrospective of clips from her films and TV appearances, prepared by David Yarnell and Harrison Engle, were shown. There was a mural of stills of Bancroft's life and career on the Academy's main floor. Among those who spoke were Bernie Brillstein, Gordon Davidson, Kathy Bates, Robert Allan Ackerman and Toni Howard. Brillstein said he was 25 when he wrote the biography for the 25-year-old Bancroft when she was Anna Italiano and a new William Morris Agency client. They had remained close friends. Davidson, who set her in the Mark Taper Forum's *The Mystery of the Rose Bouquet*, said that Bancroft and Brooks remained strong supporters of the theater. Davidson said he always knew when they were in the house because he could hear their laughter. That night, the lights at the Odyssey Theater in Los Angeles were dimmed in her honor.

On June 27, 2005, Brooks organized a private memorial for his wife at Manhattan's St. James. Theater. Again he instructed the attendees, "If any of you are grieving, keep it to yourself." Around 100 guests attended. Speakers included Arthur Penn, Mike Nichols, Patty Duke, Sidney Lumet, Frank Langella, Matthew Broderick and Nathan Lane. Paul Simon played a solo acoustic version of the song "Mrs. Robinson."

Bancroft was remembered at the 57th Annual Primetime Emmy Awards at the Shrine Auditorium in Hollywood on September 18, 2005. Archive footage of her was included in the In Memoriam section.

In the January 6, 2006, *Entertainment Weekly*, Patty Duke wrote that Bancroft was the ultimate dramatic actress and had a wicked sense of humor, so it wasn't a surprise to Duke that Bancroft would marry Mel Brooks. Duke commented that the actress taught her by example, not by lecture, the ethics and discipline of the theater. She said that Bancroft was also one of the sexiest creatures who ever lived. Without being too obvious, Duke stole as much as she could from her behavior.

Hollywood paid one last tribute to the actress when she was featured in the In Memoriam sequence at the 78th Annual Academy Awards (March 5, 2006): Footage was shown of *The Miracle Worker* and *The Graduate*.

Frank Langella's memoir *Dropped Names: Famous Men and Women as I Knew Them* (2012) features a chapter on Bancroft. In October 2012, the Victoria & Albert Museum in London held a major exhibition of the jewelry of Harry Winston. Entitled "Hollywood Costume," it included those worn by Bancroft in *The Graduate*.

Archive footage of Bancroft appeared in "Mel Brooks: Make a Noise," the May 20, 2013, episode of PBS's biographical documentary series *American Masters* In it there are three interviews with Bancroft, with none of the sources identified. After Bancroft's death is covered, there is a black-and-white portrait of her with Brooks.

Max Brooks was interviewed in article in the *New York Times* on June 21, 2013. Writer Taffy Brodesser-Akner said that the 41-year-old Max looked like his mother and the accompanying photograph shows that Max has her eyes. He reported that when he was conceived, Bancroft was 40, and she was told that this was her last chance to have a child. She decided to forgo amniocentesis. No matter the risks, the actress would have the baby. When Max was young, his parents wouldn't let him join his classmates on field trips. His mother's explanation was that she feared a guy would try and take him by tempting him with a Hershey bar. Brooks had a hard time in elementary school when he found that he could not read. Though his teachers didn't believe him, preferring to see him as another bratty child of celebrities, Bancroft did. She had him tested for learning disabilities when he was eight, and they learned that he had dyslexia. To help, Bancroft took his textbooks to the School for the Blind and had them recorded onto audiotape. Max said it was hard for her to be a mom, to give up her career to raise him, because *she* didn't have much of a mom.

Max reported on the illness of his mother in March 2005. He said his father sat up all night with Bancroft at Mount Sinai as she awaited her next chemotherapy treatment. He would often take his father to dinner and listen to him say: "She's going to be fine. She's going to be fine." But two months later, Bancroft died.

The Italian biographical documentary *Focus: Anne Bancroft*, telecast on June 6, 2015, told of the outstanding life and career of Bancroft and included the perspective of a family friend, Italian comedian and director Ezio Greggio.

Bancroft was portrayed by Serinda Swan in the 2017 television series *Feud*, the story of the rivalry between Joan Crawford (Jessica Lange) and Bette Davis (Susan Sarandon). Swan appeared in one scene in the episode "And the Winner Is… (The Oscars of 1963)," where Bancroft was in New York doing *Mother Courage and Her Children* and is visited by Crawford, who asks her to accept the Best Actress Oscar on her behalf if she wins.

Appendix: Stage, Film and Television Performances

Stage

Dates are for Bancroft's run, not the run of the show.

Two for the Seesaw (January 16, 1958–June 28, 1959). Booth Theatre, New York. Part: Gittel Mosca.

The Miracle Worker (October 19, 1959–February 5, 1961). Playhouse Theatre, New York. Part: Annie Sullivan.

Mother Courage and Her Children (March 28–May 11, 1963). Martin Beck Theatre, New York. Part: Mother Courage.

The Devils (November 16–December 28, 1965). Broadway Theatre, New York. Part: Sister Jean of the Angels.

The Skin of Our Teeth (June 21–July 5, 1966). Berkshire Theater Festival, Stockbridge, Massachusetts. Part: Sabina.

The Little Foxes (October 26–December 16, 1967). Vivian Beaumont Theatre, New York. Part: Regina Giddens.

A Cry of Players (July 24, 1968–unknown). Berkshire Theater Festival, Stockbridge, Massachusetts. Part: Anne.

A Cry of Players (November 14, 1968–February 15, 1969). Vivian Beaumont Theatre, Broadway. Part: Anne.

John and Abigail (July 1969–unknown). Berkshire Theater Festival, Stockbridge, Massachusetts. Part: Abigail.

An Evening with Anne Bancroft (July, 12, 1970). Berkshire Theater Festival, Stockbridge, Massachusetts. Part: Herself.

Golda (November 14, 1977–February 13, 1978). Morosco Theatre, New York. Part: Golda Meir.

Duet for One (December 17, 1981–January 2, 1982). Royale Theatre, New York. Part: Stephanie Abrahams.

Mystery of the Rose Bouquet (November 16–December 17, 1989). Mark Taper Forum, Los Angeles. Part: unnamed

The Occupant (Previews in February 2002 though dates unknown–late March 2002). Peter Norton Space, New York. Part: Louise Nevelson.

Squeeze Box (July 29—September 12, 2004). Acorn Theater, New York. Producer.

Film

Don't Bother to Knock (1952). Part: Lyn Lesley.
Treasure of the Golden Condor (1953). Part: Marie.
Tonight We Sing (1953). Part: Emma.
The Kid from Left Field (1953). Part: Marion Foley.
Demetrius and the Gladiators (1954). Part: Paula.
Gorilla at Large (1954). Part: Laverne.
The Raid (1954). Part: Katy Bishop.
A Life in the Balance (1955). Part: Maria Ibinia.
New York Confidential (1955). Part: Katherine Lupo.
The Naked Street (1955). Part: Rosalie Regalzyk.
The Last Frontier (1955). Part: Corinna Marston.
Walk the Proud Land (1956). Part: Tianay.
Nightfall (1957). Part: Marie Gardner.
The Girl in Black Stockings (1957). Part: Beth Dixon.
The Restless Breed (1957). Part: Angelita.
The Miracle Worker (1962). Part: Annie Sullivan.
The Pumpkin Eater (1964). Part: Jo Armitage.
7 Women (1966). Part: Dr. D.R. Cartwright.
The Slender Thread (1965). Part: Inga Dyson.
The Graduate (1967). Part: Mrs. Robinson.

The Twelve Chairs (1970). Part: uncredited cameo.
Young Winston (1972). Part: Lady Jennie Randolph Churchill.
Blazing Saddles (1974). Part: Uncredited cameo.
The Prisoner of Second Avenue (1975). Part: Edna Edison.
The Hindenburg (1975). Part: Ursula.
Silent Movie (1976). Part: Herself.
Lipstick (1976). Part: Carla Bondi.
The Turning Point (1977). Part: Emma Jacklin.
Fatso (1980). Director and Part: Antoinette.
The Elephant Man (1980). Part: Mrs. Kendal.
To Be or Not to Be (1983). Part: Anna Bronski.
Garbo Talks (1984). Part: Estelle.
Agnes of God (1985). Part: Mother Superior Miriam Ruth.
'night, Mother (1986). Part: Thelma Cates.
84 Charing Cross Road (1987). Part: Helene Hanff.
Torch Song Trilogy (1988). Part: Ma Beckoff.
Bert Rigby, You're a Fool (1989). Part: Meredith.
Love Potion No. 9 (1992). Part: Madame Ruth.
Honeymoon in Vegas (1992). Part: Bea.
Mr. Jones (1993). Part: Dr. Catherine Holland.
La Femme Nikita aka *Nikita* (1990). Part: Amanda.
Malice (1993). Part: Mrs. Kennsinger.
How to Make an American Quilt (1995). Part: Gladiola Joe.
Home for the Holidays (1995). Part: Adele.
Dracula: Dead and Loving It (1995). Part: Madame Ouspenskaya aka Gypsy Woman.
G.I. Jane (1997). Part: Lillian DeHaven.
Antz (1998). Part: The Queen (Voice).
The Sunchaser (1996). Part: Dr. Renata Baumbauer.
Great Expectations (1998). Part: Ms. Nova Driggers Dinsmoor.
Critical Care (1997). Part: Nun.
Mark Twain's America in 3D (1998). Part: Narrator.
Up at the Villa (2000). Part: Princess San Ferdinando.
Keeping The Faith (2000). Part: Ruth Schram.
HeartBreakers aka *HeartBREAKers* (2001). Part: Barbara.
In Search of Peace—Part One: 1948-1967 (2001). Part: Golda Meir (Voice).
Delgo (2008). Part: Empress Sedessa Graleon (Voice).

Television

AS ANNE MARNO

Studio One (April 17, 1950) "The Torrents of Spring." Part: Gemma.
The Goldbergs (1950–1951, exact dates unknown) "Mother-in-Law." Part: Joyce.
Studio One (May 29, 1950) "The Man Who Had Influence."
Studio One (December 4, 1950) "Letter from Cairo."
Lux Video Theatre (December 25, 1950) "A Child Is Born." Part: Leah.
Suspense (February 6, 1951) "Night Break."
Ford Theater Hour (February 23, 1951) "The Golden Mouth."
Studio One (April 2, 1951) "Wintertime." Part: Lisa Berzins.
Danger (May 1, 1951) "The Killer Scarf." Part: Heidi.
The Adventures of Ellery Queen (May 10, 1951) "The Chinese Mummer Mystery."
Suspense (July 31, 1951) "A Vision of Death." Part: Aurora Stone.
Danger (August 14, 1951) "A Murderer's Face."
Armstrong Circle Theatre (September 18, 1951) "Flame Out."
The Web (September 26, 1951) "The Customs of the Country."
Lights Out (October 22, 1951) "The Deal." Part: Helen.

AS ANNE BANCROFT

Omnibus (December 6, 1953) "The Capital of the World." Part: The Sister.
Kraft Television Theatre (December 16, 1953) "To Live in Peace."
Lux Video Theatre (November 25, 1954) "A Medal for Benny." Part: Lolita.
Your Favorite Story (December 26, 1954) "The Waltz."
Lux Video Theatre (June 23, 1955) "Forever Female." Part: Sally.
Lux Video Theatre (February 23, 1956) "Hired Wife." Part: Kendal Browning.
Lux Video Theatre (June 21, 1956) "The Corrigan Case." Part: Ann Sommers.
Climax! (July 12, 1956) "Fear Is the Hunter." Part: Audrey.
Climax! (July 19, 1956) "No One to Cry With." Part: Intermission Guest.
The Alcoa Hour (October 11, 1956) "Key Largo." Part: Alegre.
Playhouse 90 (January 17, 1957) "So Soon to Die." Part: Isobel Waring.
Playhouse 90 (March 7, 1957) "Invitation to a Gunfighter." Part: Julie Bickford.
Lux Video Theatre (March 28, 1957) "Black Angel." Part: Cathy.
Climax! (April 18, 1957) "The Mad Bomber." Part: Elena.
The Alcoa Hour (July 7, 1957) "Hostages to Fortune." Part: Giselle.
Dick Powell's Zane Gray Theatre (November 15, 1957) "Episode in Darkness." Part: Isabelle Rutledge.

The Arlene Francis Show (February 7, 1958) Part: Herself.
The Frank Sinatra Show (February 21, 1958) "A Time to Cry." Part: Carol Welles.
The Jack Paar Show (February 20, 1959). Part: Herself.
Night-Beat (March 6, 1959). Part: Herself.
The Jack Paar Show (March 27, 1959). Part: Herself.
The Jack Paar Show (April 9, 1959). Part: Herself.
The Jack Paar Show (May 8, 1959). Part: Herself.
The Jack Paar Show (January 14, 1960). Part: Herself.
Perry Como's Kraft Music Hall (February 24, 1960). Part: Herself.
The 14th Annual Tony Awards (April 24, 1960). Part: Herself.
Person-to-Person (June 10, 1960). Part: Herself.
The Jack Paar Show (August 11, 1960). Part: Herself.
The Jack Paar Show (September 29, 1960). Part: Herself.
Gala Adlai on Broadway (October 18, 1960). Part: Herself.
The Jack Paar Show (October 27, 1960). Part: Herself.
Perry Como's Kraft Music Hall (November 30, 1960). Part: Herself.
Perry Como's Kraft Music Hall (February 22, 1961). Part: Herself.
The 15th Annual Tony Awards (April 16, 1961). Part: Herself.
Perry Como's Kraft Music Hall (April 4, 1962). Part: Herself.
Perry Como's Kraft Music Hall (May 23, 1962). Part: Herself.
What's My Line? (July 1, 1962). Part: Herself.
Password (July 3 or 10, 1962). Part: Herself.
What's My Line? (April 7, 1963). Part: Herself.
Theatre of Tomorrow (May 19, 1963). Part: Herself.
The Jack Paar Show (June 7, 1963). Part: Herself.
Bob Hope Comedy Special (February 14, 1964). Part: Herself.
36th Annual Academy Awards (April 13, 1964). Part: Herself.
18th Tony Awards (May 24, 1964). Part: Herself.
Perry Como's Kraft Music Hall (October 29, 1964). Part: Herself.
The Chrysler Theatre (November 9, 1964). "On the Outskirts of Town." Part: Faye Benet Garret.
What's My Line? (November 15, 1964). Part: Herself.
The Hollywood Palace (February 6, 1965). Part: Herself.
22nd Annual Golden Globes Awards (February 8, 1965). Part: Herself.
37th Annual Academy Awards (April 5, 1965). Part: Herself.
ABC Stage 67 (March 16, 1967). "I'm Getting Married."
39th Annual Academy Awards (April 10, 1967). Part: Herself.
Bob Hope Comedy Special (March 20, 1968). Part: Herself.
40th Annual Academy Awards (April 10, 1968). Part: Herself.
22nd Tony Awards (April 21, 1968). Part: Herself.
Kraft Music Hall (April 30, 1969). Part: Herself.
Annie, the Women in the Life of a Man (February 18, 1970). Parts: Various.
22nd Primetime Emmy Awards (June 7, 1970). Part: Herself.
This Is Tom Jones (September 25, 1970). Part: Herself.
Arthur Penn, 1922, Themes and Variants (Date unknown, 1970). Part: Herself.
Annie and the Hoods (November 27, 1974). Parts: Various.
Dinah! (December 3, 1974). Part: Herself.
Dinah! (March 21, 1975). Part: Herself.
Jesus of Nazareth (April 3 and 10, 1977). Part: Mary Magdalene.
34th Annual Golden Globe Awards (January 29, 1977). Part: Herself.
The Stars Salute Israel at 30! (May 8, 1978). Part: Herself.
Lørdagshjørnet aka *The Saturday Corner* (September 2, 1978). Part: Herself.
Mickey's 50 (November 19, 1978). Part: Herself.
The Muppets Go Hollywood (May 16, 1979). Part: Herself.
Good Morning America (February 1, 1980). Part: Herself.
Marco Polo (May 16–19, 1982). Part: Marco's Mother.
53rd Annual Academy Awards (March 31, 1981). Part: Herself.
That Was The Week That Was (April 21, 1985). Part: Herself.
58th Annual Academy Awards (March 24, 1986). Part: Herself.
44th Golden Globe Awards (January 31, 1987). Part: Herself.
Good Morning America (February 23, 1989). Part: Herself.
Freddie & Max (November 12, 1990—unknown). Part: Maxine Chandler.
American Playhouse (May 20, 1992). "Mrs Cage." Part: Mrs. Cage.
Neil Simon's Broadway Bound (March 23, 1992). Part: Kate.
65th Annual Academy Awards (March 29, 1993). Part: Herself.
Oldest Living Confederate Widow Tells All (May 1 and 3, 1994). Part: Lucille Honicut Marsden.
The Mother (October 24, 1994). Part: Mrs. Fanning.

The Simpsons (December 18, 1994). "Fear of Flying." Part: Dr. Zweig (Voice).

The 10th Annual American Comedy Awards (March 6, 1996). Part: Herself.

Homecoming (April 14, 1996). Part: Abigail.

49th Primetime Emmy Awards (September 14, 1997). Part: Herself.

The Annual Museum of Television and Radio Gala (October 19, 1997). Part: Herself.

70th Annual Academy Awards (March 23, 1998). Part: Herself.

AFI's 100 Years ... 100 Movies: America's Greatest Movies (June 16, 1998). Part: Herself.

Living with Cancer: A Message of Hope (September 25, 1998). Part: Narrator.

The American Film Institute Salute to Dustin Hoffman (April 22, 1999). Part: Herself.

Deep in My Heart (February 14, 1999). Part: Geraldine Eileen Cummins.

The Charlie Rose Show (April 15, 2000). Part: Herself.

The Rosie O'Donnell Show (May 5, 2000). Part: Herself.

The Living Edens (November 8, 2000). "Anamalai: India's Elephant Mountain." Part: Narrator.

Haven (February 11 and 14, 2001). Part: Sara aka Mama Gruber.

Late Show with David Letterman (March 13, 2001). Part: Herself.

2001 Tony Awards (June 3, 2001). Part: Herself.

Exhale with Candice Bergen (November 16, 2001). Part: Herself.

The 100 Greatest Films (November 24, 2001). Part: Herself.

The Roman Spring of Mrs. Stone (May 4, 2003). Part: Contessa.

Curb Your Enthusiasm (March 14, 2004). "Opening Night." Part: Herself.

Bibliography

Ambrose, Jennifer. *Claire Danes*. Chicago: ECW Press, 2000.

Arnold, Jeremy. "The Kid from Left Field (1953)." Turner Classic Movies. Retrieved March 13, 2015, from http://www.tcm.com.

Badham, John, and Craig Modderno. *I'll Be in My Trailer*. Studio City, CA: Michael Weise Productions, 2006.

Baker, Roy Ward. *Director's Cut: A Memoir of 60 Years in Film and Television*. Cornwall, UK: MPG Books, 2000.

Basinger, Jeanine. *Anthony Mann (Wesleyan Film)*. Middletown, CT: Wesleyan University Press, 2007.

Beaver, Jim. "Frank Perry." *Films in Review*, vol. XXXII, no. 9, 1981: 544–546.

Blake, Robert, and Roger Lewis. *Churchill*. New York: Oxford University Press, 1993.

Blottner. Gene. *Columbia Noir: A Complete Filmography, 1940-1962*. Jefferson, NC: McFarland, 2015.

_____. *Universal-International Westerns, 1947–1963: The Complete Filmography*. Jefferson, NC: McFarland, 2000.

Bogdanovich, Peter. *John Ford*. Berkeley/Los Angeles/London: University of California Press, 1978.

_____. *Who the Devil Made It: Conversations with Legendary Film Directors*. New York: Random House, 1997.

Borgnine, Ernest. *Ernest Borgnine: My Autobiography*. London, UK: Aurum Press, 2013.

Bosworth, Patricia. *Jane Fonda: The Private Life of a Public Woman*. New York: Mariner Books, 2012.

Braun, Eric. *Doris Day*. Great Britain: Weidenfeld and Nicolson, 2010.

Bret, David. *Doris Day: A Reluctant Star*. London: Aurum Press, 2008.

_____. *Joan Crawford: Hollywood Martyr*. Cambridge, MA: Da Capo, 2006.

Burstein, Don. *Secrets of Mary Magdalene*. London, UK: Weidenfeld & Nicolson, 2006.

Burstyn, Ellen. *Lessons in Becoming Myself*. New York: Riverhead Books, 2006.

Capua, Michelangelo. *Janet Leigh: A Biography*. Jefferson, NC: McFarland, 2013.

_____. *Yul Brynner: A Biography*. Jefferson, NC: McFarland, 2006.

Carr, Jay. "The Last Frontier (1956)." Turner Classic Movies. Retrieved March 7, 2015, from http://www.tcm.com.

Chandler, Charlotte. *Not the Girl Next Door: Joan Crawford, a Personal Biography*. New York: Simon & Schuster, 2008.

Chennault, Nicholas. "The Last Frontier." *Great Western Movies*. Retrieved March 7, 2015, from http://www.thegreatwesternmovies.com.

Chierichetti, David. *Mitchell Leisen: Hollywood Director*. Los Angeles, CA: Photoventures Press, 1995.

Clarke, James. *Virgin Film: Ridley Scott*. London, UK: Random House, 2002.

Colt, Henri, and Silvia Quadrelli, and Friedman Lester. *The Picture of Health: Medical Ethics and the Movies*. New York: Oxford University Press, 2011.

Considine, Shaun. *Bette and Joan: The Divine Feud*. London: Sphere, 1989.

Crick, Robert Alan. *The Big Screen Comedies of Mel Brooks*. Jefferson, NC: McFarland, 2002.

Cunningham, Frank R. *Sidney Lumet: Film and Literary Vision*. Lexington: University Press of Kentucky, 2015.

Cypert, Rick. *The Virtue of Suspense: The Life and Works of Charlotte Armstrong*. Cranbury, NJ: Associated University Presses, 2008.

Daniel, Douglass K. *Tough as Nails: The Life and Films of Richard Brooks*. London, UK: University of Wisconsin Press, 2011.

Darby, William. *Anthony Mann: The Film Career*. Jefferson, NC: McFarland, 2009.

Davis, Ronald L. *John Ford: Hollywood's Old Master*. Norman: University of Oklahoma Press, 2014.

Dearborn, Mary V. *Mailer: A Biography*. Boston, New York: Houghton Mifflin Harcourt, 2001.

Del Vecchio, Deborah. *Beverly Garland: Her Life and Career*. Jefferson, NC: McFarland, 2012.

Desser, David, and Lester T. Friedman. *American Jewish Filmmakers*. Urbana: University of Illinois Press, 2004.

Devlin, William. *The Philosophy of David Lynch*. Lexington: University Press of Kentucky, 2011.

Dillon-Malone, Aubrey. *Sacred Profanity: Spirituality at the Movies*. Santa Barbara, CA: ABC-CLIO, 2010.

Dixon, Wheeler W. *Collected Interviews: Voices from Twentieth-Century Cinema*. SIU Press, 2001.

Douglas, Edward. *Jack: The Great Seducer: The Life and Many Loves of Jack Nicholson*. New York: HarperEntertainment, 2004.

Duke, Patty, and Kenneth Turan. *Call Me Anna. The Autobiography of Patty Duke*. New York: Bantam Books, 1987.

Dunaway, Faye. *Looking for Gatsby*. New York: Pocket Books, 1995.

Ellis, Lucy. *Tom Jones Close Up*. London: Omnibus Press, 2009.

Emery, Robert J. *The Directors: The Films of Norman

Jewison. Media Entertainment Inc./American Film Institute, 1997.

_____. *The Directors: Sydney Pollack*. Media Entertainment, Inc., 1997.

_____. *The Directors: Take One, Volume 1*. New York: Big Show Entertainment, 2002.

Epstein, Dwayne. *Lee Marvin: Point Blank*. Tucson, AZ: Schaffner Press, 2013.

Eyman, Scott. *Print the Legend: The Life and Times of John Ford*. New York: Simon & Schuster, 2015.

Fahy, Thomas. *Considering Aaron Sorkin: Essays on the Politics, Poetics and Sleight of Hand in the Films and Television Series*. Jefferson, NC: McFarland, 2005.

French, John. *Robert Shaw: The Price of Success*. London: Nick Hern, 1993.

Friedkin, William. *The Friedkin Connection: A Memoir*. New York: HarperCollins, 2013.

Fusco, Joseph. *The Films of Mamie Van Doren*. Albany, GA: BearManor Media, 2010.

Gallagher, Tag. *John Ford: The Man and His Films*. Berkeley/Los Angeles/London: University of California Press, 1988.

Geisinger, Elliot. *Urban Living: Funny and Formidale*. Professional Films/Robbins Nest, 1975.

Geist, Kenneth. *Pictures Will Talk: The Life and Films of Joseph L. Mankiewicz*. New York: Da Capo, 1978.

Gibson, William. "Second wind." *Theatre Arts*, vol. XLII, no. 10, 1959: 17, 20.

Goodall, Nigel. *Winona Ryder: The Biography*. Andrews UK Limited, 1998.

Gott, Ted, and Kathryn Weir. *Gorilla*. London, UK: Reaktion Books, 2013.

Granger, Farley, with Robert Calhoun. *Include Me Out: My Life from Goldwyn to Broadway*. New York: St. Martin's Press, 2008.

Grant, Barry Keith. *Invasion of the Body Snatchers*. London: Palgrave Macmillan, 2010.

Grobaty, Tim. *Location Filming in Long Beach*. Charleston, SC: The History Press, 2012.

Harland-Smith, Richard. "Don't Bother to Knock (1952)." Turner Classic Movies. Retrieved March 1, 2015, from http://www.tcm.com.

_____. "The Hindenburg (1975)." Turner Classic Movies. Retrieved April 1, 2016, from http://www.tcm.com.

_____. "The Honey Pot (1967)." Turner Classic Movies. Retrieved August 14, 2016, from http://www.tcm.com.

Harpur, Tom. *Born Again: My Journey from Fundamentalism to Freedom*. Ontario, Canada: Thomas Allen Publishers, 2011.

Harris, Mark. *Pictures at a Revolution: Five Movies and the Birth of the New Hollywood*. New York: Penguin, 2009.

_____. *Scenes from a Revolution: The Birth of the New Hollywood*. Great Britain: Canongate Books, 2008.

Haskell, Molly. *From Reverence To Rape: The Treatment of Women in the Movies*. New York: Penguin: 1974.

Haskins, Susan. *Mary Magdalene: Truth and Myth*. Great Britain: HarperCollins, 1993.

Haspiel, James Robert. "Anne Bancroft: The Odyssey of Ruby Pepper." *Films in Review*, vol. XXX1, no. 1, 1980: 1–20.

Hawes, William. *Live Television Drama, 1946–1951*. Jefferson, NC: McFarland, 2001.

Heller-Nicholas, Alexandra. *Rape-Revenge Films: A Critical Study*. Jefferson, NC: McFarland, 2011.

Hemingway, Mariel. *Out Came the Sun: Overcoming the Legacy of Mental Illness, Addiction, and Suicide in My Family*. New York: Regan Arts, 2015.

Hill, Ona L. *Raymond Burr: A Film, Radio and Television Biography*. Jefferson, NC: McFarland, 1999.

Hirsch, Foster. *A Method to Their Madness: The History of the Actors Studio*. Cambridge, MA: Da Capo Press, 2001.

_____. *Otto Preminger: The Man Who Would Be King*. New York: Alfred A. Knopf, 2007.

Holston, Kim R. *Susan Hayward: Her Films and Life*. Jefferson, NC: McFarland, 2002.

Hughes, David. *The Complete Lynch*. London: Virgin, 2001.

Hunter, Allan. "Post-Graduate." *Films and Filming*, no. 392, May 1987: 11–13.

Isenberg, Barbara. *Tradition! The Highly Improbable, Ultimately Triumphant Broadway-to-Hollywood Story of Fiddler on the Roof, the World's Most Beloved Musical*. New York: St. Martin's Press, 2014.

Jewison, Norman. *This Terrible Business Has Been Good to Me: An Autobiography*. New York: Thomas Dunne Books, 2005.

Jones, Jenny M. *The Annotated* Godfather: *The Complete Screenplay with Commentary on Every Scene, Interviews, and Little-Known Facts*. New York: Black Dog & Leventhal, 2009.

Kalat, David. "The Twelve Chairs." Turner Classic Movies. Retrieved March 30, 2016, from http://www.tcm.com.

Kalfatovic, Mary C. (Edited by LaGumina, Salvatore J., et al.) *Italian American Experience: An Encyclopedia*. New York: Routledge, 1999.

Kinnard, Roy, and Tony Crnkovich. *The Films of Fay Wray*. Jefferson, NC: McFarland, 2005.

Knapp, Laurence F., and Andrea F. Kulas. *Ridley Scott: Interviews*. University Press of Mississippi, 2005.

Krampner, Jon. *Female Brando: The Legend of Kim Stanley*. New York: Back Stage Books, 2006.

Landazuri, Margarita. "The Helen Morgan Story (1957)." Turner Classic Movies. Retrieved July 23, 2016, from http://www.tcm.com.

Larkins, Bob. *The Films of Audie Murphy*. Jefferson, NC: McFarland, 2004.

Leachman, Cloris, with George Englund. *Cloris*. New York: Kensington Books, 2009.

Lenihan, John H. *Showdown: Confronting Modern America in the Western Film*. Urbana: University of Illinois Press, 1980.

Lennon, J. Michael. *Norman Mailer: A Double Life*. New York: Simon & Schuster, 2014.

Lentz, Robert J. *Lee Marvin: His Films and Career*. Jefferson, NC: McFarland, 1999.

Levine, Suzanne Jill. *Manuel Puig and the Spider Woman: His Life and Fictions*. Madison: University of Wisconsin Press, 2001.

Lin, Selina. *A&E Biography: Patty Duke*. A & E Television, 2003.

Linson, Art. *What Just Happened? Bitter Hollywood Tales from the Front Line*. New York: Grove Press, 2008.

Lombardi, Frederic. *Allan Dwan and the Rise and Decline of the Hollywood Studios*. Jefferson, NC: McFarland, 2013.

Longworth. James L. *TV Creators: Conversations with America's Top Producers of..., Volume 1*. Syracuse: Syracuse University Press, 2000.

Lowe, Barry. *Atomic Blonde: The Films of Mamie Van Doren*. Jefferson, NC: McFarland, 2008.

Lumet, Sidney. *Sidney Lumet: Interviews*. Jackson: University Press of Mississippi, 2006.

Macfarlane, Malcolm, and Ken Crossland. *Perry Como:*

A Biography and Complete Career Record. Jefferson, NC: McFarland, 2012.

MacLaine, Shirley. *Sage-ing While Age-ing*. New York: Simon & Schuster, 2007.

Malone, Peter. *Screen Jesus: Portrayals of Christ in Television and Film*. Plymouth, UK: Scarecrow Press, 2012.

Maltin, Leonard. Miracle Revisited. March 2, 2014. Retrieved August 11, 2016, from http://www.leonardmaltin.com.

Marriott, James. *Horror Films*. London: Virgin Books, 2004.

Marvin, Betty. *Tales of a Hollywood Housewife: A Memoir by the First Mrs. Lee Marvin*. Bloomington, IN: iUniverse, 2011.

Mayer, Geoff. *Roy Ward Baker*. Manchester, UK: Manchester University Press, 2004.

McFarlane, Brian. *Screen Adaptations: Great Expectations: A Close Study of the Relationship Between Text and Film*. London: Methuen Drama, 2008.

McGowan, Todd. *The Impossible David Lynch*. New York: Columbia Press University, 2007.

McKay, James. *The Films of Victor Mature*. Jefferson, NC: McFarland, 2012.

McKinney, Devin. *The Man Who Saw a Ghost: The Life and Work of Henry Fonda*. New York: St. Martin's Press, 2012.

Meehan, Paul. *Horror Noir: Where Cinema's Dark Sisters Meet*. Jefferson, NC: McFarland, 2010.

Melear, Mary Anne. "The Miracle Worker (1962)." Turner Classic Movies. Retrieved May 25, 2015, from http://www.tcm.com.

Mell, Eila. *Casting Might-Have-Beens: A Film by Film Directory of Actors Considered for Roles Given to Others*. Jefferson, NC: McFarland, 2005.

Mellen, Joan. *Marilyn Monroe. Pyramid Illustrated History of the Movies*. New York: Pyramid, 1973.

Meyer, Janet L. *Sydney Pollack: A Critical Filmography*. Jefferson, NC: McFarland, 2008.

Mirisch, Walter. *I Thought We Were Making Movies, Not History*. Madison: University of Wisconsin Press, 2008.

Moral, Tony Lee. *The Making of Hitchcock's The Birds*. Harpenden: Kamera Books, 2013.

Mordden, Ethan. *Open a New Window: The Broadway Musical in the 1960s*. New York: Macmillan, 2015.

Morgan, Kim. Nightfall (1957). *Film Noir of the Week*. Retrieved March 30, 2015, from http://www.noirofheweek.com.

Nathanson, Paul, and Katherine E. Young. *Spreading Misandry: The Teaching of Contempt for Men in Popular Culture*. Quebec City, Canada: McGill-Queen's University Press, 2001.

Nixon, Rob. "The Last Hunt (1956)." Turner Classic Movies. Retrieved March 15, 2015, from http://www.tcm.com.

Odell, Colin. *David Lynch*. Harpenden: Oldcastle Books, 2010.

Olson, Greg. *David Lynch: Beautiful Dark*. Plymouth, UK: Scarecrow Press, 2008.

Palin, Michael. *Halfway to Hollywood: Diaries 1980–1988 (Volume Two)*. New York: St. Martin's Press, 2009.

Paris, Barry. *Audrey Hepburn*. London: Orion, 1992.

Parrill, William B. *Ridley Scott: A Critical Filmography*. Jefferson, NC: McFarland, 2011.

Passafiume, Andrea. "Agnes of God (1985)." Turner Classic Movies. Retrieved April 10, 2016, from http://www.tcm.com.

_____. "The Prisoner of Second Avenue." Turner Classic Movies. Retrieved March 27, 2016, from http://www.tcm.com.

Penn, Arthur, and Michael Chaiken, and Paul Cronin. *Arthur Penn: Interviews*. Jackson: University Press of Mississippi, 2008.

Pykett, Derek. *British Horror Film Locations*. Jefferson, NC: McFarland, 2008.

Quinn, Eleanor. "Two for the Seesaw (1962)." Turner Classic Movies. Retrieved May 21, 2015, from http://www.tcm.com.

Quirk, Lawrence J., and William Schoell. *Joan Crawford: The Essential Biography*. Lexington: University Press of Kentucky, 2002.

Rapf, Joanna E. *Sidney Lumet Interviews*. Jackson: University Press of Mississippi, 2006.

Raw, Laurence. *The Ridley Scott Encyclopedia*. Plymouth, UK: Scarecrow Press, 2009.

Reid, John. *CinemaScope One: Stupendous in 'Scope*. Lulu, 2004.

Reid, John Howard. *Big Screen Bible Lore: Hollywood's Religious Films & Other Biblical Movie Epics*. Lulu, 2013.

_____. *Cinemascope 3: Hollywood Takes The Plunge*. Lulu, 2006.

Reinhartz, Adele. *Bible and Cinema: Fifty Key Films*. New York: Routledge, 2013.

Reyes, Luis, and Peter Rubie. *Hispanics in Hollywood: A Celebration of 100 Years in Film and Television*. Hollywood, CA: Lone Eagle Publishing, 2000.

Rickey, Carrie. *An Evening with David Lynch*. Bryn Mawr Film Institute. September 30, 2014. Viewed on YouTube, April 15, 2015.

Rich, John. *Warm Up the Snake: A Hollywood Memoir*. Ann Arbor: University of Michigan Press, 2006.

Robinson, Harlow. *The Last Impresario: The Life, Times, and Legacy of Sol Hurok*. New York: Viking, 1994.

Rodley, Chris. *Lynch on Lynch*. London: Faber & Faber, 2005.

Sammon, Paul K. *Ridley Scott: Close Up: The Making of His Movies* (Close-Up Series). New York: Da Capo, 1999.

Santas, Constantine, et al. *The Encyclopedia of Epic Films*. Lanham, MD: Rowman & Littlefield, 2014.

Santopietro, Tom. *Considering Doris Day*. New York: Macmillan, 2008.

Schaberg, Jean. *The Resurrection of Mary Magdalene: Legends, Apocrypha, and the Christian Testament*. New York: The Continuum International Publishing Group, 2004.

Segaloff, Nat. *Arthur Penn: American Director (Screen Classics)*. Lexington: University Press of Kentucky, 2011.

Sheen, Erica, and Annette Davison. *The Cinema of David Lynch: American Dreams, Nightmare Visions*. London: Wallflower Press, 2004.

Sheward, David. *Rage and Glory: The Volatile Life and Career of George C. Scott*. Milwaukee, WI: Applause Theatre & Cinema Books, 2008.

Shipman, David. *The Great Movie Stars: The International Years*. New York: St. Martin's Press [1973, 1972].

Silver, Alain, et al. *Film Noir: The Encyclopedia*. New York, London: Overlook Duckworth, 2010.

Simon, Neil. *The Play Goes On: A Memoir*. New York: Simon & Schuster, 2011.

Simons, John L., and Robert Merrill. *Peckinpah's Tragic Westerns: A Critical Study*. Jefferson, NC: McFarland, 2011.

Sinyard, Neil. *Jack Clayton*. Manchester, New York: Manchester University Press, 2000.

Smith, Gary Allen. *Epic Films: Casts, Credits and Commentary on More Than 350 Historical Spectacle Movies*. Jefferson, NC: McFarland, 2004.

Smith, Glenn D., Jr. *Something on My Own: Gertrude Berg and American Broadcasting, 1929–1956*. Syracuse, NY: Syracuse University Press, 2007.

Smith, Imogene Sara. *In Lonely Places: Film Noir Beyond the City*. Jefferson, NC: McFarland, 2011.

Smith, Richard Harland. "Walk the Proud Land (1956)." Turner Classic Movies. Retrieved March 22, 2015, from http://www.tcm.com.

Smith-Rowsey, Daniel. *Star Actors in the Hollywood Renaissance: Representing Rough Rebels*. New York: Palgrave Macmillan, 2013.

Soares, Emily. "Blazing Saddles (1974)." Turner Classic Movies. Retrieved March 24, 2015, from http://www.tcm.com.

Solomon, John. *The Ancient World in the Cinema*. New Haven: Yale University Press, 2001.

Spoto, Donald. *Marilyn Monroe: The Biography*. New York: Rowman & Littlefield, 1993.

Stafford, Jeff. "The Girl in Black Stockings (1957)." Turner Classic Movies. Retrieved March 29, 2015, from http://www.tcm.com.

_____. "Nightfall (1957)." Turner Classic Movies. Retrieved March 30, 2015, from http://www.tcm.com.

_____. "Seven Women (1966)." Turner Classic Movies. Retrieved March 8, 2016, from http://www.tcm.com.

_____. "The Slender Thread (1965)." Turner Classic Movies. Retrieved July 4, 2015, from http://www.tcm.com.

Steinem, Gloria. *Marilyn: Norma Jean*. New York: Open Road Media, 2013.

Stern, Richard C., Clayton N. Jefford, and Guerric DeBona. *Savior on the Silver Screen*. Mahwah, NJ: Paulist Press, 1999.

Sterritt, David. "The Pumpkin Eater." Turner Classic Movies. Retrieved June 8, 2015, from http://www.tcm.com.

Stoehr, Kevin L., and Michael C. Connolly. *John Ford in Focus: Essays on the Filmmaker's Life and Work*. Jefferson, NC: McFarland, 2007.

Studlar, Gaylyn, and Matthew Bernstein. *John Ford Made Westerns: Filming the Legend in the Sound Era*. Bloomington, Indianapolis: Indiana University Press, 2001.

Sweeney, Kevin. *Henry Fonda: A Bio-bibliography*. Westport, CT: Greenwood Publishing Group, 1992.

Thompson, Nathaniel. "Demetrius and the Gladiators (1954)." Turner Classic Movies. Retrieved March 4, 2015, from http://www.tcm.com.

Van Doren, Mamie, with Art Aveilhe. *Playing the Field*. New York: Putnam's, 1987.

Wallach, Eli. *The Good, the Bad, and Me: In My Anecdotage*. Orlando, FL: Houghton Mifflin Harcourt, 2005.

Weaver, Tom. *Double Feature Creature Attack: A Monster Merger of Two More Volumes of Classic Interviews*. Jefferson, NC: McFarland, 2003.

_____. *It Came from Horrorwood: Interviews with Moviemakers in the SF and Horror Tradition*. Jefferson, NC: McFarland, 2004.

Whitehead, J. W. *Appraising The Graduate: The Mike Nichols Classic and Its Impact in Hollywood*. Jefferson, NC: McFarland, 2010.

Wilder, Gene. *Kiss Me Like a Stranger: My Search for Love and Art*. New York: St. Martin's Griffin, 2005.

Wills, Brian Steele. *Gone with the Glory: The Civil War in Cinema*. Lanham, MD: Rowman & Littlefield, 2011.

Wood, Bret. "The Elephant Man." Turner Classic Movies. Retrieved April 15, 2015, from http://www.tcm.com.

Wood, Robin, and Richard Lippe. *Arthur Penn*. Detroit: Wayne State University Press, 2014.

Zimmerman, Steve. *Food in the Movies*. Jefferson, NC: McFarland, 2009.

Index

Numbers in ***bold italics*** indicate pages with photographs.

ABC Stage 67: I'm Getting Married 82–83
Ackerman, Robert Allan 146, 173, 175
The Actors Studio 7, 28, 43, 45, 50, 53, 56, 58, 61, 71, 74, 77, 81, 114, 125, 126, 134, 161, 162
The Adventures of Ellery Queen: The Chinese Mummer Mystery 8
AFI's 100 Years ... 100 Movies: America's Greatest Movies 163
Agnes of God 2, 98, 132–134, ***133***, 137
Albee, Edward 169, 170
The Alcoa Hour: Hostages to Fortune 34
The Alcoa Hour: Key Largo 29
America at the Movies 114
The American Film Institute Salute to Dustin Hoffman 163
American Masters: Mel Brooks: Make a Noise 176
American Playhouse: Mrs. Cage 146–147
Andrews, Julie 70, 77
Annie and the Hoods 105–106, 128
Annie, the Women in the Life of a Man 96–98, 128
Antz 157, 171
The Arlene Francis Show 42
Armstrong Circle Theatre: Flame-Out 8–9
Arthur Penn, 1922– : Themes and Variants 99
The Assassin 144–146
Attenborough, Richard 100, 101
An Audience with Mel Brooks 130
The August 114

Bacall, Lauren 86, 87, 94, 125
Barker, Lex 26, 27, 28
Basehart, Richard 30, 31, 32
Benny, Jack 93, 105, 128
Bert Rigby, You're a Fool 141
Blazing Saddles 103
Bob Hope Comedy Special 71, 92–93
Bob Hope's Women I Love: Beautiful and Funny 71
Bogart, Paul 139, 148, 149
Brady, Scott 28, 29
Bridges, Lloyd 15, 42
Broderick, Matthew 139, 140, 169, 175
Brooks, James L. 131, 172, 173\
Brooks, Max 102–103, 106, 115, 117, 128, 130, 131, 138, 143, 146, 160, 166, 170, 172, 174, 175, 176
Brooks, Mel 1, 2, 18, 56–58, 63, 66, 67, 68, 71, 72–73, 80, 81, 82, 87, 88, 89, 90, 92, 93, 94, 95, 96, 102, 103, 105–106, 108, 114, 115, 116, 117, 118, 119, 122, 123, 125, 128, 129–130, 131, 137, 138, 139, 141, 146, 153, 154, 155, 156, 157, 160, 161, 163, 165, 166, 168, 169, 170, 172, 173, 174, 175, 176
Bruce, Lenny 58
Burstyn, Ellen 102, 105, 108, 126, 127–128, 137, 151, 152, 153

Cacoyannis, Michael 78
Cameron, Ken 150, 151
Chrysler Theatre: Out on the Outskirts of Town 73
Clayton, Jack 68, 70
Climax!: Fear Is the Hunter 27
Climax!: No One to Cry With 27
Climax!: The Mad Bomber 32
Coe, Fred 30, 31, 32, 33, 34, 37, 38, 39, 40, 41, 42, 44, 48, 50, 58, 59, 67, 91, 99
Crawford, Joan 67, 87, 123, 176
Critical Care 8, 161
Cronyn, Hume 148, 149
A Cry of Players 93–95
Curb Your Enthusiasm: Opening Night 174
Curtis, Simon 151, 152

Danger: A Murderer's Face 8
Danger: The Killer Scarf 8
Daves, Delmer 13, 16
Davis, Bette 1, 67, 176
Day, Doris 29, 87
Deep in My Heart 163–164
The Deer Park 43
Delgo 171–172
DeLuise, Dom 95, 96, 108, 119, 121, 123
Demetrius and the Gladiators 16, 18
The Devils 1, 77–78, 80–81, 89
Dick Powell's Zane Grey Theatre: Episode in Darkness 34–35
Don't Bother to Knock 10, ***11***–12, 14, 50
Dracula: Dead and Loving It 155–156
Duet for One 1, 102, 126–***127***
Duke, Patty 46, 47, 48, 49, 50, 53, 58, 59, 63, 67, 73, 175
Durning, Charles 128, 129, 154, 155
Dwan, Allan 28, 29

84 Charing Cross Road 1, 2, 137–138
The Elephant Man 2, 119, ***124***–125, 126, 127, 137
Ericson, Jon 9, 10, 12
An Evening with Anne Bancroft 98

185

Fatso 1, 2, 95, 114, 119–123, **121**, 166
Ferrari-Ferreira, Mario 34, 39
Ferrer, Jose 128, 129
Feud 176
Fierstein, Harvey 139, 140, 141
Finch, Peter 69
Fletcher, Louise 108, 131
Focus: Anne Bancroft 176
Fonda, Henry 33, 34, 36, 37, 38, 39, 40, 41–42, 44, 60
Fonda, Jane 102, 108, 118, 132, 133, 134
Ford, John 74, 76–77
Ford Theater Hour: The Golden Mouth 7
Frank, Melvin 103, 106
The Frank Sinatra Show: A Time to Cry 42
Freddie & Max **143**–144
Fregonese, Hugo 19, 20
Friedkin, William 102, 126, 127–128
Funny Girl (stage) 66, 68

Gala Adlai on Broadway 54
Garbo, Greta 19, 130
Garbo Talks 8, 130–131, 140
Gardner, Ava 68, 87
G.I. Jane 156–157
Gibson, William 30, 31, 32, 33, 36, 37, 38, 39, 40, 41, 42, 44, 45, 48, 50, 59, 60, 67, 81, 91, 93, 94, 95, 115, 116, 117, 118, 123, 126
The Girl in Black Stockings 27–28
Godfrey, Peter 22, 27, 28
Golda 1, 115–116, 117, 118, 168
The Goldbergs 5–6
Good Morning America 138, 139, 141
Gorilla at Large 16, **17**–18
The Graduate 1, 84–**85**, 86–91, 92, 93, 95, 114, 150, 155, 163, 176
Granger, Farley 22, 23
Grant, Lee 31, 42, 44, 98, 103
Great Expectations 159–**160**
Great Performances: The Mother 2, 151–152

Hackman, Gene 157, 167
Harris, Julie 1, 30, 50
Haven 167–168
Hayward, Susan 16, 29, 87
Heartbreakers 153, 167
Henry, Buck 84, 86–87
Hepburn, Audrey 59, 87, 102
Hepburn, Katharine 67, 93
Heston, Charlton 6, 99
The Hindenberg 106–**107**, 108, 133

Hoffman, Dustin 84, 86, 88, 89, 91, 93, 150, 163
Hollywood: The Gift of Laughter 128
Home for the Holidays **154**–155
Homecoming 157–158
Honeymoon in Vegas 144
Hope, Bob 55, 71, 93
Hopkins, Anthony 101, 124, 137, 138
How to Make an American Quilt 152–153
Hughes, Tresa 48, 117

In Search of Peace—Part One: 1948-1967 169

The Jack Paar Show 44, 54, 68
Jesus of Nazareth 109–111, 123
Jewison, Norman 98, 132, 133–134
Johnson, Alan 128, 129
Jones, David 137, 138
Jones, Harmon 15, 16

Kazan, Elia 53, 60–61
Keeping the Faith 165–166
Keller, Helen 42, 44, 45, 46, 47, 53, 59, 61, 126
The Kid from Left Field **15**–16
Kraft Music Hall 95
Kraft Television Theatre: To Live in Peace 19
Kulik, Buzz 22, 24, 27

Lane, Diane 150, 151
Lane, Nathan 163, 169, 174, 175
Lange, Jessica 118, 176
Langella, Frank 81, 84, 89–90, 92, 93–94, 95, 96, 175
The Last Frontier 23–24
The Last Hunt 24, 28
Leigh, Janet 13, 21, 64, 131
Leighton, Margaret 75, 92
Leisen, Mitchell 14
Lemmon, Jack 54, 103, 104–105, 106
A Life in the Balance 18, 20, **21**
Lights Out: The Deal 9, 67
Lipstick 109
The Little Foxes 1, 91, 92, 107
Living with Cancer: A Message of Hope 163
Lombard, Carole 128, 129
Lørdagshjørnet aka The Saturday Corner 118
Love Potion No. 9 142–143
Lovingkindness 166, 167
Lumet, Sidney 8, 130, 131, 140,161, 175
Lux Video Theatre: A Child Is Born 7
Lux Video Theatre: A Medal for Benny 22

Lux Video Theatre: Forever Female 24
Lux Video Theatre: Hired Wife 26
Lux Video Theatre: The Black Angel 32
Lux Video Theatre: The Corrigan Case 27
Lynch, David 124

MacLaine, Shirley 60, 64, 102, 111, 113, 114, 131
Magnani, Anna 43, 65, 99, 110, 161
Mailer, Norman 43, 58
Malice 149–150
Mann, Anthony 23
Marcello Mastroianni: I Remember, Yes I Remember 161
Marco Polo 125–126
Mark Twain's America in 3D 163
Marvin, Lee 18, 43, 91
Mason, James 69
Mature, Victor 16, 23, 24
May, Martin A. 18–19, 20–21, 23, 24, 25, 29, 39
McCarthy, Kevin 39, 43
Meir, Golda 115, 116, 117–118, 131, 168
Mickey's 50 118
The Miracle Worker (film) 1, 31, 44, **59**–60, 61–63, 64, 70, 91, 99, 114, 136, 163, 176
The Miracle Worker (stage) 1, 31, 35, 42, 44–**49**, 50–51, 52, 53, 54, 55, 57, 58, 98, 106, 114, 126
The Miracle Worker (television) 31, 44
Mirkin, David 153, 167
Mirren, Helen 170, 171
Mr. Jones 144, **145**
Mitchell, Cameron 16, 18
Mommie Dearest 67, 123
Monroe, Marilyn 1, 10, 11, 12, 16
Moreau, Jeanne 68, 87, 145
Mother Courage and Her Children 1, 65, 66, 67, 176
The Muppets Go Hollywood 123
Mystery of the Rose Bouquet 1, 142, 169, 175

The Naked Street 22–23
Neal, Patricia 45–46, 70–71, 74, 76, 87
Negulesco, Jean 14, 15
Neil Simon's Broadway Bound 2, 148–149
New York Confidential 21–22
Newman, Paul 53, 108
Nichols, Mike 57, 84, 86, 87, 88, 89, 90, 91, 92, 103, 175
Night-Beat 44

'night, Mother 1, 134–137, **135**, 139, 155
Nightfall 26–27
Norman, Marsha 134, 136
Norton, Edward 165, 166

The Occupant 1, 169–170
Oldest Living Confederate Widow Tells All 150–151
Omnibus: The Capital of the World 19
Orbach, Jerry 148, 149

Page, Geraldine 50, 65, 67, 71, 87, 98, 102, 108, 132, 134, 137
Paget, Debra 16, 24
Password 64
Penn, Arthur 31, 32, 36, 37, 38, 39, 40, 42, 43, 44, 45, 46, 47, 48, 50, 51, 59, 60, 63, 67, 80, 81, 89–90, 91, 115, 117, 123, 126, 175
Perry Como's Kraft Music Hall 52–53, 54–56, 61, 63, 73
Person-to-Person 53
Playhouse 90: Invitation to a Gunfighter 31, 32
Playhouse 90: So Soon to Die 30
Pleshette, Suzanne 49, 61
Point of No Return see *The Assassin*
Poitier, Sidney 58, 71, 78, 79, 93
Pollack, Sydney 78, 80
Preminger, Otto 12, 16, 30
The Prisoner of Second Avenue 54, 103–**104**, 105, 106, 109, 128
The Producers (musical) 166, 168–169, 173, 174
The Producers (1967 film) 56, 58, 66, 82, 89, 92, 95, 166
The Producers (2005 film) 174
The Pumpkin Eater 1, 68, **69**–71, 73, 77, 98

Raft, George 148, 149
The Raid 19
Randolph, Ann 173
Reiner, Carl 57, 105, 108, 123, 141, 161, 175
The Restless Breed 28–29

Rich and Famous (play) 60, 64
Robards, Jason 77, 80
Robbins, Jerome 65, 66, 68
Roberts, Julia 87, 147
Roiphe, Anne 166
The Roman Spring of Mrs. Stone 170–171
Rose, Charlie 32, 49, 90, 122, 129–130, 162, 165, 166–167
The Rosie O'Donnell Show 167
Ross, Herbert 111, 113, 114, 140
Ross, Katharine 84, 86, 89
Rouse, Russell 21, 22
Russell, Rosalind 26, 48, 87
Ryder, Winona 152, 153

Schaffner, Franklin J. 5, 6, 7
Scott, George C. 92, 106, 107
Scott, Ridley 156, 157
7 Women 1, 74–**75**, 76–77
Shogun 126
Silent Movie 108, 118
Silver, Ron 130, 131
Simon, Neil 2, 103, 105, 148
The Simpsons: Fear of Flying 153, 167
The Skin of Our Teeth 1, 81
The Slender Thread 1, 78–**79**, 80
Smith, Maggie 69, 127
Spacek, Sissy 134, 136, 137
Spanglish 172–173
Squeeze Box 173
Stanley, Kim 1, 30–31, 50, 143
The Stars Salute Israel at 30! 118
Steiger, Rod 6–7
Studio One: Letter from Cairo 6
Studio One: The Man Who Had Influence 6
Studio One: The Torrents of Spring 5
Studio One: Wintertime 7–8
Sullivan, Annie 35, 42, 44, 45, 50, 53, 55, 59, 61, 126
The Sunchaser 158–159
Suspense: A Vision of Death 8
Suspense: Night Break 7

Taylor, Elizabeth 1, 53, 59, 88, 91, 96, 99, 111
Taylor, Robert 24, 57
Terms of Endearment 129, 131

That Was The Week That Was 134
Theatre of Tomorrow 68
This Is Tom Jones 98
To Be or Not to Be 2, 106, 122, 128–130, 155, 163
Tonight We Sing 13–15
Torch Song Trilogy 9, 139–141
Treasure of the Golden Condor 12–13, 16
The Turning Point 1, 111–114, **112**, 118
The Twelve Chairs 58, 95–96
Two for the Seesaw (film) 1, 42–43, 52, 53, 60
Two for the Seesaw (stage) 1, 30, 31, 32, 33–34, 35, 36–**42**, 43, 44, 45, 48, 52, 56, 57, 64, 72, 74, 91, 175

Up at the Villa 162–163, 166, 167
Ustinov, Peter 93, 98

Van Doren, Mamie 27, 28
Verdon, Gwen 30, 150
Von Sydow, Max 126, 127

Walk the Proud Land **25**–26
Wallach, Eli 14–15, 166
Wayne, David 14, 15
Weaver, Fritz 39
Weaver, Sigourney 123, 167
The Web: The Customs of the Country 9
What Ever Happened to Baby Jane? 67
What's My Line? 64, 66–67, 73
Widmark, Richard 10, 11, 12
Wilder, Gene 66, 105
Windsor, Marie 27, 28
Wise, Robert 60, 107
Wogan 137, 138

Young Winston 99–**100**, 101
Your Favorite Story: The Waltz 22

Zanuck, Darryl F. 10–11, 15
Zeffirelli, Franco 109, 110, 111, 123

www.ingramcontent.com/pod-product-compliance
Ingram Content Group UK Ltd.
Pitfield, Milton Keynes, MK11 3LW, UK
UKHW050523150426
5217IPUK00026B/1774